MATTERING PRESS

Mattering Press is an academic-led Open Access publisher that operates on a not-for-profit basis as a UK registered charity. It is committed to developing new publishing models that can widen the constituency of academic knowledge and provide authors with significant levels of support and feedback. All books are available to download for free or to purchase as hard copies. More at matteringpress.org.

The Press' work has been supported by: Centre for Invention and Social Process (Goldsmiths, University of London), European Association for the Study of Science and Technology, Hybrid Publishing Lab, infostreams, Institute for Social Futures (Lancaster University), OpenAIRE, Open Humanities Press, and Tetragon Publishing.

We are indebted to the ScholarLed community of Open Access, scholar-led publishers for their companionship and extend a special thanks to the Directory of Open Access Books and Project MUSE for cataloguing our titles.

MAKING THIS BOOK

Books contain multitudes. Mattering Press is keen to render more visible the otherwise invisible processes and people that make our books. Our gratitude goes to our readers, for books are nothing without them, and our supporters for helping us keep our commons open. We thank the editors and contributors, and the reviewers Huub Dijstelbloem and Lucy Suchman. We thank Steven Lovatt for copy-editing; Alice Ferns for manuscript formatting; Tetragon Publishing for typesetting and design; Julien McHardy for cover design; Will Roscoe for our website and for maintaining our books online; Anna Dowrick for caring for the book's promotion and its community of readers and contributors; and Julien McHardy and Endre Dányi, who acted as production editors of this book.

SENSING IN/SECURITY

Sensors as Transnational
Security Infrastructures

EDITED BY

NINA KLIMBURG-WITJES,
NIKOLAUS POECHHACKER,
GEOFFREY C. BOWKER

The book has received funding from the Excellence Initiative of the German Federal and State governments, the Department of Science and Technology Studies, University of Vienna, and the Endowment Fund of Geoffrey C. Bowker, Bren Professor, UC Irvine.

ISBN: 978-1-912729-10-4 (pbk)
ISBN: 978-1-912729-11-1 (ebk)
DOI: http://doi.org/10.28938/9781912729111

CONTENTS

LIST OF FIGURES

CONTRIBUTORS

ERIK AARDEN is a postdoctoral researcher at the Department of Science, Technology, and Society Studies of the University of Klagenfurt. His research has focused on the distributive implications of the governance of genetic diagnostics in Western Europe, and the social and political dimensions of medical tissue and data collection in the United States, Singapore, and India. Erik has previously held positions at Maastricht University (the Netherlands), RWTH Aachen University (Germany), Harvard University (US) and the University of Vienna (Austria). He currently works on a project on transnational European research infrastructures and their relation to European integration and identity.

ILIA ANTENUCCI is currently completing her PhD at the Institute of Culture and Society, Western Sydney University. Her research interests are in the intersections of technologies, government and security. In her PhD research, she investigated the making of 'smart' city projects in Cape Town (South Africa) and New Town Kolkata (India). Challenging mainstream narratives of smart cities, she focuses on the ways in which computing infrastructures distribute borders across the urban space and reconfigure security as well as value extraction. At the moment, Ilia is also working with her colleague Andrea Pollio on a book on the making of a digital ecosystem in Cape Town.

CIARA BRACKEN-ROCHE is an Assistant Professor of Criminology in the Department of Law at Maynooth University, and Adjunct Professor in the Department of Criminology at the University of Ottawa. She completed her PhD in the Surveillance Studies Centre at Queen's University. Her current project explores the adoption and use of drone technologies in Canada and Ireland with a specific focus on their application by policing and public safety agencies. Her ongoing research agenda focuses on the relationship between governance and technology, and the social implications of technocratic governance. Her work has been funded by SSHRC in Canada and the IRC in Ireland.

GEOFFREY C. BOWKER is Chancellor's Professor and Donald Bren Chair at the School of Information and Computer Sciences, University of California at Irvine, where he directs the Evoke Laboratory, which explores new forms of knowledge expression. Recent positions include Professor of and Senior Scholar in Cyberscholarship at the University of Pittsburgh iSchool and Executive Director, Center for Science, Technology and Society, Santa Clara. Together with Leigh Star he wrote *Sorting Things Out: Classification and its Consequences*; his most recent books are *Memory Practices in the Sciences* and (with Stefan Timmermans, Adele Clarke and Ellen Balka) the edited collection: *Boundary Objects and Beyond: Working with Leigh Star*. He is currently working on big data policy and on scientific cyberinfrastructure; as well as completing a book on social readings of data and databases. He is a founding member of the Council for Big Data, Ethics and Society.

RACHEL DOUGLAS-JONES is an Associate Professor of the Anthropology of Data and Infrastructures at the IT University of Copenhagen. She is the Head of the Technologies in Practice research group, and she co-directs the ETHOSLab. In her research she is interested in sites of technological mediation and valuation, and she publishes her work in science and technology studies, anthropological and computer science venues.

MASCHA GUGGANIG is a postdoctoral researcher at the Munich Center for Technology in Society, Technical University Munich, where she is part of the Innovation, Society & Public Policy research group. Her work looks at epistemological differences and knowledge politics in food, agriculture, and the environment. For many years, she has also been committed to furthering visual, arts-based and multimodal methodologies. She received her PhD in anthropology at the University of British Columbia, and was a visiting fellow in the STS

Program at Harvard University. Currently she is a visiting scholar at Cornell University's Department of Science and Technology Studies.

NINA KLIMBURG-WITJES is a postdoctoral researcher at the Department of Science & Technology Studies, University of Vienna. In her work at the intersection of science and technology studies and critical security studies, she explores the role of technological innovation and knowledge practices in securitization processes, with a particular focus on sensors and space technologies. Tracing the entanglements between industries, political institutions, and users, Nina is interested in how visions about sociotechnical vulnerabilities are co-produced with security devices and policy, and how novel security technologies interact with issues of privacy and democracy.

FRANCIS LEE is an associate professor of Technology and Social Change at Chalmers University of Technology. He works in the interdisciplinary tradition of science and technology studies. His research focus lies on the politics of information infrastructures and knowledge production. Of particular concern for Francis is how information infrastructures – such as AI, algorithms, or big data – become part of constructing a diversity of objects in society. For example, he is interested in how disease outbreaks are constructed with algorithms, or how risky people are constructed and tracked using different types of information infrastructures.

EVAN LIGHT is an Assistant Professor and Coordinator of the Bilingual Communications Program at York University's Glendon Campus. He studies surveillance and privacy, communication policy and international border spaces. His work has appeared in a variety of peer-reviewed journals in North America, Latin America and Europe. Evan's Snowden Archive-in-a-Box, an offline archive of the Edward Snowden documents, has been exhibited in Canada, Germany, Serbia and Italy.

KATJA MAYER was trained as sociologist and works at the intersection of science-technology-society. Her research focuses on the powers of social scientific methods. Currently she is immersing herself in data practices in computational social science and data science. Katja is an advocate of open access to scientific knowledge production and open policies for science and technology. Until the end of 2018 she was a postdoctoral researcher at the Technical University in Munich. Currently she is a senior researcher at the Centre for Social Innovation in Vienna working on science policy issues. Furthermore, Katja is Elise Richter Fellow at the University of Vienna, Department of Science and Technology Studies.

FENWICK MCKELVEY is an Associate Professor in Information and Communication Technology Policy in the Department of Communication Studies at Concordia University. He studies the digital politics and policy. He is the author of *Internet Daemons: Digital Communications Possessed* (University of Minnesota Press, 2018) winner of the 2019 Gertrude J. Robinson Book Award and co-author of *The Permanent Campaign: New Media, New Politics* (Peter Lang, 2012) with Greg Elmer and Ganaele Langlois.

JAN-HENDRIK PASSOTH is Professor for Sociology of Technology and Head of the Science and Technology Studies Group at the European New School of Digital Studies of the European University Viadrina in Frankfurt / Oder. He explores the ongoing digital transformation of our lives, working environments and institutions; focusing on the entanglements between infrastructures, datafication and communication. He writes about the social and cultural role of software, data and algorithms and works in close collaboration with projects in computer science, mathematics and software engineering.

ANNALISA PELIZZA is Professor of Science and Technology Studies at the University of Bologna. Before, she was Associate Professor at the Science, Technology and Policy Studies department of the University of Twente, where she is now Visiting Professor. Annalisa studies how information systems entail broader but unnoticed transformations in the modern order of authority, buried in technical minutiae. Her work adopts tools proper to science and technology studies to investigate data infrastructures and security in international relations.

She has been the recipient of several European Commission scientific grants and currently leads the 'Processing Citizenship' (http://processingcitizenship. eu) research group, funded by the European Research Council.

NIKOLAUS POECHHACKER is a researcher at the Institute for Public Law and Political Science, University of Graz. Before his academic life, he worked as an IT professional. In his research, he is studying the relationship between democratic institutions, social order, and algorithmic systems in various domains, bringing together perspectives from media theory, science and technology studies, computer science, and sociology. Most recently, he is exploring the impact of algorithmic procedures and digital legal technologies on the legal system.

EL IBLIS SHAH, chair of the 'Conference on Informational Violence' at Aden Academy of Science, researches the politics of machine networks and coded symbolic representations. His interest in the crypto-speleological realms of media and his liminal research on control technologies focuses on human sacrifice and encoded belief. In a foundational text on algorithmic regimes, *Cannibalistic Capitalism and Alien Algorithms*, El Iblis Shah analysed the rule of terror through invisible formulas and the infectious power of logic spells. For many years, the elusive author of *The Book of Half-Truths* predicted the return of the repressed in haunted digital futures.

LUCY SUCHMAN is a Professor Emerita of Anthropology of Science and Technology at Lancaster University. Her work at the intersections of anthropology and feminist science and technology studies engages cultural imaginaries and material practices of technology design, with a focus on demilitarisation and social justice.

A.R.E TAYLOR is an anthropologist based at the University of Cambridge. He works at the intersection of digital anthropology, media archaeology and the history of technology. His research concentrates on imaginaries of digital collapse and on the material and temporal dimensions of data storage and security. He is an Editorial Assistant for the *Journal of Extreme Anthropology* and a founder of the Cambridge Infrastructure Resilience Group (CIRG), a network of researchers exploring critical infrastructure protection in relation to global catastrophic risks. He is also a founding member of the Social Studies of Outer Space (SSOS) Research Network. His research interests include: data futures, digital preservation, outer-space, techno-apocalyptic narratives and pre-digital nostalgia.

MARTIN TIRONI is Associate Professor, School of Design at the Pontifical Catholic University of Chile. He holds a PhD from Centre de Sociologie de l'Innovation (CSI), École des Mines de Paris, where he also did post-doctorate studies. He received his Master degree in Sociology at the Université Paris Sorbonne V and his BA in Sociology at the Pontifical Catholic University of Chile. He was Visiting Fellow (2018) at the Centre for Invention and Social Process (CISP), Goldsmiths, University of London (UK). He is currently involved in a 3-year research project (FONDECYT) which focuses on the processes de datafication of individuals and urban spaces.

MATÍAS VALDERRAMA is a sociologist with a Master in Sociology from the Pontificia Universidad Católica de Chile. His main areas of interest include digital culture, science and technology studies, digital methods, social network analysis and surveillance studies. He is currently working as a researcher at the School of Design of the Pontificia Universidad Católica de Chile, conducting research projects on digital technologies and datafication in Chile.

GODERT JAN VAN MANNEN built his first computer at the age of 12. Five years later, he was hired by the Dutch Ministry of Defense as a security consultant. Godert Jan has worked for several Dutch intelligence agencies and co-founded a cyber security company, which became one of the biggest private IT-Security companies in the Netherlands. Amongst his clients are the Dutch National Cyber Security Centre (NCSC), part of the National Coordinator for Security and Counterterrorism (NCTV), national internet service providers, mayor investments banks, and several Dutch ministries.

WOUTER VAN ROSSEM is a PhD candidate in the Department of Science, Technology, and Policy Studies at the University of Twente in the Netherlands. He studied computer science at the Vrije Universiteit Brussel and worked for several years as a software engineer in different organizations. His current PhD research is part of the European Research Council funded project Processing Citizenship. He also takes part in the Dutch Graduate School Science, Technology and Modern Culture (WTMC).

JULIA VELKOVA is an assistant professor in Technology and Social Change at the Department of Thematic Studies (TEMA-T) at Linköping University. With a background in media and communication studies, her work lies at the intersection of media studies, science and technology studies and cultural studies of digital media. Her current research is focused on the politics and temporalities of media infrastructures, digital excess and ruination and the intersection of the data economy with energy politics.

JUTTA WEBER is a science and technology studies scholar, philosopher of technology and professor for media studies at the University of Paderborn. Her research focuses on computational technoscience culture(s) asking how and for whom the non/human actors work. She has been visiting professor at several universities including Uppsala (Sweden), Vienna (Austria) and Twente (the Netherlands). Recent publications include: *Technosecurity Cultures*. Special Issue of 'Science As Culture' (with Katrin Kämpf, March 2020); *Tracking and Targeting: Sociotechnologies of (In)security*. Special Issue of 'Science, Technology & Human Values' 42:6, 2017 (with Karolina Follis und Lucy Suchman) For more see www.juttaweber.eu

CHRIS WOOD is an artist interested in the effects of technology on space, time and ontology. Recent work involves tarot readings based on the position of GPS satellites and an AI algorithm trained to speak in tongues. A parallel career in radio production influences his work, with the majority of his projects realized through sound. He holds a PhD from Queen Mary University of London and has exhibited internationally. For examples of work, visit http://chriswood.art

ACKNOWLEDGEMENTS

This book grew out of conversations that began at the workshop 'Sensor Publics: workshop on the politics of sensing and data infrastructures' which took place at Technical University Munich in April 2017. We would like to thank all the speakers and participants, and especially Laurie Waller for co-organizing this event and Jennifer Gabrys for her wonderful keynote. The conversation on sensors as infrastructures of in/security continued in multiple places, among them during panels at 4S in Boston, EASST in Lancaster, and 4S in New Orleans and we are thankful to all participants for the excellent discussions! We wish to thank all contributing authors for their persistent engagement and dedication through all steps of this project as well as Erik Aarden, Huub Dijstelbloem, Ulrike Felt, Nina Frahm, Mascha Gugganig, Alexander Klimburg, Matthias Leese, Peter Müller, Paul Trauttmansdorff, Sarah Schönbauer, Pouya Sepehr, Jan-H. Passoth, Sebastian Pfotenhauer, Godert-Jan Van Manen and Renate v. Otto for their warm support of this endeavour, and Lucy Suchman for her wonderful foreword to this book! A final thank you to Julien McHardy and Endre Dányi of Mattering Press for their excellent, creative and thoughtful advice along the way.

FOREWORD

Writing this Foreword amidst daily news reports of the COVID-19 outbreak affords a very particular context for thinking about transnational security infrastructures. Events beginning in November of 2019 have made it abundantly clear that surveillance and control can be life-saving resources under circumstances of pandemic disease. Yet while population monitoring as a defence against exceptional threats to public health seems at once newly relevant, it is also clearly insufficient without the political will and organisational effectiveness required for the mass mobilisation of both preparation and response. Moreover, it is now clear that the effects of the pandemic disclose and amplify insecurities arising from more longstanding and systemic threats to planetary health and individual well-being.

Sensing technologies are, arguably, a quintessential kind of human/machine hybridity. On the one hand, like other infrastructural devices, sensor technologies must be designed to operate automatically so that once installed, they run continuously. Sensing technologies reflexively constitute the world as the kinds of data that they can sense. In most instances, moreover, their sensory capacities are radically different from our own; their ability to register signals undetectable by the human sensorium is central to their value. On the other hand the significance of what is sensed, and in the service of whom, is an entirely human affair.

This rich and extensive collection of studies examines sensors and sensing at the intersections of critical security studies and science and technology studies. The trope of in/security signals that insecurity and security are mutually constituted, and that states of one or the other do not objectively exist in any straightforward sense. Deployed in the name of securitisation, sensing technologies are enrolled in particular technopolitical regimes and associated designations of what constitutes a threat and to whom. Working through the generative frame of infrastructure, these studies track the conditions of possibility that enable specific, technologically-enhanced sensoria of threat detection and the worlds that they render legible and, as importantly, illegible. Far from seamless, their extent and redundancies nonetheless ensure remarkable degrees of continuity in operation. Notable for their scalability, electronic sensoria are engaged in processes ranging from rendering micro-organisms as genetic signatures, to monitoring whole-earth planetary transformations.

A crucial topic for these studies is the question of who feels threatened and who feels protected by regimes of surveillance, and how apparatuses deployed in the name of securitisation are at the same time generative of insecurity, in the ways that they presume and figure a threat. Contemporary security infrastructures, we are reminded, are deeply indebted to their military and colonial histories, which set the terms for who is in a position to monitor and administer whom. We learn how very different the resulting effects (and affects) are if surveillance from the air is done in the name of protecting those on the ground, or for purposes of rendering them as targets. It matters as well what the relations are between those who are positioned as vulnerable (for example, the wealthy in the so-called war on crime), and those who are figured as the threat (for example, the 'unlawful combatant' in the war on terror). We learn about the work of fear (whether of burglary or extrajudicial assassination) and the promise of protection to those that the apparatus figures as deserving. As vendors search for new markets, military technologies like the Predator B drone, developed to identify targets for attack abroad, are reimagined as a critical security infrastructure required to safeguard citizens at home.

Media accounts of technological developments typically conflate references to actually and already existing infrastructures and more speculative projects. Crucially, these conflations are performative, contributing to widespread acceptance of the fact that 'it's only a matter of time' before that imaginary is more than a prototypical reality. Too often discussions around the proliferation of embedded sensing share with discourses of technological progress the naturalisation of sociotechnical developments. In the voice of the disinterested observer, the 'advance' of technology is described as if it were a kind of *force majeure*. The increasing presence of sensors in our built environments is not the result of an autonomously unfolding process, however, but rather of concerted actions on the part of those bodies (persons, agencies, corporations, states) invested in their proliferation. However large the investment, the proliferation is not inevitable.

The authors collected here ground their engagement with security infrastructures in empirical studies, which in turn make evident the political and practical contingencies that characterise actual projects. Countering discourses of seamless integration and linear development, these studies attend to the fragmented, boundary-constructing processes and very differentially distributed effects of infrastructuring. Transnational private/public partnerships carry discourses of the 'smart city,' promoting standardisation under the sign of innovation. Technological solutions searching for their problems, the imaginaries and technological devices involved travel across sites (for example, the Israeli Skystar 180 aerostatic surveillance balloon travels via College Station, Texas, to become one of a suite of surveillance technologies adopted in Santiago, Chile; US multinationals set the stage for 'smart city' projects of India and South Africa.) While technophiles defend these investments, those on the front lines of their operation frequently express scepticism regarding their efficacy. Enacted within the layered historical/political/economic realities of the target territory, standardised visions are torqued and hybridised, furthering unequal access to resources. The smart city and the biometric border are conjoined through schemes for profiling and risk assessment. We hear as well about devices for the (partial) detection of (messy), noncoherent surveillance infrastructures, themselves parasitic on the military lineages of GPS. And we are treated to the graphic-novel arabesques of visual vignettes, offered as a counter-genre for infrastructural inversions of both surveillance infrastructures and the media for their tracking and analysis.

As infrastructural studies have taught us, sensing at once requires and enacts delineations of similarity and difference, sorting and classification. Seeing is always *seeing as*. Infrastructural inversion as method underscores the importance of attending both to the labours and politics of creating accountable relations between data and worlds, and that which escapes the data sensorium. For and by whom are infrastructures themselves rendered variously visible (for example, to those who build, maintain and operate them) and invisible (to those who are their subjects/objects)? What modes of knowledge and action live in the digital sensorium's blind spots and exceed its capacities of registration? What would it mean to re-engage the sensorium in deeper awareness of its politics? As the contributors to this collection suggest, new digital infrastructures rematerialise already existing social orderings, and are re/generative of dominant cultural, historical, political, and economic relations. At the same time, the configuration of sociotechnical infrastructures of in/security is always fragmented and open to contestation. Perhaps most importantly, then, we need to recover the partiality and contingency of surveillance technologies and their associated in/securities to recognise the forms of life that escape them and the different possibilities for knowing and world-making that those lifeworlds both demand and enable.

LUCY SUCHMAN
Saltspring Island, British Colombia

I

SENSING IN/SECURITY: AN INTRODUCTION

Nina Klimburg-Witjes, Nikolaus Poechhacker and Geoffrey C. Bowker

There are more automated sensors perceiving our environment and the elements that constitute it than there are living human beings.

Tironi 2017: 2

ALMOST ANYTHING AND ANYONE CAN BECOME A SENSOR, GATHERING AND transmitting data about our world. Sensors are omnipresent and increasingly important elements in constituting and controlling contemporary societies in many domains of our lives. Built into (smart) cities, communication devices, and our clothes, attached to our bodies, to drones, satellites and cars, sensors have become our mostly invisible companions. Invested with ideals ranging from 'invisible computing', the 'Internet of Things', 'global transparency', or 'algorithmic governance', 'these automatic electromechanical labourers, at the fringe of our awareness, control the world around us. At times, they even control us. Yet they are now so familiar, so mundane, that we hardly notice' (Townsend 2014: xi). In/security is one of the domains that we now find equipped, imagined and measured with sensors.

The contributions in this volume bring together science and technology studies (STS) and critical security studies (CSS) to examine in/security, sensors and sensing. By bringing these fields together, we aim to extend long-standing STS concerns with infrastructuring to emergent modes of surveillance and securitization enabled by sensing practices and digital infrastructures. We set out by exploring many by now classical STS issues such as monitoring, registering, representation and visualization (Amoore 2009; Dijstelbloem and Broeders 2015; Vertesi 2014; Dumit 2003; Witjes and Olbrich 2017; Ruivenkamp and Rip 2014); issues of technological mediation and human/non-human networks (Callon and Muniesa 2005; Law 1994; Poechhacker and Nyckel 2020); infrastructures (Larkin 2013); the politics of knowledge and expertise (Ezrahi 2012; Shapin and Schaffer 2011); issues of classification and categorization (Bowker and Star 2000; Star and Ruhleder 1996; Star 1998; Suchman 1994; Barry 2001); group formation and data politics (Edwards et al. 2011; McCosker and Graham 2018; Ruppert 2011); as well as questions concerning the shaping of societies, states and technologies (Bijker and Law 1992; Jasanoff 2004; Felt 2015; Hecht 2009; Scott 2001; Mitchell 2011), with a particular view towards sensors as security infrastructures.

Most sensing activities operate in the background and do not require active or direct registration by those who are monitored (see Andrejevic and Burdon 2014). Sometimes, however, it is deliberately made clear that we are being sensed, or made sense of by devices. Questions about the in/visibility of sensors drives this book: how do sensors shape and how are they being shaped by the environment in which they are placed, and by the processes they (attempt to) render visible (see Frith 2019)? Sensors pick up some data and not others, depending on which data their designers consider relevant. Materially, sensors register only what they are designed to measure (Helmreich 2019). In the case of security-related sensors, sensors pick up data that their designers take to indicate a security threat. Sensor design and deployment, in this way, takes part in constructing and delineating the phenomena that are to be sensed and governed. Sensors actively produce data traces by enacting otherwise contingent realities. Acts of sensing reduce the multiplicity of potential ontologies to a singular reality that the specific sensing regime can register. This translation of reality excludes enactments and actors that escape the sensing regime, making sensing always also a political act (Law 2002; Callon 1986).

Our aim with this volume is to draw attention to the ways in which sensors are integrated into the environment and how they produce different forms of in/security through processes of exclusion and inclusion. STS and CSS alike have observed a shift of security regimes from 'evidenced-based identification and assessment of danger informed by a causal logic and reliant on empirical analysis' (Suchman, Follis, and Weber 2017: 2) towards a predictive and risk-based evaluation of potential threats (Amoore 2013). However, the notions of causal logic and empirical evidence have been problematized in STS and neighbouring fields for some time now as emergent qualities of sociotechnical arrangements. Processes of inclusion and exclusion thus produce security and insecurity alike: Security as a performed and shared form of knowledge, insecurity as becoming the subject of security regimes. This distinction can then also be discussed along the lines of becoming visible *for* someone or becoming visible *as* someone. In each case, the production of sensory in/visibility creates a dialectic relation between security and insecurity.

A SHORT SENSOR JOURNEY

To illustrate the abundance of sensors built into our everyday practices and experiences, let us take you on a brief journey through sensing infrastructures, each enacting and interacting with the world in its own way. First, switch on your smartphone's augmented Global Positioning System (GPS). You are no longer alone, and you will no longer get lost, as you are now sensed by apps like Google Maps using a flock of satellites circling the Earth in a series of orbits designed to optimize coverage at any given moment. Each satellite contains an atomic clock, constantly emitting electromagnetic signals carrying an almanack of information about the positions the satellite is supposed to be in. Your device uses these pieces of information to triangulate its position, thereby embedding you in a military-commercial geopolitical infrastructure of ground antennae and data centres with its own (post)colonial legacy (see Oldenziel 2011). While satellites might help you on your way, they also continuously observe, measure and monitor the Earth. In terms of security, they are situated at the intersection of technologies of militarized intelligence, and technologies of human rights, as both are used to reify security threats posed by adversarial countries or groups. For instance, commercial satellite imagery is increasingly used by non-state actors like human-rights activists and think tanks as a tool to hold perpetrators accountable for human rights violations and mass atrocities. At the same time, government agencies are still powerful in determining what is visible and to whom (see Wang et al. 2013; Witjes and Olbrich 2017). Although seen by many as omnipresent surveillance technology from above (Parks 2005; Herrscher 2014; Shim 2016; Hong 2013), the satellite gaze can be hampered by cloud cover as well as by limited windows of observation due to geocentric orbits (Zirker 2013). However, within multi-modal sensing networks, if one sensor is hindered in its function, another is likely to take over.

We have now reached the oceanside, where wave buoys provide local measures that satellites – using scanning radar altimeters, scatterometers, and synthetic aperture radar – cannot (Helmreich 2019: 5). The buoy, as Helmreich suggests, could 'be read as a symptom of how ocean politics have been enabled by national, military, and corporate infrastructures of measure, with buoys looking like harmless bystanders even as they concretize real relations of territorial domination in ocean space' (2019: 5). Following anthropology underwater, we encounter multiple sensor networks: Collaboratively, they monitor physical or environmental conditions, such as pressure, sound, temperature, etc. and transmit data to the underwater node. The data are transmitted to a surface buoy via a wired link, and eventually received at an onshore or surface sink via radio communication, thus enabling computation to become environmental (Gabrys 2016) and the environment to become computational (Helmreich 2019). This assemblage can be utilized in many scenarios from environmental monitoring and deep-sea exploration to flood and tsunami alerts, from navigation and communication to underwater warfare (see Starosielski 2015; Oreskes 2003; Mort 2002).

From here, we are bound to the airport, a site where sensors and security-related sensory networks condense, sensing our bodies, belongings and biometrics in multiple ways. At the check-in counter, we are asked to show our passports with now mandatory biometric fingerprint data, detected by a tiny scanner that governs both the mobility and enclosure of bodies (Amoore 2016), turning surveillance into a form of 'social sorting' (Lyon 2003a, 2003b; Leese 2016;

Cunningham and Heyman 2004). At the smart border, we are likely to go through the procedure of body scanning – shortly after its introduction re-labelled to 'security scanners', thus distracting our attention from the vulnerability of human bodies rendered visible with the promise of increased security (Bellanova and Fuster 2013). These security devices 'illuminate the body with short-wavelength radio waves [...] and form an image from the reflected radio waves [...] to create a two-dimensional image of the body' (European Commission 2010: 8) that highlights metallic and non-metallic objects.

This journey has illustrated some of the many instances where sensing devices are employed in the name of security; from satellites to underwater networks, biometric scanners and radars. As with so many sensing technologies, that were first developed for the military (see also Chapter 11 on 'Drones as political machines' by Bracken-Roche, this volume), what is being sensed and how we are subjected to different sensing regimes is at least ambivalent, and so are the meanings and the consequences of being sensed; seeing (like) a drone means something different if you are in suburban US house or a village in Pakistan (see Gusterson 2017).

No matter where we go, stories about sensors as actors in techno-societies are complicated, multiple and political. Not surprisingly, then, sensors have come to the foreground in contemporary academic and policy debates about the relations between data, security and politics. Some authors have even postulated that we live in a 'sensor society that is constituted by the devices we use to work, communicate and play with, and which double as probes capturing the daily lives of people, things, environments, and their interactions' (Schermer 2008 cited in Andrejevic and Burdon 2014: 6). In STS research, sensors are not new objects, whether in the assembling of controlled experimental setups, the design and implementation of 'large technical systems' (Hughes 1987; Summerton 1994) or the production of novel measuring instruments (Gramaglia and Mélard 2019; Gabrys 2016), sensors have been widely studied as 'lively' devices that detect, inscribe, capture and record; if not always explicitly as 'sensors' (Waller and Witjes 2017; Gabrys 2019, 2009; Gabrys and Pritchart 2018; Helmreich 2019; Suchman, Follis, and Weber 2017; Edwards 2004, Walford 2017; Spencer et al. 2019).

SENSOR PRACTICES — PRACTICING SENSING

In a technical sense, sensors are devices that capture and record data which are then transmitted, stored, analysed and linked to other data sets. Oscillating between civilian, police and military domains, sensors are inscription devices (Latour and Woolgar 1986). Inscription devices were originally conceptualized in science studies as crucial elements of laboratory equipment that 'transforms pieces of matter into written documents' (Latour and Woolgar 1986: 51), thus creating a reference to the reality in question. Sensors, however, often are no longer part of a confined laboratory space, but are crucial elements in the 'production of security in 'laboratory' conditions' (Amicelle et al. 2015: 299). As such, sensors enable new forms of interacting with the world at a distance through sociotechnical infrastructures mediating between actors across space (Latour 1999). In short, sensing infrastructures include not only mechanical sensing, but a delicate interplay between humans, artefacts, and discourses (Gabrys and Pritchard 2018). As much work on knowledge infrastructures in STS and beyond has shown, conceptualizing raw data as neutral and objective is a bad idea (Bowker 2008; Gitelman 2013). Because data is always processed, and subject to infrastructures, sensors do not only produce 'raw data' but also problematize the relation between epistemic practices and their environment (Waller and Witjes 2017).

This volume aims to explore some of the complex and often invisible political, cultural and ethical processes that contribute to the development of sensors and their data infrastructures (see Bowker et al. 2010; Edwards 2010; Star 1999). By doing so, it shows how sensors reduce complexity and selectively produce a version of the world measured. As such, the power of sensor networks not only 'work[s] through the sensory capacity of artifacts' (Kim 2016: 400), but through the embeddedness of sensory capacity in a broader sociotechnical network. While making sensing activities possible in the first place, this embeddedness allows for the sense-making of multiple data traces produced through sensing practices by collecting and combining them in what Latour (1987) called centres of calculation. Sensing traces are thereby not just collected in one centre of calculation – keeping the chains of translations stable – but are compared and calculated in multiple centres, where their meaning is re-interpreted and re-stabilized (see Egbert 2019).

Through the sensors discussed in this volume, we perceive the world like a security regime, producing probabilities and possibilities alike (Amoore 2013). Monitoring and measuring people, processes, and practices, sensors are framed as a means to increase security by diminishing uncertainty and enabling action against perceived, known, and unknown threats and risks. Sensors – as infrastructural actors – thus produce, standardize, and enact a certain notion of security. They transform diffuse ideas of a dangerous and threatening world into an experienceable and graspable entity; we might say, they perform ontological politics (Mol 1999). Yet, the visibility that is produced through sensors, creates also invisibilities, depending who gets included or excluded in the broader sensing regime. Sensors are becoming part of a knowledge/power configuration that is built on the distinction of in/visibility (Foucault 1979; 1991). In this sense, new sensory infrastructures re-materialize already existing social orderings, and are re/generative of dominant cultural, historical, political, and economic relations. Sensors are shaping what type of 'politics take hold along with these technologies' (Gabrys 2016: 18), as novel modes of data gathering lead to 'new configurations of engagement, relationality, sensing, and action' (Gabrys 2016: 23). For the realm of security this means that novel forms of sensing might not only inform security politics and practices, but enable novel understandings of what security is and ought to be in a specific context: while each sensor is tasked to transmit data that are thought to be relevant for security purposes, the processes of measuring and monitoring render certain issues visible that might have been hidden before, thus co-constructing novel or previously unexpected security issues. Often, the enactment of security rests on prediction through algorithmic means (Suchman et al. 2018). In what Mackenzie (2015) called the production of prediction, machine learning systems and similar applications enact the world so that they can sort, reorder and find patterns (see Dow Schüll 2014). As such, the method of machine learning builds practices that resolve the inherent indexicality of data usage in algorithms, consequently connecting the abstract formulations of computer code to an experienced world (Ziewitz 2017).

THINKING SECURITY THROUGH AND WITH SENSORS

To approach security as a social practice of sensing embedded in broader socio-political contexts, critical security studies can provide valuable insights into how security is thought and enacted in different settings, and how it continuously involves constructions of insecurity (Aradau and Van Munster 2008; Buzan et al. 1998; c.a.s.e. collective 2006; Huysmans 2000). Work in this field has done much to show that security fears are not *out there* to be discovered, but are constructed in the process of securitization (Buzan et al. 1998). Security is here understood as a discourse of power that can be invoked to frame a particular object or subject as a vital threat to society, the state, or public order. This has broader political effects and legitimizes the use of extraordinary measures to tackle the perceived threat. This call to engage with the practices enacted in the name of managing risk and uncertainty is also met by Amoore's work on the politics of possibility. Not accepting discourses of a global risk society (Beck 1992) in which we enter an age of uncertainty, she argues that it is not so much a question of whether or how the world is more dangerous but how specific representations of risk, uncertainty, danger, and security are distinctively writing the contours of the world (Amoore 2013: 7). The figure becomes the ground. Security as predictive technoscience, as Suchman et al. (2018: 2) have elaborated, rests on an 'apparatus of distinction' (Perugini and Gordon 2017: 2) that turns the suspect/enemy into an anticipatory target with the help of information based on real-time tracking, data mining, and the imagination of an omnipotent sensorium (see Latour and Hermant 2006).

To study security critically thus requires a focus on practices and the modes of governing they shape and promote (Amichelle et al. 2015; Huysmans 2006). Recent work in CSS linked to the 'material turn' of the field has shifted the focus from discourse to technologies and materialities; and from conceiving 'security' in terms of performative constructions to networks and associations. In this line of work the 'technologization' of security (Ceyhan 2008) and the logics and rationale that are undergirding security practices has received increased attention (see Amichelle et al. 2015: 295). This shared interest in the materiality and ontology of security issues and the mutual influences of technological devices and security practices is precisely what has spurred an inspiring and engaged conversation between STS and CSS (see Valkenburg and van der Ploeg 2015; Bellanova and Duez 2012; Jeandesboz 2016; Schouten 2014; Klimburg-Witjes and Wentland 2021; Leese 2016).

As a contribution to this exchange, this volume is a joint effort of scholars at the intersection of STS and CSS to come to terms with the messy and complicated properties of sensors as important and powerful elements[1] of security infrastructures. The following chapters can be read as attempts to exemplify the processes and practices of sensing in/security visible. Engaging with the multiple entanglements of sensing practices, data infrastructures and in/security in different parts of the world, they empirically explore the contingencies of sensory knowledge, standardization process of security infrastructures and transgressions of boundaries between civilian and military spheres. They address the question of how sensors shape, shift, and constitute domains of national and international security policy and by this, explore the role of sensor infrastructures in the constitution of and mediation between state and non-state actors.

Coming from various academic lineages, the authors in this volume speak to these themes from multiple perspectives using a variety of case studies from various regions. In jointly presenting their views on sensing in/security, the authors seek to illuminate some of the shared concerns from different fields about surveillance, control, social sorting, border practices and social exclusion and envisioned security futures as enabling and enabled by sensing infrastructures.

MAKING SENSE OF SENSING IN/SECURITY: INTRODUCING THE CHAPTERS

The issue of in/visibility is particularly relevant in the chapters that explore the ways in which sensors and their data infrastructures are either deliberately kept out of sight, physically hidden, underground, in remote areas, hidden from attention, behind technical terms, or powerfully deployed to create climates of in/security among those being or assuming to be sensed. Martin Tironi and Matthias Valderrama's account of aerial surveillance in Chile addresses the latter. The authors show how the skies over modern cities have been increasingly occupied by new flying monitoring and datafication devices. Over the past ten years, a climate of fear and insecurity has developed in Chile, a feeling that is also widespread in Las Condes, one of the country's wealthiest municipalities. Inspired by the techno-imaginary of Smart Cities, the local government has introduced a series of *innovative* and *dynamic* surveillance technologies as part of its efforts to manage and secure urban spaces and wage *war on crime*. However, residents and local organizations have protested the use of these technologies, citing profound over-surveillance and questioning the use of these security devices.

Drawing on qualitative interviews and participant observation, Tironi and Valderrama propose that vertical surveillance capacities must be analysed not only in terms of the surveillance and control they generate but also the affective atmospheres that they deploy in urban space and the ways in which these atmospheres are activated or resisted by residents. Reflecting on aerial sensing technologies, they show how these open up an affective mode of governance by air in an effort to establish atmospheres or micro-climates in which one experiences (un)expected sensations such as safety, disgust or indifference. The air, they argue, emerges as an ambience that must be controlled and securitized by the use of a series of aerial sensors and technologies that generate a vertical distancing between control rooms and the experiences of entities that coexist with/under the aerial gaze of such technologies of sensing in/security (see Adey 2010; Graham and Hewitt 2013; Klauser 2010; Weizman 2002).

Sensing infrastructures are increasingly disseminating and performing across the urban space techniques that are specific to borders, and especially to *smart* borders, such as algorithmic profiling, biometrics recognition, scanning, and screening. Drawing on fieldwork in New Town Kolkata in India, Ilia Antenucci explores how, in contrast with popular narratives of smart cities as seamless inter-connected spaces, the processes of urban digitization entail bordering practices. These work through the sensing networks and devices that are becoming more and more embedded in everyday life – bus shelters, water and electricity meters, garbage bins, home automation, apps etc. She discusses the political effects of ubiquitous sensing networks from two perspectives. First, it is suggested that sensing infrastructures introduce a new distribution of the sensible (Rancière 2000), setting boundaries between the different aspects of reality and perception, and measuring them incessantly; in this sense, the border operates at an ontological and epistemic level. Second, the chapter goes beyond the paradigm of surveillance/dataveillance to look at the nexus between algorithmic modelling, preemption and security decisions (Amoore 2013; De Goede et al. 2014) in the government of digital cities. This chapter contributes to an understanding of algorithms as creating new regimes of visibility that are politically charged.

At the same time, a new regime of invisibility is created – one of the code strings and operative systems that process urban data, crucial components remain largely inaccessible not only to citizens but also to the city agencies that are expected to act upon data. In their essay, A.R.E. Taylor and Julia Velkova show how data centres facilitate and make possible the work of sensing media, the tracking and collection of data and the production of metric cultures while remaining curiously absent in discussions of digital security infrastructures. Their piece introduces readers to the sterile technological spaces where sensor data is secured. As a critical intervention in recent scholarship that understands data centres as striving to remain invisible (see Holt and Vonderau 2015: 75), Taylor and Velkova draw on empirical work inside the buildings that store the vast volumes of sensor data now produced on a daily basis. They show how data is persistently imagined in terms of 'flows', like a constantly moving and circulatory form that never stays still – an imaginary that overlooks its situatedness, and the static, unmoving sites of digital information storage and accumulation where different technologies of sensing – human, mechanical and digital – intersect. Following Taylor and Velkova into the data centre, we understand how data centres are not just enablers of new sensor-based security regimes, but the sensory mirrors of the quantified, metrified societies that they infrastructurally help produce.

These chapters are in conversation with two of the three Visual Vignettes that both invite the observer to explore the cities' hidden, invisible and secretive sensing infrastructure. The Visual Vignettes in this volume are a method by which sensing technologies can be differently seen, accessed, and understood, both by analysts and those with whom we as scholars might wish to share our work. Making Visual Vignettes for sensor stories brings novel forms of research communication into conversation with novel forms of sensing. Finding ways to communicate about our wired, and wireless world is a task of demonstrating the mutual co-constitution of security and insecurity.

The first vignette by Evan Light, Fenwick Mackelvey and Simon Hackbarth explores how International Mobile Subscriber Identity (IMSI) catchers, commonly known as StingRays allow users to determine which mobile phones are being used in a given location, to intercept phone calls, text messages and Internet traffic, and to send fake text messages. The past ten years, the authors argue, have seen a rise in the use of IMSI catchers by police departments, intelligence agencies and any number of non-state actors to monitor mobile phones. More recently, both commercial and non-commercial systems and products have emerged that aim to detect the use of IMSI catchers – so-called IMSI catcher catchers. IMSI catchers repurpose mobile telephone infrastructure as a surveillance device. Rather than embedding surveillance in mobile standards, IMSI catchers are technically a hack, collecting data not meant to be technically shared by our phones with anybody but a legitimate network provider. Drawing on the concept of infrastructural parasitism (Gehl and McKelvey 2019), they approach IMSI catchers as a parasitic surveillance device wherein the vulnerabilities and weaknesses in infrastructure might entice intelligence agencies and others. They argue that infrastructural weaknesses become opportunities for spying and surveillance as IMSI catchers feed on vulnerabilities in wireless code just as the Edward Snowden disclosures revealed how the 5 Eyes exploited vulnerabilities and the interconnection points of the global Internet (see Musiani 2015). Rather than seeing infrastructure as one coherent system, the parasite invites thinking of infrastructure as a plurality of technical projects that coexist with each other in a parasitic chain (see Serres 1980). Inspired by Anna Tsing's work on the Matsutake mushrooms and their pickers that prototypes a landscape story which 'requires getting to know the inhabitants, human and not human', they look for IMSI catchers within this urban environment, as transient objects that, only by getting to know their enabling environment and human contact points, become possible to discover.

Chris Wood then invites us to walk with satellites and explore the meanings held within the GPS satellite network (typically hidden behind the hegemony of user interfaces). He contends that rather than being concentrated in the ways an individual interacts with technical objects and interfaces, an experience of space is held by the multiple human and non-human objects which form GPS infrastructures. Wood uses walking workshops which leverage GPS diagnostic tools to speculate on themes and phenomenologies across such networks. In doing so, this Visual Vignette brings our attention back to the infrastructure by leveraging architecture to create an experience where GPS fails, thereby inspiring reflection on how meaning emerges across the entire network, rather than being concentrated in the hands of the user. To make GPS infrastructure visible, Wood chooses architectural sites that have the potential to disrupt its usually smooth operation, such as spaces with limited lines of sight with the sky (e.g. narrow streets or building complexes with covered walkways and underpasses). During the walk, each person was given an android smartphone running an app which reverse-engineers the process of locating to show participants where the satellites are in relation to them. After walking around the site individually for some time, the attendees reconvened and drew and wrote responses to the experience around perceptions of infrastructure and surveillance. By gaining insights into how a hidden but essential technology operates, we are enabled to reflect on that technology's implications.

The theme of sensor-based knowledge and related processes of infrastructuring is the focal point of Francis Lee's and Erik Aarden's chapter, respectively, that both focus on the different enactments of health security, legitimizing political actions on the grounds of contingent knowledge production. A fact that is not new in STS or CSS, but one that deserves special attention when it comes to the analysis of security regimes. Written during the global COVID-19 pandemic, these two chapters are timelier than we hoped they were. Drawing from post-ANT sensitivities and fieldwork at the European Center for Disease Control (ECDC), Lee discusses how different practices of sensing and making sense of the world have been used to argue for or the distribution of responsibility in the case of a salmonella outbreak. By utilizing the method of genetic sequencing and finding genetic similarities between geographically distributed mutations of the bacteria, the team at the ECDC concluded that the disease had its origin in a specific country. Yet, this mode of sensing had been contested on the grounds of another sensing practice, following the bacterium through transport routes and logistical infrastructure. Applying what Lee calls shoe-leather epidemiology, the opposition argued that there is no identifiable causal link connecting the outbreak and the country. Thus, different sensing practices and infrastructures had been brought in place to support different political claims in global health security regimes.

Similarly, Aarden uses the case of the Million Death Study (MDS) in India to show how human sensors are deployed and sensitized in order to create new forms of national health statistics. This new form of infrastructuring, he argues, brings into opposition two distinct matters of concern within the existing health security regime: first, the increasingly prevalent discourse on global health security with its focus on 'exceptional events that may be anticipated with jointly developed digital sensing methods' (Aarden, this volume). This marks an interesting shift in governance practices, as it means a transition from classical biopolitical governance towards the effort to prepare for singular and unpredictable events (Collier and Lakoff 2008). Thus, the MDS marks an attempt to contest a security regime that is built towards 'politics of possibility' (Amoore 2013). Second, the MDS applies a distinct form of sensing in contestation to the established clinical system. Combining interviewer skills for, what the study calls, verbal autopsies with standards for interpretation and machine learning applications, MDS is hoped to 'access data on causes of death closer to the source and interpret that data more accurately' (Aarden, this volume). More accurately here means also overcoming the bias towards urban regions inherent to the clinical system at the time. MDS sensing infrastructure contests not only the way of sensing but also what is managed within the health security regime, highlighting health issues of the rural households and those of low socioeconomic status.

In the case of ECDC, as well as the Million Death Study, the different sensing infrastructures are becoming each other's brick wall and object of demolition. Providing different enactments as socio-political arguments for or against something, the focus shifts to the interplay of these diverse assemblages as infrastructures of contestation, where different enactments must be managed through negotiations (Mol 2002).

Discursive visions and perceptions of the world, entangled with the usage of technologies, are equally important to understanding how social orders are established. The idea of visions of an (un-)foreseeable future often drives the reordering of security regimes, as Jutta Weber explores in her essay on 'wild cards' as challenging traditional security doctrines. By focusing on highly unlikely, but potentially devastating events, a shift of orientation towards risky futures becomes the new mode of ordering in regard to thinkable interventions – also reflected in national security programmes. With that, another boundary is renegotiated: the way the (vision of a) future influences contemporary security orders. 'Thinking the unthinkable' creates future risks that call for action in the present. This dystopic performance of a potential future as a mode of establishing a social order has been reflected in STS research for some time now (Jasanoff and Kim 2009). With her contribution, Weber points at a specific form of reordering the present – not only by probable or possible events but also towards highly unlikely ones through the description of these wild cards. Sensing and making sense of the future and the present, in this case, works fundamentally different than in algorithmic or calculative forms of knowledge production – challenging our assumptions of what a sensor is and can be. Enacting security risks through wild-cards goes beyond the notion of probability and realizes non-calculative politics of possibility (Amoore 2009).

This question of how the future is being made sense of through sensors is also one that drives the Visual Vignette by Katja Mayer and El Iblis Shah. They explore the notion of human sensors and an interesting genealogy of prediction within security domains, based on the practice of consulting occult seers during the cold war to create predictions in a politically tense and potentially unforeseeable situation. Prediction, aside from risk calculation, became a fascinating element of security order, as they argue. The ways in which they provocatively put the spiritual human and an alternative construction of the future and security side by side, questions the dominance and the apparent objectivity of predictions, thereby creating a space to reflect on often implicit assumptions about practices of future taming and future-making.

In their chapter Visual Vignette as a format, Mascha Gugganig and Rachel Douglas-Jones situate it within the shifting grounds of STS's knowledge infrastructures and discuss its affordances for work in STS. While their project originates in the anthropological embrace of multimodal, imaginative work (Collins, Durrington and Gill 2017, Elliott and Culhane 2017), the authors put their experimental engagements with analysis and communication of research in conversation with efforts to work across media that are simultaneously gaining prominence in STS (Ballestero and Winthereik, 2021; Dumit 2017; Jungnickel 2020; Le Bot and Noel 2016). Gugganing and Douglas-Jones then review the capacities of the *Sensing In/Security* Visual Vignettes to bring forward critical aspects of our sociotechnical world, and offer a guide for those who might be inspired to experiment with the format and its potentials of working with images alongside text, and to stay with the dissonance produced when a conventional tool (Powerpoint) is pressed into alternative, imaginative use.

The (supposed) invisibility of sensors and sensing infrastructures in the making of security issues and politics has provoked us to engage with the issue of representation in research and the form, normativity, and power of written words in more experimental ways. The three Visual Vignettes in this book all aim at breaking up the 'division of labour' of text as content and image as its illustrator as they engage the reader/viewer to critically reflect and rethink the dialectic between visuals and text. The genre of Visual Vignettes considers research, data analysis and dissemination tools as methodological infrastructure. It challenges us to reconsider the norms of common research, writing and communication practices that have defined STS, often borrowed and readapted from neighbouring disciplines. Methodological infrastructures, like all infrastructures are made and remade, leak and break and get fixed and repurposed. As such, this format allows us to make sense of sensors by creating new forms of visibility and tangibility, reflecting the multi-modal data that sensors capture, transmit and are part of.

The third major theme of this volume, sensors as boundary infrastructures and bordering practices, is addressed by Annalisa Pelizza and Wouter Van Rossem, who take up the question of reordering security and its boundary infrastructures by focusing on a network of migration hotspots. In this fascinating account, the authors combine empirical insights and a textual experiment to explore how 'architectures of sensor networks and trans-national security orders' can influence each other. First, the hotspots are what the authors call nodes of equivalence, where standards and procedures are homogenized, creating a space of comparability, connecting diverse national and transnational actors. Second, new forms of boundaries of responsibilities are drawn, and new forms of labour divisions between sensors at the periphery, i.e. migration hotspots, and centres of calculation are established. The double movement of renegotiating borders within the system of border security infrastructures and, at the same time, the blurring of boundaries between national security regimes shows the potential impact of sensor networks on social order(s).

In her chapter, Bracken-Roche contributes to the discussion of sensors and the renegotiation of boundaries and borders by showing how drones do not obey traditional bounds of state and security. The transgression of traditional boundaries between different spatial and political spaces is thereby the result of the economic interests of industrial actors. Drones, as sensing devices, transitioned from the military domain into the realm of civic applications – performing a securitization of risk and publics through technologies constructed for military needs. Bracken-Roche argues that domestic drones are commonly framed by industry groups as benign sensing technologies as compared to militarized drones, while at the same time security professionals deploy particular narratives about drones to suit economic and political agendas. The chapter highlights how drones in Canada, in both civilian and military applications, represent a technological zone (Barry 2001, 2006) and how these sensing machines dramatically shape public spaces and impact individuals across various contexts.

Aiming towards an at least temporary demolition of disciplinary borders, the experimental chapter by Jan-Hendrik Passoth, Geoffrey C. Bowker, Nina Klimburg-Witjes and Godert Jan van Manen addresses questions of, and experiments with, possible forms of engagements between social science, hacking and security policy through a conversation on 'Infrastructures, Security and Care' over the course of two years. Their aim is (at least) two-fold: First, they explore novel ways of listening to, and discussing and engaging with people who are experts on sensors outside of academia – yet explicitly not in a sense of an extraction of knowledge and information, which almost always creates the risk of patronizing or exploiting the *expert engineer*, but as a form of mutual exchange of perspectives, questions, and issues. Second, the contribution is an experiment with novel formats, looking for ways to integrate these engagements into an academic, edited volume while being sensible to the different work logics as well as the different disciplinary logics of crediting (academic) work and the challenges that bear for traditional processes of academic peer-review.

CONCLUSION

Sensors and sensing infrastructures are neither neutral nor innocent but imbricated in politics on all levels, from international migration to sensing (genetic) evidence for disease outbreaks, from biometric to aerial surveillance, from huge data centres to satellites to tiny cell phone sensors eavesdropping on our conversations. Sensors often do invisible work, while simultaneously making (perceived) threats experienceable. We might thus say that where there are sensors, there is also governance. But then, where are the control rooms, and how are agencies arranged between people, things and politics in sensing security infrastructures? Building on and linking work from science and technology studies, security studies, critical data studies, sociology, and anthropology, this edited volume tackles these questions as it seeks to understand the role of sensors in the making of transnational security infrastructures. Sensors contribute to the production of in/security in manifold ways, producing in/visibilies and modes of in- and exclusion. Sensing realties raises questions of what is being sensed in which way, and visible to whom. Sensing therefore draws boundaries on different levels, sorting actors into sensed populations, regulating access to sense-making tools, or producing discipline through the visibility of sensing processes. The relation between in/visibility and in/security is thereby not always straightforward. Becoming the target of a weaponized security system creates insecurity without a dash. However, being excluded from sensing regimes based on lack of health insurance creates – as the current pandemic painfully demonstrates – vast insecurities. In/securities thereby are the result of in- and exclusion processes of at least three different dimensions, which are reflected in the collection of this book. In/visibility of sensing, sensing as knowledge production, and the construction of (new) borders.

First, *the in/visibility of sensing devices and possible processes of infrastructural inversion*. Here, we bring together work in STS on the (in)visibility of infrastructures with studies interested in security and surveillance. Research in STS and adjacent fields on the nexus of visualization and materiality has continuously engaged with questions of how 'things are made visible' and 'which things are made visible', and investigates 'the politics of visible objects' (Kuchinskaya 2014; Rose and Tolia-Kelly 2012: 4). The emergence of sensors is connected to the social orders they co-constitute. Yet, STS has not only attended to the tendencies of infrastructures to fade into the background, but indeed also shown that there is movement, a process in which some (parts of) infrastructures become visible whereas other (parts) become invisible. Thus, an important question to raise is: when do we make these infrastructures of sensing visible and to what end? Sensors tend to become invisible or so much part of our daily life that the enactment of in/security only becomes visible to certain stakeholders, while others are only included as objects of inquiry, but excluded from the sensor data informed security discourse. Visibility thus becomes not an effect, but an issue, as surveillance 'has become increasingly unaccountable and less and less visible to ordinary people' (Lyon 2015).

Second, the collection contributes to work interested in the *social construction of sensor-based knowledge and related processes of infrastructuring*. As Star (2002: 116) put it: 'One person's infrastructure is another's brick wall, or in some cases, one person's brick wall is another's object of demolition'. Through different sensing practices, different versions of the sensed world are created, including or excluding issues, people, sensations, and geographical places, creating the basis for different argumentations and rationales. As such, sensing infrastructures are always political, as they enact varying matters of concern (Latour 1999). Taking up on this observation, the contributions of this volume exemplify how the different ways of sensing become the basis for making or contesting political arguments on security issues. This dynamic is illustrated by health infrastructures and the question of sensing health incidents. Political and health care systems have a tremendous impact on how the tests are distributed and how the distribution of the virus is made visible.

Lastly, the book engages with *sensors as boundary infrastructures and bordering practices*. Information streams and communication structures are often integral elements of the way a state or other big institutional setting is organized (Mukerji 2011). Sensor infrastructures are no exception. They play an important role in the production of political entities, social orders and the production of manifold boundaries by moments of performative integration of actors. This integration – and with it also always moments of exclusion – can be explored from at least two different perspectives. Starting from the idea of infrastructuring (Pipek et al. 2017), the spread of trans/national networks defines moments of connect-ability and the forms of possible interactions between different elements within these networks. Are you using the same protocols, the same standards (Bowker and Star 1999), and is the distribution of tasks compatible with the broader systemic practices? With the production of transnational sensor infrastructures, national boundaries seem to be pierced and weakened while other boundaries are produced.

This collection contributes to a growing literature on the diverse processes of both securitization and normalization as integral to these infrastructures, along with their performativity in the making of boundaries and borders. Instead of solely focusing on the specific sensory devices and their consequences, the book engages with the emergence of sensing infrastructures and networks, and how sensing devices become invested with socio-political significance. By paying attention to sensors as an important part of the material equipment of in/security practices, this collection unpacks sensing as situated practices of constructing, reconfiguring, stabilizing and disrupting in/security. As such, it encourages us to be both critical and hopeful that networks of in/security withstand drives to build all-encompassing surveillance regimes. There are always modes of contingency and practice which exceed the panopticon – which is necessarily always incomplete, but whose power is multiplied by beliefs that it is all-encompassing. Securing our futures entails living joyfully with insecurity.

NOTES

1 Within STS and related fields approaches like ANT or new materialism make the case that the distinction between singular objects and a broader structure of which they are part, i.e. being something or being part of something is not a pre-given quality of the actors involved but emerges out of the situated enactment – including the seemingly innocent observer (Barad 2007; Latour 1996; Mol 2002).

REFERENCES

Adey, P. (2010). Vertical Security in the Megacity: Legibility, Mobility and Aerial Politics. *Theory, Culture & Society* 27(6): 51–67.

Amicelle, A., Aradau, C., and Jeandesboz, J. (2015). Questioning Security Devices: Performativity, Resistance, Politics. *Security Dialogue* 46(4): 293–306.

Amoore, L. (2006). Biometric Borders: Governing Mobilities in the War on Terror. *Political Geography* 25(3): 336–351.

—— (2008). *Risk And The War On Terror*. London; New York: Routledge.

—— (2009). Lines of Sight: On the Visualization of Unknown Futures. *Citizenship Studies* 13(1): 17–30.

—— (2011). Data Derivatives: On the Emergence of a Security Risk Calculus for Our Times. *Theory, Culture & Society* 28 (6): 24–43.

—— (2013). *The Politics of Possibility: Risk and Security Beyond Probability*. Durham, NC: Duke University Press.

Andrejevic, M., and Burdon, M. (2015). Defining the Sensor Society. *Television & New Media* 16(1): 19–36.

Aradau, C. (2010). Security that Matters: Critical Infrastructure and Objects of Protection. *Security Dialogue* 41(5): 491–514.

Armstrong, D. (2019). The Social Life of Data Points: Antecedents of Digital Technologies. *Social Studies of Science* 49(1): 102–117.

Ballestero, A., Winthereik, B. R. (2021). *Experimenting with Ethnography: A Companion to Analysis*. Durham, NC: Duke University Press.

Barad, K. (2007). *Meeting the Universe Halfway: Quantum Physics and the Entanglement of Matter and Meaning*. Durham: Duke University Press.

Barry, A. (2001). *Political Machines: Governing a Technological Society*. London; New York: Bloomsbury Academic.

—— (2006). Technological Zones. *European Journal of Social Theory* 9(2): 239–253.

Bates, J., Lin, Y.-W., and Goodale, P. (2016). Data Journeys: Capturing the Socio-Material Constitution of Data Objects and Flows. *Big Data & Society* 3(2): 1–12.

Beck, U. (1992). *Risk Society: Towards a New Modernity*. SAGE Publications.

Belcher, O. (2019). Sensing, Territory, Population: Computation, Embodied Sensors, and Hamlet Control in the Vietnam War. *Security Dialogue* 50(5): 416–436.

Bellanova, R., and Fuster, G. G. (2013). Politics of Disappearance: Scanners and (Unobserved) Bodies as Mediators of Security Practices. *International Political Sociology* 7(2): 188–209.

Bijker, W. E., Carlson, W. B., and Edwards, P. N. (1997). *The Closed World: Computers and the Politics of Discourse in Cold War America*. Cambridge, MA: The MIT Press.

Bijker, W. E., and Law, J. (1992). *Shaping Technology/Building Society: Studies in Sociotechnical Change*. Cambridge, MA: The MIT Press.

Bowker, G. C. (2014). Big Data, Big Questions: The Theory/Data Thing. *International Journal of Communication* 8(2043): 5.

Bowker, G. C., Baker, K., Millerand, F., and Ribes, D. (2010). Toward Information Infrastructure Studies: Ways of Knowing in a Networked Environment. In J. Hunsinger, L. Klastrup, and M. Allen (Eds), *International Handbook of Internet Research*. Springer, Dordrecht: Springer, pp. 97–117.

Bowker, G. C., and Star, S. L. (2000). *Sorting Things Out: Classification and Its Consequences*. Cambridge, MA: The MIT Press.

Broeders, D., and Hampshire, J. (2013). Dreaming of Seamless Borders: ICTs and the Pre-Emptive Governance of Mobility in Europe. *Journal of Ethnic and Migration Studies* 39(8): 1201–1218.

Callon, M. (1986). The Sociology of an Actor-Network: The Case of the Electric Vehicle. In M. Callon, J. Law, and A. Rip (Eds), *Mapping the Dynamics of Science and Technology: Sociology of Science in the Real World* (pp. 19–34). Basingstoke: Palgrave Macmillan UK.

—— (1991). Techno-Economic Networks and Irreversibility. In J. Law (Ed.), *A Sociology of Monsters: Essays on Power, Technology and Domination*. London: Routledge, pp.132–161.

Callon, M., and Law, J. (1989). On the Construction of Sociotechnical Networks: Content and Context Revisited. *Knowledge and Society* 8: 57–83.

Callon, M., and Muniesa, F. (2005). Peripheral Vision: Economic Markets as Calculative Collective Devices. *Organization Studies* 26(8): 1229–1250.

Collier, S. J., and Lakoff, A. (2015). Vital Systems Security: Reflexive Biopolitics and the Government of Emergency. *Theory, Culture & Society* 32(2): 19–51.

Collins, S. G., Durington, M., and Gill, H. (2017). Multimodality: An Invitation: Multimodal Anthropologies. *American Anthropologist* 119(1): 142–146.

Dijstelbloem, H., and Broeders, D. (2015). Border Surveillance, Mobility Management and the Shaping of Non-Publics in Europe. *European Journal of Social Theory* 18(1): 21–38.

Dumit, J. (2017). Game Design as STS Research. *Engaging Science, Technology and Society* 3: 603–612.

—— (2003). *Picturing Personhood. Brain Scans and Biomedical Identity*. Princeton, NJ: Princeton University Press.

Edwards, P. N., Mayernik, M. S., Batcheller, A. L., Bowker, G. C., and Borgman, C. L. (2011). Science Friction: Data, Metadata, and Collaboration. *Social Studies of Science* 41(5): 667–690.

Egbert, S. (2019). Predictive Policing and the Platformization of Police Work. *Surveillance & Society* 17(1/2): 83–88.

Elliott, D., and Culhane, D. (2017). *A Different Kind of Ethnography: Imaginative Practices and Creative Methodologies*. Toronto: University of Toronto Press.

Ezrahi, Y. (2012). *Imagined Democracies: Necessary Political Fictions*. Cambridge: Cambridge University Press.

Felt, U. (2015). Keeping Technologies Out: Sociotechnical Imaginaries and the Formation if Austria's technopolitical identity. In S. Jasanoff and S.-H. Kim (Eds), *Dreamscapes of Modernity: Sociotechnical Imaginaries and the Fabrication of Power*. Chicago, IL: Chicago University Press, pp. 103–125.

Foucault, M. (1979). *The Will to Knowledge, The History of Sexuality: Volume 1* (R. Hurley, transl.). London: Penguin.

—— (1991). Governmentality. In *The Foucault effect: Studies in governmentality*. Chicago, IL: University of Chicago Press, pp. 87–104.

Gabrys, J. (2014). Programming Environments: Environmentality and Citizen Sensing in the Smart City. *Environment and Planning D: Society and Space*, 32(1): 30–48.

—— (2016). *Program Earth: Environmental Sensing Technology and the Making of a Computational Planet*. Minneapolis, MN: University of Minnesota Press.

Gabrys, J., and Pritchard, H. (2018). Sensing Practices. In R. Braidotti and M. Hlavajova (Eds), *Posthuman Glossary*. London: Bloomsbury, pp. 394–395.

Gehl, R., and McKelvey, F. (2019). Bugging Out: Darknets as Parasites of Large-Scale Media Objects. *Media, Culture & Society* 41(2): 219–235.

Graham, S., and Hewitt, L. (2013). Getting off the Ground: On the Politics of Urban Verticality. *Progress in Human Geography* 37(1): 72–92.

Goede, M. D. (2012). *Speculative Security*. Minneapolis, MN: University of Minnesota Press.

Gitelman, L. (2013). *Raw Data is an Oxymoron*. Cambridge, MA: The MIT Press.

Graham, S. (n.d.). Foucault's Boomerang: The New Military Urbanism. OpenDemocracy. <https://www.opendemocracy.net/en/opensecurity/foucaults-boomerang-new-military-urbanism/> [accessed 30 May 2019].

Haggerty, K. D., and Ericson, R. V. (1999). The Militarization of Policing in the Information Age. *Journal of Political and Military Sociology* 27(2): 233.

Hecht, G. (2006). Nuclear Ontologies. *Constellations* 13(3): 320–331.

Helmreich, S. (2019). Reading a Wave Buoy. *Science, Technology, & Human Values*, 42(5): 737-761

Hilgartner, S. (1992). The Social Construction of Risk Objects. In L. Clarke and J. F. S. Jr (Eds), *Organizations, Uncertainties, And Risk*. Boulder: Westview Press.

Holt, J., and Vonderau, P. (2015). 'Where the Internet Lives': Data Centers as Cloud Infrastructure. In L. Parks and N. Starosielski (Eds), *Signal Traffic: Critical Studies of Media Infrastructures*. Champaign, IL: University of Illinois Press, pp. 71–93.

Huysmans, J. (2011). What's in an Act? On Security Speech Acts and Little Security Nothings. *Security Dialogue* 42(4–5): 371–383.

Jensen, C. B. (2008). Power, Technology and Social Studies of Health Care: An Infrastructural Inversion. *Health Care Analysis* 16(4): 355–374.

Jungnickel, K. (2020). *Transmissions: Critical Tactics for Making and Communicating Research*. Cambridge, MA: The MIT Press.

Klauser, F. R. (2010). Splintering Spheres of Security: Peter Sloterdijk and the Contemporary Fortress City. *Environment and Planning D: Society and Space* 28(2): 326–340.

Klimburg-Witjes, N. & Wentland, A (2021). Hacking Humans? Social Engineering and the Construction of the "Deficient User" in Cybersecurity Discourses. *Science, Technology and Human Values*. https://journals.sagepub.com/doi/full/10.1177/0162243921992844

Kim, E.-S. (2016). The Sensory Power of Cameras and Noise Meters for Protest Surveillance in South Korea. *Social Studies of Science* 46(3): 396–416.

Latour, B. (1987). *Science in Action: How to Follow Scientists and Engineers Through Society*. Cambridge, MA: Harvard University Press.

—— (1996). On Actor-Network Theory. A Few Clarifications plus more than a Few Complications. *Soziale Welt* 47(4): 369–381.

—— (1999). On recalling ANT. In J. Law and J. Hassard (Eds), *Actor Network Theory and After*. Oxford: Wiley-Blackwell, pp. 15–26.

—— (2005). *Reassembling the Social: An Introduction to Actor-Network Theory*. Oxford; New York: Oxford University Press.

Latour, B., and Woolgar, S. (1986). *Laboratory Life: The Construction of Scientific Facts* (2nd ed.). Princeton, NJ: Princeton University Press.

Latour, B., and Hermant, E. (2006). *Paris: Invisible City*. <http://www.bruno-latour.fr/sites/default/files/downloads/viii_paris-city-gb.pdf>.

Larkin, B (2013). The Politics and Poetics of Infrastructure. *Annual Review of Anthropology* 42(1): 327–343.

Law, J. (1994). *Organizing Modernity: Social Ordering and Social Theory*. Hoboken, NJ: Wiley-Blackwell.

—— (2009). Seeing Like a Survey. *Cultural Sociology* 3(2): 239–256.

—— (2002). *Aircraft Stories: Decentering the Object in Technoscience*. Durham, NC: Duke University Press.

Law, J., and Mol, A. (2001). Situating Technoscience: An Inquiry into Spatialities. *Environment and Planning D: Society and Space*,19(5): 609–621.

Leese, M. (2016). Exploring the Security/Facilitation Nexus: Foucault at the 'Smart' Border. *Global Society* 30(3): 412–429.

Le Bot, J., and M. Noel. (2016). 'Making and Doing' at 4S Meeting (Denver): Let's extend the experiment! *EASST Review* 35(1). <https://easst.net/article/making-and-doing-at-4s-meeting-denver-lets-extend-the-experiment/> [accessed 24 March 2020].

Lyon, D. (2002). Everyday Surveillance: Personal Data and Social Classifications. *Information, Communication & Society* 5(2): 242–257.

Lyon, D. (2003). *Surveillance as Social Sorting: Privacy, Risk, and Digital Discrimination.* London; New York: Routledge.

Mackenzie, A. (2017). *Machine Learners: Archaeology of a Data Practice.* Cambridge, MA: The MIT Press.

Martin, L. L. (2010). Bombs, Bodies, and Biopolitics: Securitizing the Subject at the Airport Security Checkpoint. *Social & Cultural Geography* 11(1): 17–34.

McCosker, A., and Graham, T. (2018). Data Publics: Urban Protest, Analytics and the Courts. *M/C Journal* 21(3). <http://journal.media-culture.org.au/index.php/mcjournal/article/view/1427>.

Mitchell, T. (2011). *Carbon Democracy: Political Power in the Age of Oil.* London; New York: Verso.

Mol, A. (2002). *The Body Multiple: Ontology in Medical Practice.* Durham, NC: Duke University Press.

Mukerji, C. (2011). Jurisdiction, Inscription, and State Formation: Administrative Modernism and Knowledge Regimes. *Theory and Society* 40(3): 223–245.

Musiani, F. (2015). Practice, Plurality, Performativity, and Plumbing: Internet Governance Research Meets Science and Technology Studies. *Science, Technology, & Human Values* 40(2): 272–286.

Parks L. and Starosielski N. (2015) *Signal Traffic: Critical Studies of Media Infrastructures.* Champaign, IL: University of Illinois Press.

Poechhacker, N., and Nyckel, E.-M. (2020). Logistics of Probability. Anticipatory Shipping and the Production of Markets. In M. Burkhardt, K. Grashöfer, M. Shnayien, and B. Westerman (Eds), *Explorations of Digital Cultures.* Lüneburg: Meson Press.

Pelizza, A. (2016). Developing the Vectorial Glance: Infrastructural Inversion for the New Agenda on Government Information Systems. *Science, Technology, & Human Values* 41(2): 298–321.

Pipek, V., Karasti, H., Bowker, G. C. (2017). A Preface to 'Infrastructuring and Collaborative Design'. *Computer Supported Cooperative Work (CSCW)* 26(1–2): 1–5.

Ruivenkamp, M., and Rip, A. (2014). Nanoimages as Hybrid Monsters. in C. Coopmans, J. Vertesi, M. Lynch and S. Woolgar (Eds), *Representation in Scientific Practice Revisited.* Cambridge, MA: The MIT Press: 177–200.

Ruppert, E. (2011). Population Objects: Interpassive Subjects. *Sociology,* 45(2): 218–233.

—— (2012). The Governmental Topologies of Database Devices. *Theory, Culture & Society* 29(4–5): 116–136.

Ruppert, E., Isin, E., and Bigo, D. (2017). Data Politics. *Big Data & Society* 4(2): 1–7.

Salter, M. B. (2004). Passports, Mobility, and Security: How Smart Can the Border Be? *International Studies Perspectives* 5(1): 71–91.

Schüll, N. D. (2014). *Addiction by Design: Machine Gambling in Las Vegas*. Princeton, NJ: Princeton University Press.

Serres, M. (1980). *The Parasite*. Grasset: Paris.

Slota, S. C., and Bowker, G. C. (2016). *How Infrastructures Matter*. In U. Felt, R. Fouché, C. A. Miller, and L. Smith-Doerr (Eds), *The Handbook of Science and Technology Studies*. Cambridge, MA: The MIT Press, pp. 529–554.

Spencer, M., Dányi, E., and Hayashi, Y. (2019). Asymmetries and Climate Futures: Working with Waters in an Indigenous Australian Settlement. *Science, Technology, & Human Values* 44(5): 786–813.

Star, S. L., and Ruhleder, K. (1996). Steps Toward an Ecology of Infrastructure: Design and Access for Large Information Spaces. *Information Systems Research* 7(1): 111–134.

Star, S. L., and Bowker, G. C. (2002). How to Infrastructure? In Leah A. Lievrouw and Sonia Livingstone (Eds), *The Handbook of New Media: Social Shaping and Consequences of ICTs*. London: Sage, pp. 151–162.

Star, S. L. (1995). The Politics of Formal Representations: Wizards, Gurus, and Organizational Complexity. In: S. L. Star (Ed.), *Ecologies of Knowledge: Work and Politics in Science and Technology*. Albany, NY: SUNY Press, pp. 88–118.

Starosielski, N. (2015). *The Undersea Network*. Durham, NC: Duke University Press.

Tironi, M. (2017). Regimes of Perceptibility and Cosmopolitical Sensing: The Earth and the Ontological Politics of Sensor Technologies. *Science as Culture* 27(1): 1–7.

Trischler, H., and Weinberger, H. (2005). Engineering Europe: Big Technologies and Military Systems in the Making of 20th Century Europe. *History and Technology* 21(1): 49–83.

Tufekci, Z. (2014). Engineering the Public: Big Data, Surveillance and Computational Politics. *First Monday* 19(7). <https://firstmonday.org/article/view/4901/4097>.

Valkenburg, G. (2017). Security Technologies Versus Citizen Roles? *Science as Culture* 26(3): 307–329.

Vertesi, J. (2015). *Seeing Like a Rover: How Robots, Teams, and Images Craft Knowledge of Mars*. Chicago, IL: University of Chicago Press.

Walford, A. (2017). Raw Data: Making Relations Matter. *Social Analysis* 61(2): 65–80.

Waller, L., and Witjes, N. (2017). Sensor Publics: Report from a Workshop on the Politics of Sensing and Data Infrastructures. *EASST Review* 36(2). <https://easst.net/article/sensor-publics-report-from-a-workshop-on-the-politics-of-sensing-and-data-infrastructures/>.

Walters, W. (2011). Rezoning the Global: Technological Zones, Technological Work, and the (Un-)Making of Biometric Borders. In V. Squire (Ed.), *The Contested Politics of Mobility: Borderzones and Irregularity*. London: Routledge.

Wang, B. Y., Raymond, N. A., Gould, G. and Baker, I. (2013). Problems from Hell, Solution in the Heavens? Identifying Obstacles and Opportunities for Employing Geospatial

Technologies to Document and Mitigate Mass Atrocities. *Stability: International Journal of Security & Development* 2: 1–18.

Weizman, E. (2002). Introduction to the Politics of Verticality. *Open Democracy* 23. < https://www.opendemocracy.net/en/article_801jsp/>

Winner, L. (1980). Do Artifacts Have Politics? *Daedalus* 19(1): 121–136.

Witjes, N., and Olbrich, P. (2017). A Fragile Transparency: Satellite Imagery Analysis, Non-State Actors, and Visual Representations of Security. *Science and Public Policy* 44(4): 524–534.

Ziewitz, M. (2017). A Not Quite Random Walk: Experimenting with the Ethnomethods of the Algorithm. *Big Data & Society* 4(2): 1–13.

Zureik, E., and Hindle, K. (2004). Governance, Security and Technology: The Case of Biometrics. *Studies in Political Economy* 73(1): 113–137.

2

MICROCLIMATES OF (IN)SECURITY IN SANTIAGO: SENSORS, SENSING AND SENSATIONS

Martin Tironi and Matías Valderrama

ABSTRACT

Over the past ten years, a climate of fear and insecurity has developed in Chile. Despite the low homicide and crime victimization rates, Chileans generally feel unsafe. This feeling is widespread in Las Condes, one of the country's wealthiest municipalities. Inspired by the techno-imaginary of Smart Cities, the local government has introduced a series of 'innovative' and 'dynamic' surveillance technologies as part of its effort to manage and secure urban spaces and wage the 'war on crime'. These measures include the deployment of aerostatic surveillance balloons more recently, highly sophisticated drones that deliver 'personalized warnings' in parks and streets. These drones and balloons offer the municipality a new vertical perspective and allow it to have a *presence* in the air so that it can give the residents a feeling of security. However, residents and local organizations have protested the use of these technologies, citing profound over-surveillance and raising important questions about the use of these security devices. In this chapter, we argue that vertical surveillance capacities must be analysed not only in terms of the surveillance and control that they generate, but also the affective atmospheres that they deploy in the urban space and the ways in which these atmospheres are activated or resisted by residents. We reflect on how these technologies open up an affective mode of governance by air in an effort to establish atmospheres or micro-climates in which one experiences (un)expected sensations such as safer, disgusted or indifferent.

KEYWORDS: Drones, video surveillance, security, affective atmosphere, Santiago.

INTRODUCTION: THE OCCUPATION OF THE URBAN SKY

The skies over modern cities are increasingly occupied by new flying devices of monitoring and datafication. Cities are investing significant amounts of resources in order to test this type of 'smart solutions' based on mass data recording under the promise of greater levels of efficiency and public safety. This form of intervening in and surveilling the city 'from above', using devices such as drones, helicopters, satellites or aerostatic balloons, has given rise to a series of studies that seek to understand their impacts on urban life (Adey 2010; Klauser 2013; Arteaga Botello 2016). Stephen Graham (2012, 2016), has argued that this expansion of the practices of tracking, identifying and setting targets of suspicion in spaces of daily life speak to the increasing militarization of urban management and security. Within this process one can situate the intensification of what has been called 'politics of verticality' in which control is not limited to two dimensions, instead governments try to cover a three-dimensional volume of urban space. The air emerges as an ambience that must be controlled and securitized by the use of a series of aerial sensors and technologies that generate a vertical distancing between control rooms and the experiences of entities that coexist with/under the aerial gaze of such technologies (Adey 2010; Graham and Hewitt 2013; Klauser 2010; Weizman 2002).

In dialogue with this discussion of the urban effects of this new form of surveilling urban life from the sky, this chapter analyses the case of Santiago and its recent incorporation of aerostatic balloons and drones to surveil the municipality of Las Condes, one of Chile's wealthiest areas. Described as pilot projects and experimental initiatives, these surveillance devices were introduced within a frame of a 'war on crime' mobilized by the right wing, attempting to improve the climate of insecurity and fear that every inhabitants supposedly perceive on a daily basis. In spite of criticism and opposition from citizen groups, these technologies are viewed as a great 'success' by those responsible for their introduction[1] and have begun to be evaluated by other cities in Chile.

Based on an ethnographic study of the process of implementation and operation of aerostatic balloons and drones in Las Condes, we argue that these technologies' vertical capacities should not only be analysed in terms of the surveillance and control that they generate, as tends to be the case in the literature, but also in terms of the atmospheres (Anderson 2009; Adey et al. 2013; McCormack 2008, 2014) that they deploy in the urban space. Adopting an approach from Science and Technology Studies and perspectives informed by the affective turn, we analyse these surveillance technologies as atmospheric interventions in the city. We seek to move beyond the idea of the fixed 'impacts' of security technologies on the city to examine how the presence of these flying video surveillance devices in the urban sky participates in the deployment of what we will call atmospheres or microclimates of (in)security.

This analysis is particularly relevant in the Latin American context, where there is a growing militarization of the modes of securing urban spaces, particularly through the use of transnational aerial surveillance devices (Arteaga Botello 2016). It is necessary to problematize the belief that technological solutions are imported from the North to Latin America as stable black boxes with preset qualities and functions. We demonstrate the importance of studying how these aerial surveillance devices are re-created and re-signified in local contexts, considering the entanglements, knowledges and situated frictions that are produced. We seek to contribute to the discussion of sensing security in the urban space in the Global South, showing that spaces and individuals are not only 'surveilled' through monitoring practices and data infrastructures, but also with sensors and devices that activate different levels of affectations that tacitly condition emotions and atmospheres of (in)security.

Specifically, the chapter describes two displacements. The first is related to how the drones and balloons form part of an experimental political strategy to make residents' atmospheres and sensations more manageable with regard to security. The individuals responsible for the technology argue that the war on crime is not won solely by improving statistics, it requires intervention oriented towards influencing people's sensations and sensibilities. Second, in regard to the effort to produce sensations of security among residents, we analyse the multiple feelings and situated forms of knowledge (Haraway 1988) that the surveilled individuals experiment in the everyday coexistence with the flying devices. These registers reveal how the attempt to make and sense the city secure are exceeded by contingent and indeterminate modes of inhabiting and weaving together atmospheres, in which experiences, materialities, representations and affects mingle. In other words, the work to condition atmospheres of security among the population are far from being lineally and uniformly deployed, and are instead the result of specific entanglements and micro-resistances distributed in diverse agencies and contexts.

ATMOSPHERES AND THE CITY

A cluster of publications mainly based on cultural geography and non-representational theory have emerged in the past several years that are interested in understanding territory and technologies beyond their physical or discursive qualities, emphasizing the need to incorporate the sensorial and affective dimensions that they involve (Thrift 2004; Anderson 2009; Bisell 2010). The consideration of affects in the construction of spatiality, environments and urban practices pays attention to how emotions and affectivities shape perspectives, forms of behaving and doing, deploying peculiar modes of production and appropriation of space. While this approach has been particularly important for examining infrastructures and practices of urban mobility (Bisell 2010; Merriman 2016; Simpson 2017; Tironi and Palacios 2016), it also has begun to be used in surveillance studies to explore how technologies oriented towards the control of spaces and populations install particular atmospheres in the space (Adey et al. 2013; Adey 2014; Ellis et al. 2013; Klauser 2010).

A relevant concept for this work is 'affective atmospheres' (Anderson 2009; Ash and Anderson 2015; Bissell 2010; McCormack 2008, 2014; Stewart 2011).

Understood as heterogeneous and ambiguous configurations in which the presences and absences, the visible and invisible are connected, this concept reveals that the issue of affects goes far beyond a purely subjective matter and is rooted in material and social circumstances, bodies and imaginaries, creating realities that influence how people feel and act (Bissell 2010). The qualities of affective atmospheres cannot be reduced to words or numbers because they circulate and are felt through various senses, involving sight, smell, taste, sound and any other form that affects bodies, both human and non-human. Affective atmospheres manifest themselves performatively before they are manifested through discourse. Prior to a conscious discourse, the concept of affective atmospheres presents as circulatory, pre-narrative: 'they are neither fully subjective nor fully objective but circulate in an interstitial place in and between the two' (Adey et al. 2013: 301).

Exploring the idea of atmosphere, McCormack (2008) suggests that this concept is commonly defined in two ways: in a *meteorological sense* as the gaseous layer that surrounds a celestial body like the Earth and in which entities that inhabit said planet breathe and live, and in an *affective sense* as an affective situation or environment that surrounds or envelops a group of entities under a general or shared feeling or state, such as when one define a festive atmosphere during celebrations. An important element for our argument is related to the vague and diffuse nature of atmospheres: their qualities are not given and cannot be causally attributed, but are instead registered in and through sensing bodies (McCormack 2008: 413). They have the capacity to condition subjectivities and situations in a distributed and absorbing manner that is at once invisible and indeterminate (Böhme 1993; Bissell 2010). This idea is shared by Anderson (2009) considering that affective atmospheres are ambiguous because they are not only generated by the things or subjects that perceive them but are always present in the diffuse intersection or entangling of both.

This ontologically dynamic status of atmospheres requires that attention be paid to the conditions that give life to them, overcoming a vision in which the atmosphere is conceived of something 'out there'. On the contrary, it is important to explore the materiality of atmospheres, how they are sensed and experienced, and how this atmospheric sensibility affects our participation in the world. In this sense, Ingold (2012) suggests that atmospheres should be understood as a becoming-with, that is, rather than representing fixed entities, they arise from the entanglements between multiple entities or forces (humans, chemicals, weather, wind, etc.) in particular places, and are perceived in different ways by different sensing bodies. As such, the urban ceases to be a well-defined container and is woven through environments and situations that constitute the threads of the city. As Anderson put it, 'atmospheres are perpetually forming and deforming, appearing and disappearing, as bodies enter into relation with one another. They are never finished, static or at rest' (Anderson 2009: 79).

The conditioning and design of atmospheres

Atmospheres shape how people feel and think about the spaces they breathe and live so it has become of great interest how atmospheres can be 'designed', 'engineered', 'sealed off', 'intervened' or 'intensified' by different means. Through the composition of various elements, atmospheres can deeply absorb many actors in almost unnoticed ways, but in other cases they could be more notorious. As Edensor and Sumartojo (2015) argue, this may depend on the skills of professional and non-professional designers of atmospheres and how they composite, curate or manipulate different materials through design.

This point has been addressed in depth by Peter Sloterdijk in his spherology and his question about the conditions for the deployment and persistence of life on the planet. In a world where security in the largest circles from traditional theological and cosmological narratives has been lost, for Sloterdijk (2011 2016) modernity have been producing technically it's immunities by the design of interiors or spheres that protect or contain life: 'Spheres are air conditioning systems in whose construction and calibration, for those living in real coexistence, it is out of the question not to participate. The symbolic air conditioning of the shared space is the primal production of every society. Indeed – humans create their own climate; not according to free choice, however, but under pre-existing, given and handed-down conditions' (2011: 47–48).

For Sloterdijk, the twentieth century will be remembered for the development of 'atmotechnics' innovations or technologies for atmospheric design or climate creation: 'Air-design is the technological response to the phenomenological insight that human being-in-the-world is always and without exception present as a modification of "being-in-the-air"' (2009: 93). As Sloterdijk shows, the recognition of our ontological condition of being always enfolded in atmospheres in coexistence with others was directly exploited in the gas warfare, through the use of chemical weapons to make unbreathable the enemy's air. The terrorist principle of intervening the environment (the atmosphere) instead of the system (the enemy's body), was generalized to everyday life through the design of interiors like shopping malls, clinics or hotels. The hygienic cleaning of the air is no longer sought, but rather with air design it is intended to intervene directly the atmospheres of these spaces to induce pleasurable sensations in people and facilitate consumption (2009: 94). Similarly, Böhme signals the 'increasing aestheticization of reality' (1993), where we find the everyday making of atmospheres through the aesthetic work of multiple objects (like stage sets, advertising, landscapes, cosmetics, gardens, music, art, and so on) with the sentient or observer subject.

Within this growing conditioning of the air, atmospheres are becoming objects of concern for security. Based on Sloterdijk's spherology, Klauser (2010) proposes that we think about the efforts to develop an urban security agenda as an entanglement of practices, technologies and architectures of policing, surveillance and enclosure that are not only oriented to the ground but also increasingly to the air. From this view, security is becoming an atmosphere formation force, splintering the urban volume in multiple psycho-immunological spheres of protection. With the unfolding of drones and everyday security technologies, Peter Adey (2014) speculates that security becomes more alive, encompassing and immersive, registering and resembling the sensibilities of the sensing bodies in the city. Feelings of greater 'security', 'tranquillity' or 'hospitality' are intended to be engineered and contained atmospherically through the arrangement of surveillance technologies, posters, air condition, music, etc. providing new forms of sensing and controlling (Adey et al. 2013). Therefore, in the discussion of the military nature of vertical technologies for security, there is a need to turn our attention to the intervention of micro-climates through the affective relationships between the sensorial presence of these technologies and the ambiguous and diffused feelings that they may produce in everyday life.

Following this literature on the – always partial and fragile – modes of creating self-sealed atmospheres, we believe that aerial surveillance technologies are used to try to generate 'a state of being immersed in a psycho-immunological sphere of protection' (Klauser 2010: 327). Here we do not emphasize on how individuals are disciplined and/or controlled, but instead we demonstrate how the ambiguous aerial intervention activates sensations and forms of sensibility, politically and affectively configuring urban life. Following Rancière (2000), we understand politics as an ontological operation that defines the sensible, that is, what is visible and thinkable, what can be spoken and what is unspeakable or noise. But this 'partition of the sensible' (2000: 12) may operate under a regime that Rancière calls *police* in which an effort is made to distribute functions and capacities, the public and the private, that which can be perceived and named. In this sense, we will show how these aerial surveillance technologies seek to provoke specific affective atmospheres, trying to reconfigure the city's sensible distribution.

At the same time, we focus on the resistance to those efforts to design and condition atmospheres of security. The situational nature of affective atmospheres, which are constantly being built and becoming-with, requires that we examine the surveillance situations as moments in dispute and negotiation. As Edensor and Sumartojo (2015) suggest, the enfolding of an atmosphere is always conditioned by social, historical, cultural contexts as well as the personal background and trajectories of each body. Thus, rather than considering the entities absorbed or immersed in an atmosphere as passive and uncritically actors with no agency, they actively constitute their own sensory experience. They can resist, modify and charge the atmosphere with unwanted or unforeseeable tones or sensations for their designers. Therefore, is relevant to show how an atmosphere can be felted and experienced in unexpected ways by different sensing bodies.

On an empirical level, this kind of atmospheric intervention is examined using the example of the municipality of Las Condes and its increasingly introduction of sensitive and aerial technologies to fighting crime. Here we propose to understand these surveillance air balloons and drones as a way of affective atmospheres creation or air design in the sense that these security technologies modify the mood and sensibility of inhabitants. Their presence in the sky, sensing and registering urban spheres, affect how bodies feel, interact and lives in the urban space. In this sense, we wanted to explore not just what people feel about these surveillance aerial systems but also 'how they act as sensors working on the human body and generate affects in human bodies.' (Lupton 2017: 8).

This chapter is based on two periods of fieldwork. The first was conducted in 2015 and focused on aerostatic balloons, and the other took place in 2017 and was centred on the use of drones. We conducted approximately 20 interviews with key stakeholders such as municipal officers, council members who supported and opposed the use of these technologies, members of social organizations, attorneys, residents and others. In addition, ethnographic work was carried out in the urban sites where these balloons and drones were situated. We went on guided walks and had conversations with residents and visited the mobile operation centres for these technologies. Finally, the study includes a thorough review of secondary documents, including media coverage of the controversies and legal and administrative documents that were generated through the introduction and judicialization of these technologies.

THE CLIMATE OF INSECURITY AND SURVEILLANCE TECHNOLOGIES IN LAS CONDES

Although Chile has historically reported some of the lowest homicide and victimization rates in the region, a feeling of insecurity and fear has intensified over the past few years. This sensation is constantly mentioned in public opinion surveys, which suggest that people believe that crime is rising and public security appears as one of the key concerns of the population (CEP 2017). This climate of insecurity has been particularly present in the municipality of Las Condes, which is one of the wealthiest in the nation. A series of high-impact crimes took place in 2014, including ATM, jewellery store and vehicle robberies and two explosions in metro stations. City council members and residents staged *cacerolazos* – protests during which participants bang on pots and pans – and called for specific measures to be implemented to win the 'war on crime'. This feeling calls into question the low crime statistics that had been reported in the municipality at the time. Some believed that crime reporting did not manage to capture the 'real' level of criminality in the area and in the country in general due to factors such as under-reporting of crimes. For others, such as Las Condes Mayor Francisco de la Maza, citizens' fear was driven by high-impact news coverage that generated a sensation that was different from the 'reality' of crime in the municipality (Las Condes Municipal Council 2014a: 10).

In response to these events, the Municipality of Las Condes introduced a series of 'technological solutions' that would be categorized as innovative and smart in order to ensure complete, flexible surveillance of the urban space and thus reduce criminality in the area. These have included the deployment of a video surveillance system based on aerostatic balloons, algorithm-based camera control systems, facial recognition and license plate detection, citizen security app SOSAFE, panic buttons and anti-carjacking systems, lenses with integrated video cameras for guards and most recently the use of drones that provide 'personalized warnings' in public squares.

In this paper, we focus on the transnational travel and adoption of the balloons and drones for video surveillance in the municipality. Rather than cantering the discussion on the effectiveness of these aerial technologies when it comes to detecting and reducing crime or the legal aspect of the violation of privacy, our intention here is to reflect on how these technologies intervene in the urban sensibilities. We argue that these technologies have a capacity beyond that of detecting, recording and discouraging crime, an 'affective capacity' to condition atmospheres of security among residents.

Aerostatic balloons

Aerostatic surveillance balloons (for a more complete analysis, see Tironi and Valderrama 2016), were presented in September 2014 as one of the most important smart innovations of the municipality of Las Condes. Former mayor Francisco de la Maza, proposed that these 'high technology aerial cameras' be purchased as they were successfully being implemented in the university town of College Station, Texas. He argued that if the municipality had two or three of these cameras 'nearly the entire municipality of Las Condes could be surveilled' right down 'to the size of an ant' (Las Condes Municipal Council 2014b: 9). In response to this proposal, a service commission travelled to Texas to learn about the scope and characteristics of the surveillance system.

The Skystar 180 tactical aerostatic system was developed by the Israeli firm RT Aerostats, which was founded by a retired colonel who had served in Beirut and Gaza named Rami Shmueli. The device consists of a helium balloon measuring 5.7 meters in diameter that can fly up to 300 meters. A video camera with night vision that can swivel 360° degrees is hung from the device, allowing someone up to 5 kilometers away to be observed. The elements are connected by an electrical cable to a compact trailer, and the set is operated from land by two or three agents in a van or enclosure near the trailer. The corporate brochure describes the device as the perfect tool for surveilling fixed sites such as military bases, temporary military camps, strategic facilities and borders where there are high risks of hostility. While the balloons were initially designed for military use and were deployed on the Gaza Strip and more recently on the US–Mexico border, the company has expanded its scope, selling the military intelligence system to local police departments such as the College Station traffic control unit and to security services for massive events such as Rio de Janeiro's Carnival or the 2015 Climate Change convention in Paris.

After learning about the technology in College Station, the Las Condes service commission returned to Chile convinced that they should buy it. In order to bring the balloons to the Chilean context, they sought to erase or minimize the military origins of the technology, invoking it as a global, civilized tool that had been adapted for Santiago's urban context. In interviews and news pieces, the mayor, councillors and municipal directors constantly emphasized the balloons' capacity to capture evidence of crimes and to have a 'dissuasive effect' on criminal behaviour and drug trafficking when criminals recognize that they are under the gaze of the camera. In addition, it was stressed that the balloons would provide more dynamism and flexibility in surveillance and management of the public space, covering a greater visual radius. This would eliminate the need to install many fixed cameras and would decrease oversight costs, identifying broken pipes or traffic lights, crowds of people or traffic problems more quickly. Moreover, the balloons would be described as ideal for the physiognomy of the municipality because of the topography of the hills and considerable variations in altitude, which would eliminate the possibility of using traditional short-distance fixed cameras. It was argued that the terrain necessitated an aerial, vertical vision with greater range for city management.

Also, efforts were made during the negotiations to downplay the military-Israeli roots of the equipment and 'Chileanize' it, creating an alliance between RT Aerostats and the Chilean security technologies firm Global Systems, transferring knowledge and technical capacities for the use of the technology. The military intelligence functions of the balloons were removed from the bidding terms, and the equipment was described as a 'surveillance and traffic control system', and part of the financing was taken from the municipality's transit department.

Once the bid was awarded in May 2015, the Municipality of Las Condes established a rental contract with the company Global Systems for two balloons, one mobile and one fixed, and delegated their operation and maintenance to Global Systems. The importation of a foreign technology involved lack of knowledge of the device's surveillance capacities and possibilities, which meant that trainers had to travel from Israel for two months to prepare the Chilean staff behind the balloons. Two Global Systems staff members were assigned to five or six hour shifts for each balloon. They shared administrative tasks such as recording events, controlling the balloon's height, monitoring the wind and controlling the camera using a joystick.[2]

FIG. 2.1 Surveillance balloon in Las Condes

In regard to the experience of the balloon operators, surveillance is never complete or so 'intelligent' because there are no analytics or sophisticated algorithms for interpreting the images. As such, the criteria of the operators when controlling the joystick regarding what to look at and focus on become very important. Wind, climate, geographic conditions and the restrictions set by the General Civil Aeronautics Directorate or DGAC regarding maximum heights would also be important conditions for the surveillance system's capacities. For example, some of the main obstacles to visibility were the force of the wind, tree tops and high buildings, the latter generating blind spots that could not be accessed (field notes from 26 October 2015). According to one municipal director, the cameras had to follow roadways 'but it is very hard to find something on a roadway because everything is moving and the camera is moving' (Director, Municipality of Las Condes). In fact, the operators interviewed told us that they had not detected any ongoing crimes, just traffic accidents, couples having sex in public and 3-7s (people behaving suspiciously). The balloon operators believe that the devices do not reduce crime definitively, but just displace it: 'The fact that the balloon is there and the bad guys see it, persuades. I personally feel like they just go someplace where there are no cameras.' (Operator 1, Global Systems). The balloons are thus catalogued as 'just another complement' to other municipal safety policies, which the employees believe were already quite good.

Drones

The introduction of drones for video surveillance in Las Condes did not emerge as a result of a decision made at the top of the municipality's administration as was the case with the balloons, but through a proposal made by a municipal worker. A former police officer and municipal inspector from the Las Condes Security Direction was a big fan of drones and had a great deal of experience using them recreationally. Connecting his hobby to his policing of the municipality, he began to draft a proposal for using drones in public safety work. In January 2017, after word got out that the municipality of Providencia was thinking about using a drone system, the proposal began to gain traction in the mayoral administration of Joaquín Lavín. The idea was discussed on two occasions by the Municipal Council. In contrast to the case of surveillance balloons where a large amount of money was spent without an assessment of their efficiency, the council members unanimous support a 'pilot project' of drones for surveillance with an initial period of evaluation and testing.

Following a public bidding process, in March 2017 the Las Condes Municipality purchased two DJI MATRICE 600 PRO drones to the DroneStore (Zalaquett y Avendaño Ltda.), the Chilean authorized DJI dealer. Da-Jiang Innovations (DJI) is a Chinese company founded in 2006 and based in Shenzhen, widely considered China's Silicon Valley. This company has pushed the design of drones for non-military purposes such as film making, agriculture, security, search and rescue, energy infrastructure and recreational uses, becoming the world leader in the civilian drone industry. Specifically, the Matrice model was designed for industrial applications. It weighs around 9 kilos, and has an emergency parachute and a modular design that makes it easy to mount additional modules. It can travel at a maximum speed of 65 km/h and can fly autonomously for up to 32 minutes. he system also have a DJI Zenmuse Z30 camera weighing 549 grams with an optical zoom of at least 30x and digital zoom of at least 6x, which allowed for a broad range of vision.

The municipality decided to train internally the staff required to manage the new technology. The municipal inspector who contributed to the process of adopting the drones agreed to train seven operators (including five municipal inspectors) on the aerial technology. Three of these employees would go on to form part of the Municipal Aerial Surveillance Brigade, which became responsible for drone operation to support Public Security work. The Brigade's work began in April 2017, initially supporting the 'Vacation Phone' plan which consists of 'taking care of' residents' homes when they were on vacation. However, the focus quickly changed because, as the municipality explained, 'It was very difficult to take care of them or know if something happened, because we were only looking from outside of the gate, so we could only know whether or not someone had broken the gate or opened a window' (Las Condes Public Security Direction). Furthermore, the regulations regarding drone use in urban space establish that in order to surveil homes, each property owner would have to submit a notarized letter to the municipality authorizing the drones to fly over their house. This limiting factor (there could be 2,000 homes assigned to a single flight) caused the municipality to change their focus to surveillance of public squares, parks and public spaces. As a council member stated, 'The purpose of the drones ended up being the squares… there was a lot of alcohol and drug use in certain squares' (Council Member A, Las Condes). The devices became a tool for surveilling and patrolling the 15 plazas regarding which the most complaints for drug trafficking and alcohol abuse focused. The sophisticated cameras that were mounted on the drones allowed them to obtain evidence that could be used in police or prosecutor's office investigations.

The purpose of the drones' use was not the only element to undergo changes. Once introduced in Las Condes, the devices acquired new 'Chilean-style' functionalities. As one member of the brigade said, a drone is 'like a tailor-made suit' to which one can add elements in order to respond to certain requests or needs. First, in response to an announcement made by the mayor on social media, drones were equipped with speakers connected to a radio so that the operator (municipal inspector) could interact with the people who were committing crimes or required assistance. Another drone was subsequently outfitted with special LED lights for night monitoring (field notes from 13 November 2017). For the winter of 2018 a thermal camera was added to one of the drones to monitor and sanction the use of chimneys on days of high environmental pollution. The drones were thus catalogued as 'Chilean' and unique, manifesting an intervention in their design and functionalities.

The implementation of the drones was accompanied by a strong municipal communications plan to legitimate the benefits of their use. The mayor himself used Twitter to defend the measure, publishing images and videos, directly addressing questions and criticism posed by residents who were opposed to the technology. The municipality claimed that the drones had increased surveillance and optimized municipal resources, becoming more effective than a guard and more precise, flexible and inexpensive than the surveillance balloons. The media exposure of the drones was such that they were included in a local military parade.

FIG. 2.2 Military parade with drones

FIG. 2.3 Drone assembly and aerial view

The daily use of the drones is as follows: The drones are launched from five closed areas that are agreed to by the municipality and the DGAC. An operations centre is installed in each of those areas, and the drones are assembled there. Operators review the flight requirements such as battery loads, ensure that the trip memory of the drone is restarted and verify that the weather conditions are optimal. Drones are not used if it is raining or windy. They can still fly but use more energy and thus have a shorter autonomous flight time. The flight route varies but cannot exceed 500 meters from the departure area or last more than 32 minutes (battery life). The devices' actual use depends on the mission that is to be completed for that day. Specific requests submitted by the Investigation Police (PDI) require the drones to be as unobtrusive as possible, identifying the suspect and hiding their lights so that the suspects' behaviour does not change (field notes from 13 November 2017). By contrast, patrolling of public plazas to discourage people from committing crimes involves making the drone's presence known. The operators may turn on the lights or interact through the speakers in these cases. One of the drone operators said that 'often just placing the drone over the plaza makes the people causing trouble leave' (Revista Drone Chile 2017: 17). This is indicative, again, of the importance of the presence/absence of this kind of technologies in the urban sky, an issue that we will further explore in the next section.

CONDITIONING ATMOSPHERES OF SECURITY IN LAS CONDES

The analysis of the incorporation of these two technologies in the municipality of Las Condes shows how the purposes of the surveillance systems were reconfigured as they travel to Chile and were inserted into the urban space. Efforts were made to erase the military origins of the drones or balloons by trying to 'Chileanize' the technologies and give them new applications. But at a deeper level, and based on the discourses of those responsible for them, their capacities would go further than detecting or discouraging crime. They would also have a less visible or publicly recognized affective capacity. The municipality is aware that both the drones and balloons are not only a technical solution, but also an instrument that intervenes in and reconfigures the dominant 'climate of insecurity', which is associated with feelings of fear and anguish on the part of residents. For example, the municipality's Security Direction representative stated:

> Las Condes is the municipality in which crime has fallen the most over the course of this year, but people continue to feel fear. The fear that people feel does not reflect reality. Today people can say, "Yeah, the numbers are down but I am still afraid and I know there is crime because I see it." And that is a reality. It is a highly subjective matter because it is a feeling, and it is an enormous challenge to address. (Reyes 2017)

It has become necessary to try to manage and shape residents' feelings. Decreasing fear is not just a matter of operations, but is mainly sensible and environmental. This has led officials to seek out ways of managing people's feelings, combatting fear, anxiety or panic. It is not only important to manage the issue of crime using functional instruments or declaring decreases in crime rates. It also becomes necessary to manage the sensations and affective climates around people's security. The solution is not limited to increasing the number of security agents or putting more fixed cameras on corners. It involves creating secure atmospheres and making people feel that they are living in a sphere of constant protection and care.

Along this line, the Las Condes Public Security Direction has implemented various initiatives in public spaces in an effort to increase the sensation of security, such as lighting streets, erasing graffiti and installing home alarms. These measures are all meant to decrease the sensation of 'disrepair' or 'lack of protection' of certain neighbourhoods. The introduction of aerial video surveillance technologies come to constitute another step in this atmospheric conditioning agenda. The audible and/or visible presence of drones and balloons above Las Condes and the meanings attached to these technologies connected to their smart nature seek to establish an air design or conditioning of certain affective relationships between the residents and their environments, generating the sensation that they are being 'protected' or 'surveilled' on an ongoing basis. The aerial surveillance technologies are conceived by their proponents as having the ability to trigger perceptions and feelings of security among passers-by. As such, the presence of the drone was considered from the outset as a way of amplifying the presence and power of the municipality in and on the neighbourhoods. 'Some communities have told us that they want a drone to be sent there. In that sense, the drone can be assimilated *by being there*, in the sense of making its presence known.' (Las Condes Safety Direction). Similarly, during our field trips in the communities, some residents (including children) mentioned that the balloons made them feel like they were being observed, which produced a feeling of more security and tranquillity for example when they were walking at night.

These examples show the capacity of these technological devices (balloons and drones) to make some people feel emotions of security. The operations are part of an attempt to decrease crime rates but also to manage affective atmospheres. We see a form of surveillance emerge here that seeks not to internalize the norm through a certain action but to evoke and intervene in the sensations of security of the bodies, assuming that emotionally *affected* bodies can contribute to generating atmospheres or microclimates of greater security.

Excess, violence and ambiguity

The affective capacities of these technologies in regard to conditioning atmospheres are never unidimensional or confined to a single intention of those who seek to produce sensations of security. We identified feeling of displeasure, vulnerability, indifference and even insecurity in some actors, that goes against the sensations of security that were sought, but these sensations nonetheless coexists in urban space despite the intention of the municipal authorities.

An attorney from Las Condes and other residents filed a remedy of protection against the balloons, arguing that their mere presence symbolically generated the same level of displeasure as seeing military officials with machine guns in the street. The balloons' omnipotent and omnipresent observation disrupted their social lives, generating a feeling of vulnerability. He insisted on this:

> You have a military device that was built for war operated by a mayor, not even
> a mayor, by private operatives who are recording a large, unspecified number
> of people, 24 hours a day every day in public and private spaces. It seems
> the closest thing to a Western world nightmare. (Independent attorney)

Activist organizations also filed remedies of protection against the balloons and drones, denouncing the violation of privacy by these aerial technologies and limitations on freedom of movement. The devices' vertical nature simulated 'a combination of the panopticon and the Eye of Sauron' over the city (Opposition D, Derechos Digitales). According to the NGO Derechos Digitales, residents have changed their way of life because of the balloons' proximity. One of the victims had a balloon located 90 meters from her home and said:

I can imagine the clarity with which they can see my bedroom and it gives me chills. I have to keep my windows closed and I can't live the way I used to live because I feel like I am being watched 24 hours a day, seven days a week. (Garay 2015)

These descriptions seek to emphasize the negative effects of the presence and over-surveillance of these technologies, making visible the affective states of vulnerability and precarity that these devices would activate in the municipality through their mere presence in the sky. The efforts to 'militarize public safety' are also criticized in an attempt to stop the propagation of these aerial tools in other spaces.

What we could call the "pacification" or "civilization" of military equipment does not have to do with changing its name. It has to do with the disproportionate use of force.... No matter how dangerous a neighbourhood may be, you don't go in like Rambo with a machine gun firing or tank. You have to react proportionally. This is the same with the balloons. You can paint it, you can civilize it... the problem is not so much its appearance but what it is. (Opposition C, Corporación Fundamental)

A sort of military ontology is manifested that re-emerges despite the municipality's attempts to whitewash the military tints of the technologies. In addition, residents say that the technologies may inhibit criminals' actions but they may also affect the behaviours of residents in the public space because they know they are always being watched.

If you know that they may be watching you, you stop doing certain things... if I know that I am in a radius in which a drone might be surveilling me, I will behave in the way in which the drone wants me to behave. (Opposition E, Fundación Datos Protegidos)

These surveillance technologies are again ascribed a capacity for generating an affective atmosphere in their radius of vision – which is indeterminate and dynamic, changing both conducts and sensations by making the presence of these technologies visual or audible. When we asked to activist organizations about how they interpreted the adoption of these devices, some said that they were sensationalist measures 'showier than effective' (Opposition F, Derechos Digitales) because they mainly serve 'to provide the feeling that something is being done about crime' (Opposition E, Fundación Datos Protegidos). If local authorities managed to decrease crime rates, they would not have an impact for people because they would be guided more by perceptions and sensations. They thus felt that the balloons and drones were highly demonstrative technologies designed to establish a *presence* in the public space and win votes for local officials whether or not they actually reduced or displaced crime. Despite these arguments, the remedies of protection against the technologies' use have been dismissed and their operation has continued.

Parallel to the public debate of these legal remedies of protection, in our visits to Las Condes we find a multiplicity of sensations that complicate the affections that were sought to activate in the population. The residents stated that the balloons or drones did not necessarily provide security and often made them feel like they were being 'tattled on', 'as if the devil were watching'. But the opinion that was repeated most frequently in our ethnographic visits regarding the placement of the balloons and drones was that crime had continued, showing a certain indifference to their presence. 'Everything is still the same', was one of the phrases most frequently uttered by the residents of the Colón Oriente area, suggesting that drug trafficking and crime continued to take place even with the presence of the balloon: 'The people who were committing crimes were afraid in the beginning, but after a while they got used to them' (Resident from the Colón Oriente). Furthermore, due to the daily coexistence with these technologies in the sky, people demonstrated forms of situated knowledge (Haraway 1988), recognizing certain frictions, fragilities and problems that the technologies experienced in their contexts of operation. For example, some residents pointed to blind spots, mainly the tree tops that blocked their view, or technical limitations like helium charge or battery life, gusts of wind and the height restrictions that they had to follow. Others residents criticized the discriminatory capacity of these technologies, saying that both the drones and the balloons were there 'to protect the rich', speculating on where their cameras are focused. This manifests the asymmetric partition of the sensible. The position of these aerial technologies speaks of a vertically defined distribution of feelings in the urban volume that establishes certain neighbourhoods and squares as more 'dangerous', 'insecure' or 'necessary to fly over' than others, thus reproducing socioeconomic differences and accentuating processes of stigmatization and criminalization. In sum, the multiplicity of micro-climates is not represented in public debates or even imagined by those responsible for these aerial devices, who do not consider the performativity of their located and sensitive presences.

CONCLUSION

In this chapter, we have shown how the introduction of aerial surveillance technologies involves multi-sitedness relations, strategies and re-designs, both discursive and material. In the two cases analysed here, we can see an attempt to 'de-militarize' and 'de-politicize' these vertical technologies, performing them as 'civilized' tools suitable for the context of Las Condes, or even 'Chileanized' despite their transnational origins. The justification of the vertical regime of surveillance established by the municipality of Las Condes has been based on the supposed efficiency and greater capacity to surveil and identify 'suspicious' or 'conflictive' behaviours and spaces. However, we have tried to show that these technologies are not exclusively deployed for detecting or discouraging criminal acts, but also to intervene in citizen's atmospheres of security.

During our research, we were able to observe how drones and balloons are used to try to activate a governmentality based on sensations, that is, to condition and produce micro-climates of security in the population. In response to the misalignment between the quantification of crime and the way the population feels, the people who promote these technologies use them not only as a tool for conduct criminal conducts, but also to affect, intervene in and conduct citizen perceptions and sensations. As such, the devices analysed here are not only handled as technical instruments, but also as mechanisms for installing micro-spheres of psycho-immunological protection in the city (Sloterdijk

2009, 2016; Klauser 2010). Or, to cite Rancière (2000), these technologies are mobilized to reconfigure the politics of the sensible, that is, seeking to impact the 'partition of the sensible', trying to regulate the orders of the visible, the audible, utterable, and doable. Thinking about drones and balloons as the inscription of a specific politics of the sensible – which for Rancière is the reduction of the multiplicity of the idea of consensus and normalization – implies recognizing the ontological orders that these devices seek to install, influencing ways of sensing and being in the city.

If there is a tendency to disassociate the human as a sentient entity from technologies as a simple passive reflection of human will, in this chapter we have tried to demonstrate the ways in which these technologies affects the urban environment in affective terms. In other words, our analysis allows us to situate the discussion regarding security technologies beyond our understanding of them as tools for detecting a reality 'out there' to be disciplined and modulated as well as a way of deploying a vertical politics of affects that reconfigure ways of feeling, living and inhabiting the urban space.

However, it is important to note that atmospheres are always fragile and ambiguous, producing themselves in an always vague and situated manner, often indifferent to efforts to design and control them at will. The intended microclimate on the part of the municipality of Las Condes inevitably coexists with varied sensations that exceeds their programme. Many residents expressed emotions that crack open the possibility of conditioning safer atmospheres, experiencing at times displeasure, violence, discrimination or indifference. The municipality's goal of allowing residents to artificially breathe security is situated in a territory of excesses and disputes, exceeding all manner of programming. Officials can use drones and balloons to try to control the types of affects and atmospheres that are experienced in the municipality, but in their entangle-ments and frictions with their surroundings, these devices have the potential to exceed the intentions and wills of their operators (Simondon 1989), perform-ing other atmospheres and modes of feeling. In this sense, the emotions and affective atmospheres produced by the drones and balloons do not depend on their intrinsic or objective qualities, but the different agencies involved. In this sense, the bodies do not only feel the qualities of the atmospheres produced by the drones and balloons differently – they also often act in unanticipated, recalcitrant manners, complicating the ways in which agents try to condition/control the urban space.

In this chapter, we sought to recognize the importance of studying the operations of atmospheric conditioning introduced by aerial surveillance technologies and the redefinitions that this suggests for surveillance and control practices in Latin American cities (Arteaga Botello 2016). We also analysed the ways in which these atmospheres are rearranged in the process of being activated by different bodies situated in specific socio-material contexts. In this sense, far from analysing the 'security' of these technologies as a technical effect of increasing the capacity for observation and data collection, we have tried to understand it as an event that emerges from the entanglement of bodies, varied climatic forces, materialities and sensations.

NOTES

1 For example, the municipality of Las Condes awarded a prize for innovation at a seminar on Smart Cities in 2017 for the introduction of advanced technologies like the drones.

2 All of the staff assigned to monitoring the cameras were women because the spokespeople said that they would be less voyeuristic than men.

REFERENCES

Adey, P. (2010). Vertical Security in the Megacity: Legibility, Mobility and Aerial Politics. *Theory, Culture & Society* 27(6): 51–67.

—— (2014). Security Atmospheres or the Crystallization of Worlds. *Environment and Planning D: Society and Space* 32(5): 834–851.

Adey, P., Brayer, L., Masson, D., Murphy, P., Simpson, P., and Tixier, N. (2013). 'Pour votre tranquillité': Ambiance, Atmosphere, and Surveillance. *Geoforum* 49: 299–309.

Anderson, B. (2009). Affective Atmospheres. *Emotion, Space and Society* 2(2): 77–81.

Arteaga Botello, N. (2016). Política de la verticalidad: drones, territorio y población en América Latina. *Región y sociedad* 28(65): 263–292.

Ash, J., and Anderson, B. (2015). Atmospheric Methods. In *Non-Representational Methodologies*. Routledge, pp. 44–61.

Bissell, D. (2010). Passenger Mobilities: Affective Atmospheres and the Sociality of Public Transport. *Environment and Planning D: Society and Space* 28(2): 270–289.

Böhme, G. (1993). Atmosphere as the Fundamental Concept of a New Aesthetics. *Thesis eleven* 36(1): 113–126.

Las Condes Municipal Council (2014a, 2 October). Regular Session No. 832. *Las Condes*. <https://www.lascondes.cl/descargas/transparencia/alcalde_consejo/actas/secciones_ordinaria/2014/ORD_N_832_02_OCTUBRE_2014.pdf>.

—— (2014b, 25 September). Regular Session No. 831. *Las Condes*. <https://www.lascondes.cl/descargas/transparencia/alcalde_consejo/actas/secciones_ordinaria/2014/ORD_N_831_25_SEPTIEMBRE_2014.pdf>.

Edensor, T., and Sumartojo, S. (2015). Designing Atmospheres: Introduction to Special Issue. *Visual Communication* 14(3): 251–265.

Ellis, D., Tucker, I., and Harper, D. (2013). The Affective Atmospheres of Surveillance. *Theory & Psychology* 23(6): 716–731.

Garay, V. (2015). Organizaciones interponen recurso de protección contra los globos de vigilancia de Las Condes y Lo Barnechea. ONG Derechos Digitales. <https://www.derechosdigitales.org/9331/recurso-de-proteccion-contra-los-globos-de-vigilancia-en-las-condes-y-lo-barnechea/>.

Graham, S. (2011). *Cities under Siege: The New Military Urbanism*. New York: Verso.

—— (2016). *Vertical: The City from Satellites to Bunkers*. New York: Verso.

Graham, S., and Hewitt, L. (2013). Getting off the Ground: On the Politics of Urban Verticality. *Progress in Human Geography* 37(1): 72–92.

Haraway, D. (1988). Situated Knowledges: The Science Question in Feminism and the Privilege of Partial Perspective. *Feminist Studies* 14(3): 575–599.

Ingold, T. (2012). The Atmosphere. *Chiasmi International* 14: 75–87.

Klauser, F. R. (2010). Splintering Spheres of Security: Peter Sloterdijk and the Contemporary Fortress City. *Environment and Planning D: Society and Space* 28(2): 326–340.

Lupton, D. (2017). How Does Health Feel? Towards Research on the Affective Atmospheres of Digital Health. *Digital Health* 3. <https://doi.org/10.1177/2055207617701276>.

McCormack, D. P. (2008). Engineering Affective Atmospheres on the Moving Geographies of the 1897 Andrée Expedition. *cultural geographies* 15(4): 413–430.

—— (2014). Atmospheric Things and Circumstantial Excursions. *cultural geographies* 21(4): 605–625.

Merriman, P. (2016). Mobility Infrastructures: Modern Visions, Affective Environments and the Problem of Car Parking. *Mobilities* 11(1): 83–98.

Rancière, J. (2000). *La partage du sensible: esthétique et politique*. La fabrique éditions.

Revista Drone Chile (2017). Drones en tareas de seguridad y vigilancia. < http://www.revistadronechile.com/revista-digital/>.

Reyes, C. (2017). Javiera Benítez, la socióloga a cargo de enfrentar la delincuencia en Las Condes: 'La gente sigue sintiendo temor'. El Mercurio. <http://www.emol.com/noticias/Nacional/2017/08/02/869274/Javiera-Benitez-la-sociologa-a-cargo-de-enfrentar-la-delincuencia-en-Las-Condes-La-gente-sigue-sintiendo-temor.html>.

Sloterdijk, P. (2009). *Terror from the Air.* Los Angeles, CA: Semiotext(e).

—— (2011). *Bubbles, Spheres Volume I: Microspherology.* Los Angeles, CA: Semiotext(e).

—— (2016). *Foams, Spheres Volume III: Plural Spherology.* Los Angeles, CA: Semiotext(e).

Simondon, G. (1989). *Du mode d'existence des objets techniques.* Paris: Aubier.

Simpson, P. (2017). A Sense of the Cycling Environment: Felt Experiences of Infrastructure and Atmospheres. *Environment and Planning A: Economy and Space* 49(2): 426–447.

Stewart, K. (2011). Atmospheric Attunements. *Environment and Planning D: Society and Space* 29(3): 445–453.

Tironi, M., and Palacios, R. (2016). Affects and Urban Infrastructures: Researching Users' Daily Experiences of Santiago de Chile's Transport System. *Emotion, Space and Society* 21: 41–49.

Tironi, M., and Valderrama, M. (2016). Urbanisme militarisé et situation cosmopolitique. Le cas des ballons aérostatiques de surveillance à Santiago du Chili. *Revue d'anthropologie des connaissances* 10(3): 433–470. < https://www.cairn.info/resume. php?ID_ARTICLE=RAC_032_0433>.

Thrift, N. (2004). Intensities of Feeling: Towards a Spatial Politics of Affect. *Geografiska Annaler* 86B(1): 57–78.

Weizman, E. (2002). The Politics of Verticality. Open Democracy. < https://www. opendemocracy.net/ecology-politicsverticality/article_801.jsp>.

3

SMART CITIES, SMART BORDERS: SENSING NETWORKS AND SECURITY IN THE URBAN SPACE

Ilia Antenucci

INTRODUCTION

In the outskirts of Kolkata, West Bengal, a satellite township called Rajarhat New Town is being transformed into a smart city, as part of the '100 Smart Cities' programme launched by the Indian government in 2015. The township was originally designed, about thirty years ago, as a Special Economic Zone (SEZ) for the IT industry but resulted into a paradoxical space where corporate enclaves and slums, upscale hotels and unfinished constructions uneasily coexist. The projects for New Town reiterate the narrative, crafted by major commercial players, of smart cities as smoothly interconnected systems, and promise that the extensive distribution of computing technologies will turn this urban purgatory into an efficient and harmonic environment. This chapter deconstructs this storyline and draws attention to the ways in which processes of digitalization entail the distribution of border technologies across the urban space. I also discuss how these bordering processes might be constitutive of distinct politics of knowledge and aesthetic, as well as of new techniques of security and urban government.

In her work on the introduction of biometric borders in the context of post 9/11 'war on terror', Louise Amoore (2006) explains how these become ubiquitous and bring risk profiling techniques into every realm of social life. Smart borders are informed by an anticipatory logic that seeks to identify, assess and authorize (or not) individuals in such a way that 'the body itself is inscribed with, and demarcates, a continual crossing of multiple encoded borders – social, legal, gendered, racialized and so on' (2006: 337). More recently, Holger Pötzsch (2015) has described the emergence of a sociotechnical apparatus – what he calls the 'iBorder' – made of biometrics, dataveillance and AI, which generates

> bordering processes that disperse locally as well as across transnational space. In these processes, individuals become objects of governance to be analysed and assessed, but also serve as implicit contributors to the database enabling algorithm-driven mappings of patterns of behaviour and association. (Pötzsch 2015: 23)

In the past few years, studies on the introduction of smart borders have explored how digital technologies and algorithmic calculations are transforming security practices and responses to terrorism and migration movements in Europe and North America (de Goede et al. 2014; Leese 2016). At the same time, scholars have noted that smart borders are increasingly seeping into the city and neighbourhoods (Amoore 2006; Amoore, Marmura and Salter 2008) as part of new military and security paradigms, emerging in the US and UK, which problematize urban life (Graham 2012). However, work remains to be done to chart the specific, situated ways in which smart borders permeate and constitute urban environments, especially in cities outside the US and UK, where the category of military urbanism might not be equally relevant.

At the same time, critiques of smart cities abound, and point to the risks of technocratic governance, surveillance, perpetuation of inequality, or social engineering (Crang and Graham 2007; Halpern et al. 2013; Kitchin and Perng 2016). Again, Stephen Graham (2012) has pointed to the ways in which the digitalization of urban life spreads and normalizes technologies that were developed for military purposes. Overall, this critical literature has hardly ever crossed over to a more punctual and comprehensive discussion on borders in smart cities. Borders have a polysemic, heterogeneous and dynamic nature (Balibar

2002; Mezzadra and Neilson 2013). They work along, within and beyond the territorial limits of state as instruments of differential inclusion, as well as exclusion, which continuously filter and stratify the circulation of people and things. This chapter illustrates how, by creating a connected and sentient environment (Crang and Graham 2014; Thrift 2014; Gabrys 2016), digital infrastructures also perform and distribute border functions across the urban space.

In the making of smart cities, Rob Kitchin and Sung-Yueh Perng (2016) note, code becomes embedded in urban infrastructures, services and utilities, and government practices, in modalities that are always contingent and situated. Cities under digitalization can be seen as a patchwork of millions sociotechnical assemblages where code is, at once, produced through and producing multiple sets of relations with other material and discursive elements (Kitchin and Perng 2016; Dourish 2016). Empirical researches confirm how diverse and complex these relations can be. For example, Ayona Datta (2017) observes how the strategies to forge new smart citizens in the wake of India's 100 smart cities challenge merge a global imaginary of smart citizenship with the issues and struggles of postcolonial citizenship, resulting in hybrid and vernacular forms of digital engagement in Indian cities. In his work on data-driven urbanism in Delhi, Sandeep Mertia (2017) illustrates how the forms of knowledge production, forms of authority and identities in and about the city are being reconfigured through sensing/computing infrastructures in ways that are contingent and very much affected by contextual factors. The sociotechnical assemblages that compose a smart city have a political significance that demands attention. For this reason, I look at the frictions and barriers that take place around and through these assemblages from the angle of borders. The point here is neither to fetishize the notion of borders, nor to offer a fixed spatial representation of instrumented cities. Rather, looking at urban digitalization through the lens of borders is a way to attend to the distributed, situated and often microscopic relations of power that permeate smart infrastructures.

This chapter is based on the examination of planning documents, direct observation and interviews with informants involved with the process of urban digitalization at various levels. It is organized as follows: The first section explores how popular narratives of smart cities as harmonic, seamless systems have been crafted through a set of assumptions and *topoi*, in accordance with specific commercial strategies. The second section reviews the history of smart developments in New Town, and illustrates how digitalization has in fact taken place through zoning processes. In the third section, I examine the dissemination of border techniques across digitalized infrastructures, objects and apps of common use, and how the promises of smart urban harmony actually turn into the multiplication of points of control and filter in every aspect of urban life. The fourth section investigates how sensing and computing systems reconfigure categories of perception and knowledge, as well as relations, by setting boundaries and filters, and how borders are active at an ontogenetic level. In the conclusions, I situate these analyses in a broader perspective, and argue that processes of digital bordering cannot be classified merely as examples of surveillance or dataveillance. I suggest instead to look at them as infrastructures of preemption and anticipatory government.

Smart city narratives

It can be said that Smart cities of the Future will be smoother, more social, and more open than they are today.

Alexander Vancolen,
Marketing and eMobility Team Leader at Bosch Belgium[1]

Arrows in vivid colours run between skyscrapers, ports, parks and highways. Footages of people using smartphones and tablets flow quickly. Wall-size dashboards show interactive maps, graphics and figures. Smiling testimonials tell stories of success and profess their faith in a digital future. What I am describing is not a commercial video of smart city solutions released by a major provider. It is, virtually, all of them. IBM's Smarter Cities, CISCO's Smart+Connected, Microsoft's City Next, SAP Future Cities, are only some of the products on the growing market of urban digitalization. And while competing against each other to secure contracts with city governments, these and other corporate players have contributed to forge a model of smart city that is, to a large extent, homogeneous.

Their corporate documents and advertising resort to the same imaginary, the same jargon, the same visual style. The key topics in these narratives – efficiency, sustainability, resilience – are perhaps better described as *topoi*, such is the frequency and the uniformity in which they recur. In all these smart city systems, the focus is on 'breaking the silos' between different urban datasets – traffic, waste, pollution, energy, crime, social programmes, healthcare, education etc. – and creating one integrated platform for the analysis of data – a single view of the city. This is achieved by distributing IoT networks across the city, and by running analytics across disparate domains, from sensors and video cameras to social networks.

All these corporate documents present the creation of smart cities as a smooth, harmonic process, based on the assumption that more automation necessarily equals more efficiency, safety and sustainability for all; and that the integration of systems will proceed seamlessly.

Scholars have critically investigated the genesis and evolution of the predominant smart city discourse ad the underpinning commercial strategies. Donald McNeill (2015) demonstrates how the launch of IBM's Smarter Planet campaign in 2008 has signalled a substantial restructuring of the company, which sold its PC division to Lenovo in 2004 with the intention to concentrate its business in the emerging sector of IT consulting. Having identified cities as a high-potential market, IBM started to focus on aggressively promoting its solutions for urban management. Analysing these commercial strategies, Ola Söderström, Till Paasche and Francisco Klauser (2014) suggest that popular narratives of smart cities can be read as a form of 'corporate storytelling'. Drawing on the concept of 'obligatory passage point' (OPP) proposed by Michel Callon, the authors show how IBM has forged discourses 'that presents their smart technologies as the only solution for various urban problems and hence becomes an OPP'. (2014: 310). In 2011, the tech colossus officially registered the term 'smarter cities' as a trademark, while continuing Smarter Planet's powerful advertising strategy, including free consultancy for municipalities, international conferences, research papers, videos, and so on. Across these different outlets, the city is presented as a 'system of systems' – a theme then adopted by some of IBM major competitors, such as Microsoft and Cisco – and broken down into nine 'pillars', which represent the relevant sectors that have to be digitally integrated to optimize urban government. In other words, the city, along with all its issues and components, is translated in the language of data and algorithms (Söderström, Paasche and Klauser 2014: 313). Datafication and automation are associated with a number of beneficial results – transparency, efficiency, cost-effectiveness, inclusiveness, sustainability, safety and so on – up to the point that they become synonyms for better government and liveability. The processes of interconnection of infrastructures, devices, data and management practices are supposed to happen linearly and without frictions, and to be inherently virtuous. It is largely through the articulation between these discursive moves and the considerable economic power of a colossus like IBM, that the mainstream label of smart city has taken shape. As this storyline continues to be echoed among tech companies, consultants, city officers and media, the smart city is uncritically presented as a progressive, and somewhat necessary evolution of the urban condition.

The narratives of smart cities mobilized in New Town Kolkata do not deviate much from the corporate version. On the website of the India Smart Cities Mission – the government programme within which the transformation of New Town is taking place – smart cities are vaguely defined as 'clean and sustainable environments', where 'layers of smartness' are added on comprehensive infrastructural development (Smart Cities Mission, n.d). The list of technological solutions that make a city smart resembles quite closely the dominant commercial models. The city is broken down into relevant components – administrative services, waste management, energy, water, mobility, health and business – that are supposed to be equipped with digital technology and managed via analytics.

The core idea of adding 'layers of smartness' presupposes a linear development process, where technological elements and governmental practices interconnect progressively and without frictions. New Town's municipal authorities have also perpetuated this narrative throughout activities of dissemination and citizen engagement conducted with the help of consultants, such as British company Future Cities Catapult. In the workshops and events organized for the middle class residents of New Town during 2016, participants were educated about the benefits of upcoming digitalization, and invited to contribute ideas as to how to add more smart solutions to pre-selected areas of intervention – water and energy, transports, security, health, administrative services. The outcome of this 'participative' design phase is depicted as a green, harmonic landscape, of which relevant components are provided with sensing technologies and interconnected.

DIGITAL ZONING

In 2015, New Town Kolkata applied for the Smart Cities Challenge, a competition-based funding scheme launched by the Indian Government with the aim to transform 100 cities into digital and sustainable cities, and worth approximately US$ 15 billion overall. Before that, the development of New Town had progressed quite controversially.[2] The township was planned in the early nineties as a Special Economic Zone (SEZ) for the IT industry in the rural area of Rajarhat, in the north-eastern fringes of Kolkata. Strong protests rose as the former ruling Left Front government forcibly expropriated lands from farmers and villagers; thousands faced police brutality, were jailed or killed. In the following years, business parks, gated communities and luxury shopping malls began to rise alongside wastelands, villages and slums. Many of the dispossessed farmers remained in the area, living in informal settlements and taking up precarious, low-paying jobs as domestic workers, security guards, street vendors. Largely driven by speculation, the development of New Town was hampered by the financial crisis of 2008, resulting in a paradoxical urbanscape of unfinished infrastructures, unsold houses, highly securitized enclaves and stray cattle. In 2011, Ananya Roy described the township as 'the ghost town of homegrown neoliberalism, one where the ruins of the suburban middle-class dream are starkly visible' (Roy 2011: 275). Attracted by the low cost of labour and lands, several IT firms such as IBM, Tata Consultancy Services, Wipro and Accenture established branches in New Town, where they run the more basic and menial tasks of the industry such as software beta testing or business process outsourcing (Rossiter 2016). As New Town seemed to be stuck in a condition of suspended development, and disturbingly veering towards urban dystopia (Dey et al. 2013) the Smart City Challenge likely appeared to local authorities and investors as a chance to resurrect the fortunes of the township.

The Smart City Proposal (SCP) for New Town is not much of a consistent document. Developed through negotiations among several public agencies, consultants and economic stakeholders,[3] the proposal revolves around the Pan City Solution, a system of integrated digital infrastructures and software for the management of the city. On one hand, in tune with the standard vision of smart city promoted by IT firms and consultants, the SCP aims to develop a sensing urban environment, where infrastructures – from bus shelters to waste bins, from water meters to light poles – are extensively provided with sensors, GPS trackers and cameras, while several urban services are provided via mobile applications. The data sourced from sensing infrastructures are then integrated, cross-checked and processed via analytics into a single command and control room. At the same time, and quite at odds with its claim for innovation, the plan includes very basic elements of urban development – i.e., sidewalks, public toilets or street lights. Overall, Pan City looks like a sort of vernacular version of mainstream smart city projects, where the effort towards fast digitalization coexists with the need to provide basic infrastructures and services in the area. The contradiction between the aspirations towards a global model of urban development and conditions of widespread poverty, inequality and lack of essential facilities, is crucial to understand how borders intervene in the process of digitalization.

In the first stages of development of New Town, marked by political con-testations and social unrest, the implementation of digital technologies took place behind the walls of upscale private developments protected with security checkpoints, biometric identification, x-ray scan and CCTVs. Within the gates of business districts like Ecospace or Tata's Gitanjali Park, smart infrastruc-tures – high-speed Internet, security software, Building Automations Systems (BAS) that control ventilation, temperature, power systems and water through the IoT – have been running for a few years now. The informal sector is kept out from these enclaves, or only admitted inside as service workforce – clean-ers, guards, gardeners. More in general, a large part of the population of New Town still struggles to access the Internet and digital devices. According to the Internet and Mobile Association of India (IAMAI), India has approximately 450 million Internet users (IAMAI 2019), slightly more than one third of the overall population. But while technology is becoming cheaper and definitely accessible for wide strata of the population, smartphones, laptops, computers and Internet connectivity are still out of reach, at least on regular basis, for households and individuals that live in slums and work precariously in the informal sector. Between the smart world of tech companies, and the life of New Town's urban poor there is a gap of income, education and social agency that persists in the processes of urban digitalization.

At this stage, Pan City is designed as an Area Based Development (ABD). Through a digital citizen polling on the MyGov website, one district of New Town has been selected to be transformed into a smart area, where the new technologies and management systems will first be tested and implemented. The zone identified coincides with Action Areas 1A and 1C, the most densely populated in New Town, the closest to the periphery of Kolkata and to the IT hub of Salt Lake Sector V. In Action Areas 1A and 1C, the implementation of infrastructures is more advanced than in the rest of the township, urbanization appears slightly more consistent, and informal settlements have been largely cleared out. Strategic facilities, like a water treatment plant and the central bus station, are located here, as are some of New Town's most important business sites and landmarks, such as the NKDA headquarter and the monumental Biswa Bangla Gate. Meanwhile, outside the borders of the designated smart zone, large portions of New Town remain deprived of basic services and infrastructures. In Action Area II, just a few miles away, cutting-edge IT campuses are punctuated by informal markets and bustees where running water and sewerage do not reach. The landscape remains similar in the residential towers of Action Area III, a little further east, where seemingly abandoned building sites and the skeletons of unfinished towers stand out among wastelands. Such entanglements of hyper development and deprivation are far from uncommon in most megacities in the country; in fact, they can be seen as a major feature of Indian urbanization (Schindler 2014). The same applies to the increasing securitization of private and public spaces, over the past two decades, that filters the interactions between different urban worlds, while also introducing new forms of exploitation of the informal labour (Gooptu 2013). So far, at least in New Town, digitalization has not reversed these tendencies, but has rather grafted onto them. Smart developments have largely concentrated within clusters of privilege, and access to them has been restricted on the basis of class and labour control.

This overview illustrates how the making of smart New Town Kolkata is taking place through the formation of hubs and enclaves where digital implementations are concentrated. I refer to this process, which is in sharp contrast with narratives of smart cities as seamless, harmonic environments, as digital zoning. As we learn from a rich body of literature, zoning techniques are always infused with political effects and power relations. Much attention has been paid, for example, to the key role played by the creation of Special Economic Zones (SEZs) and logistical corridors in positioning countries like China and India, and South-East Asia more in general, in the global economy and political relations, as well as in transforming forms of accumulation and extraction, labour relations, normative arrangements, and lifestyles (Ong 2006; Easterling 2008; Mezzadra and Neilson 2013). There are no zones without borders; and zoning processes, be they on a larger or smaller scale, are often the occasion where techniques for monitoring and filtering the movements of people and things are tested or recalibrated. The processes of urban zoning have often been associated with the notions of enclavism (Atkinson and Blandy 2005) or enclave urbanism (Angotti 2013), to describe how the creation of gated, securitized compounds for residential, commercial or leisure purposes increasingly marks neoliberal urban developments and rising inequalities between social groups. Many elements of the development of New Town in recent years, including the creation of gated communities and business parks, can be seen as examples of enclavism. However, this category does not exhaust the complexity of the zoning processes that are associated with the smart city projects. Urban digital zones have emerged in multiple, flexible and informal manners, and have produced multifaceted effects. Some of the zones that I described in this section, such as New Town's Area Based Development and SEZs, are formally established via legal acts, while others, i.e. corporate enclaves, are demarcated *de facto*, in informal but no less effective ways, through conspicuous securitization and the restriction of access only to a certain class of citizens. These zoning processes, through which smart infrastructures are being tested and implemented, reflect the patterns of inequality and social hierarchization that have shaped the creation of New Town since the beginning. Rather than connecting the urban environment seamlessly and inclusively, as the smart city narratives promise, the processes of digitalization embed extant socio-spatial borders and produce new ones, which separate and filter the population of New Town along the lines of class and social agency.

UBIQUITOUS BORDERS

Not only are borders traced around digital infrastructures in the making of smart cities; they also become incorporated in a wide range of mundane objects and activities, and therefore ubiquitous across the urban space. The computing systems onto which smart city projects rely are, indeed, built around algorithmic techniques of classification, identification and profiling that are currently in use for the management of national borders, as well as for policing and crime investigation. The smart solutions laid out in the Pan City Solution for New Town disseminate border technologies across every domain of urban administration, from water supply to tax policies, as well as in a number of everyday obvious activities, like getting on a bus or taking out the garbage.

As mentioned in the previous sections, New Town's Area Based Development (ABD) is supposed to be the first step of the proposed smart city. Not dissimilarly from many other smart city projects, the ABD is designed as a space where ideally every house, vehicle, public area and piece of infrastructure is equipped with sensing devices, connected to the urban network, and managed via a single, central platform. According to New Town Smart City Proposal (2016), the urban components that will be integrated in the digital platform include:

- Air pollution monitoring: sensors for air quality monitoring will be installed on light poles and display real time data on LED display boards in strategic locations of the area;
- Smart parking: nine smart parking areas with parking sensors installed in light poles to collect data from the cars. At least four have been introduced

already, in partnership with Indian app Park24x7 – a mobile app that allows users to book in advance and pay for their parking online;[4]

- Sewerage and drainage monitoring: Sensor-based drainage covers will send signal to the control room on the quantity of rainfall in the area and will activate pumps to avoid water logging. More sensors will be installed to monitor sewerage and drainage and transmit the data to the Pan City control room;

- Project Zero – solid waste management: All waste collection vehicles will be equipped with GPS and tracked by the control room. Sensor-based e-bins will be installed in public areas and tracked through Off-Site Real-Time Monitoring (OSRT);

- Smart metering: All conventional meters for water and electricity will be replaced with smart meters. This will allow remote meter reading, monitoring of load profile, monitoring of tampering/pilferage by consumer from the control room. The water distribution lines will be equipped with Supervisory Control and Data Acquisition (SCADA) system, including sensor-based transducers and flow meters;

- Safety and security: CCTV cameras will be set up on light poles for 24/7 surveillance. Real-time video content analysis will be performed in the control room. 2000 intelligent street lights will be installed as well as panic buttons at key points, connected to the control room for emergency response. Drones will monitor civic services such as road conditions, street lights, littering and waste management;

- Health: Telemedicine kiosks will be installed in every block to deliver primary medical services. Healthcare for residents will be managed via mobile apps and a Smart Watch programme supported by volunteers;

- Mobility: Public vehicles including Electric buses, Autos and Totos will be monitored via GPS from the control room, while information on routes and timetable will be available on a mobile app.

The Pan City Control Centre is where data are gathered and visualized to monitor and manage all the critical components of the smart city in a holistic manner. Once processed via analytics, data turn into models and alerts and are displayed on a central dashboard which provides real-time diagnosis of urban components, from traffic congestion to the quality of the air, from water consumption to garbage disposal. In other words, in the planner's vision, the entire city becomes incorporated into a system of non-stop monitoring and risk assessment. What is commonly presented as seamless interconnection, efficiency and transparency in fact disseminates the logic and practices of border management across every domain of urban life, often on a microscopic level. Common utilities and ordinary activities become the vectors of techniques of identification, profiling and scoring. Real-time data on power consumption sent from smart meters are automatically crossed with information on housing occupancy and shared with the police, to detect potential 'illegal' residents. The network of telemedicine kiosks and health-related apps elaborate profiles on both the individual and collective levels of health or diseases in the city. Mobility apps record the itineraries of people across the city, as well as their use of public transport, cars, taxis, of other vehicles. While light poles and bus stands double as surveillance spots, drones provide bird's eye monitoring. As most of these projects are still underway – their implementation outsourced to private partners such as Intel, HP, SAP, Oracle, and the like – or even on paper only, it is too early to assess their effects on urban life. But what matters for the sake of this discussion, is that they already present the logic of the future urban environment. In the Pan City Solution, the narrative of a smoothly interconnected city translates into a landscape of ubiquitous borders. Techniques for scrutinizing and filtering are built into every bit of the urban sensing systems. Increasingly, the interactions between the population and the urban infrastructures and services are mediated by digital identification, and feed processes of algorithmic profiling and modelling.

Social media constitute a further domain of monitoring. From the Smart City Proposal, we learn that the city is negotiating with Abzooba, an Indian company specialized in Artificial Intelligence, about installing Xpresso, the company's proprietary Natural Language Processing (NLP) software, to gather and process data concerning New Town on social media (NKDA 2016: 98). NLP is a specific segment of Artificial Intelligence (AI), which makes it possible for computers to read and understand human language and process large volumes of unstructured data, such as social media content. Xpresso was originally developed to help companies analyse customer feedbacks and improve their commercial strategies accordingly. In the customized version for urban management, Xpresso will help urban authorities exploit large volume of unstructured data, such as social media content, and gain

> [...] a structured bird eye view about different aspects (Police, Transportation, Healthcare, Water, Road etc.) of city and citizen sentiment (positive, negative, neutral) about each of these aspects. (NKDA 2016: 98)

The application runs cognitive bots that are able to translate 'text into context',[5] understand the nuances of human expression and classify the intents of those who write. By generating actionable information, Xpresso provides real-time monitoring as well as an 'early warning system' to anticipate potential problems. When high percentages, temporal or spatial spikes in negative sentiment, such as anger or fear, or large number of complaints on selected topics are registered, the dashboard displays specific alerts. Authorities are able then to 'drill down' to view complaints in detail, and take 'corrective measures' (NKDA 2016: 98). A case study on the Abzooba website describes how Xpresso has been experimented before in the management of urban data.

According to the case study, Xpresso generated several benefits in urban management, including the capability to measure public opinion, make more informed decisions on new policies and better evaluate existing policies; 'safeguard the country's reputation' (*sic*) by monitoring social media conversations, and how these might affect overseas investors and tourists opinion of the country; anticipate disease outbreaks by correlating searches for specific symptoms, and improve disaster response by understanding the situation on the ground; prevent and mitigate potential crisis through 'active listening'; and 'transform security clearance process' by leveraging social media data for 'national security, background investigations, programme integrity, insider threat detection, and more'. Of course, Abzooba is not a pioneer in the field. Opinion mining and sentiment analysis are standard methods for the organization of social media content and related commercial strategies. A number of systems are being developed, not only by IT corporations, but also by academic research groups, to perform real-time sentiment analysis of discrete social media streams, that assess, for example, how urgent specific urban issues are perceived by citizens (Masdeval and Veloso 2015); the spatial distribution of intolerant discourses in Italy, or the community feelings about recovery from earthquake in the city of L'Aquila (Musto et al. 2015); or to monitor, more in general, the 'situation' of specific urban areas that emerge from topics and emotions on social media (Weiler, Grossniklaus and Scholl 2016).

The adoption of a software like Xpresso is also part, I suggest, of the bordering process that are shaping the making of the smart city. As explained earlier in this chapter, access to digital technologies in New Town remains far from universal. A considerable part of the township's population is not able to be active on social media on regular basis, or ever. In this context, monitoring the city and its citizens via social media is a form of pre-selection, or differential inclusion (Mezzadra and Neilson 2013) of the data that are relevant to urban government. In other words, only the voices that can be expressed on digital platforms count as urban data (even if for monitoring purposes only); and only those who provide data count as citizens. The example of Xpresso in New Town subverts the usual understanding of dataveillance. While common concerns are about being tracked, spied and manipulated through our immersion in digital technologies, there are groups of people that are not subject to dataveillance because their socio-economic conditions are below even that. Ned Rossiter (2016) uses the term 'post-population' to describe those who escape algorithmic control on labour or social life but pay the price for this anonymity or 'ungovernability' with extreme precariousness and vulnerable conditions, such as the dispossessed farmers and slum dwellers of Rajarhat. In the making of smart New Town then, social media emerge as the terrain of a twofold filtering process. On one hand, access to social media qualifies citizens. On the other hand, those who count as citizens (in their capacity as data providers) are subject to practices of monitoring and profiling.

The secrecy around the algorithms and code strings that process urban data – from those generated by sensing infrastructures, to social media – can be seen as a further bordering process. In the accessible documents about New

Town there is no mention of the analytics settings employed in the software that run city systems, or of the specific pools of data in use. Most likely, this information belong to the software provider, and are therefore protected by corporate cyber-security. Even city officers and agencies that have to authorize interventions and elaborate policies on the basis of analytics have no access to the raw data, or to the algorithmic settings. The ways in which the profit strategies of software providers and consultants might have informed the sourcing and processing of data; or how biases and specific understandings of social and environmental categories can be silently embedded in the calculative framework – all this is withheld from public discussion and critique. Despite promises of transparency and evidence, the operational core of smart urban management remains opaque and hidden underneath layers of digital barriers, protocols and private agreements that come with the application of smart technologies to cities.

A NEW PARTITION OF THE SENSIBLE: BORDERS AND DIGITAL ONTOGENESIS

The previous sections of this chapter have described how urban digitalization proceeds by establishing borders and zones, and by disseminating border techniques – of monitoring, measurement and filter – across infrastructures and devices of common use. But these bordering processes are active also in the sphere of perception, cognition and relations. In her book *Program Earth*, Jennifer Gabrys (2016) combines the notions of 'concrescence' formulated by Alfred North Whitehead and that of 'concretization', proposed by Gilbert Simondon, to describe how computing environments come into being. Sensing/computing systems, Gabrys claims, are more than assemblages, more than a mere aggregation of sociotechnical elements. In fact, they are able to generate new relations between elements, new forms of connection, expression, knowledge and actions; they have, in this sense, an ontogenetic quality. The making of computing environments is, therefore, a relational process, where computing becomes environmental while at the same time, the environment becomes computational. Gabrys also draws connections between this understanding of the environment and Foucault's notion of *milieu* as the field where security and government operate, and of environmentality 'as a spatial–material distribution and relationality of power through environments, technologies, and ways of life' (Gabrys 2016: 187). Hence, focusing on the borders that emerge from the processes of digitalization is a way to grasp how power relations are articulated across sensing/computing environments. As techniques of monitoring, identification, and profiling become embedded into mundane objects and infrastructure, they define a distinct terrain and distinct trajectories of government.

In his book *The Politics of Aesthetics* (2004), Jacques Rancière argues that any social order is constructed through a specific distribution of the sensible. This concept indicates modes of perception that set the boundaries between what can be seen or not seen, said and not said, heard and not heard, measured and not measured, and ultimately, between what is licit or illicit. Social roles and forms of participation are defined through specific distributions of the sensible which can, at once, include and exclude. In this sense, every social and political system is in the first place an aesthetic regime – where the term 'aesthetic' refers to what is experienced through senses – insofar as it is organized through distinct forms of perception and sensorial relations among humans, objects and nature. While Rancière's own analysis engages in a detailed examination of historical examples of politics of aesthetic, here I appropriate the notion of 'distribution of the sensible' and put it at work in a very different context, to analyse how smart technologies are increasingly performing bordering functions and reconfiguring urban life and government. The distribution of the sensible is, I argue, part of the ontogenetic processes discussed by Gabrys (2016), as changing forms of perception shape the ways in which relations unfold between the various environmental components. Looking at the reconfiguration of the senses and at the creation of new modes of existence that connect humans and things is key to understand how the computing milieu is governed.

How do sensors and analytics produce new distributions of the sensible in the city, and with what effects for the human and non-human elements involved? How is this distribution of the sensible relevant to the production of security and urban government?

When sensing technologies – in their various versions: trackers, beacons, cameras, wearables, smartphones and applications – are applied onto urban components, they enable new modalities of perception and interaction. They remodulate the patterns of attention towards the object, resource, or activity concerned. They can invite and even force attention from users, or, conversely, they might deliberately avoid it, when they are invisible. They signal that a certain component is important in the urban system. They warn that what happens around it is going to be scrutinized and assessed. Whether demanding or rejecting attention from humans, sensors are definitely attentive to selected dynamics, and at the same time, indifferent to others. In doing all this, they reconfigure the order of things, perception, thoughts and action. As described earlier in this chapter, this happens through specific techniques of monitoring and identification. Situations that could previously remain unnoticed, such as the number of people crossing the street at a certain junction, the quantity and quality of particle in the air, the amount of garbage in a bin, become, through the application of sensors, necessary points of application of the urban attention. This attention is political and unfolds simultaneously on interrelated levels. First, it demands the engagement of citizens, which are required to take part into the sensing process, by sending data, remaining aware of the information available, and behaving accordingly. At the same time, it also dictates the modalities in which this interaction can take place: through the mediation of digital devices and platforms. Second, while contributing to the monitoring activity, citizens become objects of scrutinization themselves, through the ubiquitous practices of profiling described before. Third, it marks the specific targets of urban policies and intervention: where there are sensors, there is also government. Fourth, as a whole, sensing networks produce a new map and a new definition of what is to be perceived and lived as a urban system.

The distribution of the sensible continues through analytics processes, where the performances of urban components are algorithmically broken down into factors of normality, deviation and risk, and then re-assembled into predictive models. Here again, the work of algorithms sets out distinct boundaries between what can be seen or not seen, made actionable or not. It is important to pay attention to the modalities in which analytics and modelling render urban elements, determining what is worth paying attention to, what is worth measuring. A significant epistemic move is visible here, as the very practice of measuring becomes the measure of worth itself. In other words, if something is not monitored and measured, if it is not inscribed in the computational grid, it has no worth in the smart urban system. In this sense, algorithms create new regimes of visibility and worth, which are politically charged. At the same time, a new regime of *invisibility* is created, that is the one of code strings and operative systems that process urban data. As noted earlier in this chapter, these crucial components remain largely inaccessible not only to citizens, but also to the city agencies that are expected to act upon data.

To conclude this discussion of the partition of the sensible, I maintain that the ontogenetic power that Gabrys assigns to sensing/computing environments reconfigures the order of the cognitive, aesthetic and relational processes. In other words, borders operate at an ontogenetic level, insofar as the forms of classification and filter that come with extensive datafication are able to reshape the apprehension of reality, and the relations between human and non-human elements. They reconfigure, at once the *milieu* where security and government operate; and the *modalities* through which they operate.

CONCLUSION: BEYOND DATAVEILLANCE

What emerges from the examination of New Town smart projects is an urban landscape where bordering functions – identity verification, biometrics recognition, profiling – are immanent to the development of digital infrastructures. This is evidently in contrast with popular narratives of smart cities as seamless, smoothly interconnected spaces. I have outlined three main dimensions where borders operate. The first considers the processes of digital zoning through which smart technologies are introduced and tested in the urban territory. The second one concerns the fact that practices of identification and filters are pervasively attached to objects, devices and software that are in use for everyday activities. There is, then, an ontogenetic dimension, where forms of measurement and classification enacted by sensing and computing systems are able to reconfigure cognitive categories and relational dynamics. In essence, then, border techniques are active around, across and within the sensing and computing environments, and constitute an extensive infrastructure of data sourcing, identification and profiling. These have been widely documented in literature, along with concerns on their potential political implications. These concerns have been often registered under concepts of surveillance and dataveillance (Kitchin 2014; Tufeckci 2014). Smart cities, David Lyon (2018) argues, bring along the normalization of surveillance, and metaphors like 'the new panopticon' (McMullan 2015) or the 'big brother city' (King 2016) have been mobilized in the media to describe cities governed from dashboards, where data about everyone and everything is gathered all the time and anonymity becomes impossible.

My intention is not to deny that cities are sites where dataveillance is particularly concentrated. I argue nonetheless that dataveillance is not an exhaustive framework for the analysis of data-driven urban governmentality, for two main reasons. First, despite the efforts of smart city planners, dataveillance often fails. The infinite amount of data gathered through sensing infrastructures does not automatically translates into government actions. Data are often dispersed among several different actors (states, municipalities, private firms, academic or non-academic researchers, NGOs, activists, hackers, etc. etc.) which pursue different and often conflicting agendas. This creates zones of opacity. Urban data can be so immense and fragmented that their potential in terms of actual, actionable knowledge remains largely under-exploited. Paradoxically, there might be so much dataveillance, that it makes complete dataveillance impossible. In short, data largely go wasted; or maybe, big data as such is waste, until it is dissected by algorithms, and reassembled in the form of actionable information. This is one of the problems that smart city projects like New Town are trying to address, by creating central control platforms.

But even if dataveillance is applied to the fullest extent, and no data is wasted, it still does not define a logic of urban government. Dataveillance accounts for some important aspects of data-driven environments; it is a disposition (Easterling 2010) of the sociotechnical assemblages we live in. But, as such, dataveillance does not explain how decisions are taken or strategies take form. Against the common emphasis on the *big* of big data, Louise Amoore and

Volha Piotukh (2015) demand attention for the work of *little* analytics in contemporary forms of knowledge production and government. Through specific practices of data ingestion, partitioning and memory, the heterogeneity of life is flattened and reduced to patterns of data that are *tractable* for commercial or security decisions. This is exactly the logic of urban platforms like New Town. These work for urban security not by monitoring more, but by translating what is monitored into models, such as risk alerts, and possible actions. Paradoxically, data scientist and officers in the urban control rooms might be better off with less data, but sharper analytics, than with more data without an algorithmic way through. Dataveillance does not explain new forms of urban government because it keeps the focus on the aspect of watching and on the accumulation of data, while overlooking the specific operations – scraping, skinning, connecting, drawing and, ultimately, modelling – through which algorithms make data actionable and inform decisions.

This chapter has illustrated how smart city planners in New Town seek to forge a system of urban government where, not too differently from what happens at smart borders, algorithmic calculations launched across different sets of urban data provide city officers with profiles of the performances of citizens, transports, traffic, emergency services, weather, resources, pollution, and so on. The analytics chain elaborates these data to create models of future events. In the vision of smart government, these models are the grounds for political and administrative operations. Independently of governmental projects, the same activity of profiling and modelling is undertaken by private actors, such as IoT and software providers, for commercial purposes. My point here is that the border techniques ubiquitously incorporated in urban smart technologies form a pre-emptive apparatus. This is not limited to surveillance functions and frames a specific modality in which urban government is conceived and performed. Benedict Anderson (2010) identifies pre-emption as one of the logics of anticipatory action – together with precaution of preparedness – whose specificity is that it works on undetermined, potential scenarios of the future, and that increasingly defines government in our time. Pre-emptive governance seeks to incorporate not the probability, but the imagination of future possibilities, into security procedures (De Goede 2012; Amoore 2013). Security, then, has become speculative (De Goede et al. 2014); algorithms do not predict, but think through data and build models of the future upon which present action can be taken. From this perspective, borders built within sensing/computing technologies appear as the (sometimes involuntary) infrastructure of new strategies of urban government, whose effects are only becoming to unfold.

NOTES

1 https://www.smart-circle.org/smartcity/blog/smart-cities-future-will-smoother-social-open/

2 For a detailed account of the history of New Town see Dey, I., Samaddar, R., and Sen, S. K. (2013), *Beyond Kolkata: Rajarhat and the Dystopia of Urban Imagination*. Routledge India.

3 These include: The New Town Kolkata Development Authority (NKDA), the Housing Infrastructure Development Corporation of West Bengal (HIDCO), Future Cities Catapult, Cisco, The American Chamber of Commerce in India (AmCham India), Confederation of Indian Industry (CII), National Association of Software and Service Companies (NASSCOM).

4 https://www.telegraphindia.com/states/west-bengal/app-to-fix-parking-plights/cid/1531783

5 https://www.xpressoinsights.com/about-us.html

REFERENCES

Abzooba (2018). Sentiments going viral could have adverse effects on business or governance. <https://abzooba.com/resources/case-studies/other-case-studies/sentiments-going-viral-could-have-adverse-effects-on-business-or-governance/> [accessed 17 March 2018].

Amoore, L. (2006). Biometric Borders: Governing Mobilities in the War on Terror. *Political Geography* 25(3): 336–351.

—— (2013). *The Politics of Possibility: Risk and Security Beyond Probability* Durham: Duke University Press.

Amoore, L., Marmura, S., and Salter, M. B. (2008). Smart Borders and Mobilities: Spaces, Zones, Enclosures. *Surveillance & Society* 5(2): 96–101.

Amoore, L., and Piotukh, V. (2015). Life Beyond Big Data: Governing with Little Analytics. *Economy and Society* 44(3): 341–366.

Anderson, B. (2008). Preemption, Precaution, Preparedness: Anticipatory Action and Future Geographies. *Progress in Human Geography* 34(6): 777–798.

Angotti, T., (2013). Urban Latin America: Violence, Enclaves, and Struggles for Land. *Latin American Perspectives* 40(2): 5–20.

Atkinson, R., and Blandy, S. (2005). Introduction: International Perspectives on the New Enclavism and the Rise of Gated Communities. *Housing Studies* 20(2): 177–186.

Balibar, É. (2002). What is a Border? In É. Balibar and others (Eds), *Politics and the Other Scene*. Berlin: Verso Trade, pp. 75–86.

Crang, M., and Graham, S. (2007). Sentient Cities. Ambient Intelligence and the Politics of Urban Space. *Information, Communication & Society* 10(6): 789–817.

Datta, A. (2018). The Digital Turn in Postcolonial Urbanism: Smart Citizenship in the Making of India's 100 Smart Cities. *Transactions of the Institute of British Geographers* 43(3): 405–419.

de Goede, M. (2012). *Speculative Security. The Politics of Pursuing Terrorist Monies*. Minneapolis: University of Minnesota Press.

de Goede, M., Simon, S., and Hojitnik, M. (2014). Performing Preemption. *Security Dialogue* 45(5): 411–422.

Dey, I., Samaddar, R., and Sen, S. K. (2013) *Beyond Kolkata: Rajarhat and the Dystopia of Urban Imagination*. New Delhi: Routledge India.

Dourish, P. (2016). The Internet of Urban Things. In R. Kitchin and S. Perng (Eds), *Code and the City*. London: Routledge, pp. 27–46.

Easterling, K. (2014). *Extrastatecraft: The Power of Infrastructure Space*. New York: Verso.

Foucault, M. (2007). *Security, Territory, Population*. London: Palgrave McMillan.

Gabrys, J. (2016). *Program Earth: Environmental Sensing Technology and the Making of a Computational Planet*. Minneapolis: University of Minnesota Press.

Gooptu, N. (2013). Servile Sentinels of the City: Private Security Guards, Organized Informality, and Labour in Interactive Services in Globalized India. *International Review of Social History* 58(1): 9–38.

Graham, S. (2012). When Life Itself is War: On the Urbanization of Military and Security Doctrine. *International Journal of Urban and Regional Research* 36(1): 136–155.

Halpern, O., LeCavalier, J., Calvillo, N., and Pietsch, W. (2013). Test-Bed Urbanism. *Public Culture* 25(2): 272–306.

Internet and Mobile Association of India (IAMAI) (2019). India Internet. <https://cms.iamai.in/Content/ResearchPapers/d3654bcc-002f-4fc7-ab39-e1fbeb00005d.pdf> [accessed 20 January 2020].

King, A. (2016). Is Big Brother on the Dark Side of the Smart City? *Irish Times*, 20 October. <https://www.irishtimes.com/news/science/is-big-brother-on-the-dark-side-of-the-smart-city-1.2836981> [accessed 4 July 2018].

Kitchin, R. (2011). The Programmable City. *Environment and Planning B: Planning and Design* 38(6): 945–951.

——The Real-Time City? Big Data and Smart Urbanism. *GeoJournal* 79(1): 1–14.

Kitchin, R., and Perng, S. Y. (2016). *Code and the City*. London: Routledge.

Leese, M. (2016). Exploring the Security/Facilitation Nexus: Foucault at the 'Smart' Border. *Global Society* 30(3): 412–429.

Lyon, D. (2018). *The Culture of Surveillance: Watching as a Way of Life*. Cambridge: Polity Press.

Masdeval, C., and Veloso, A. (2015). Mining Citizen Emotions to Estimate the Urgency of Urban Issues. *Information Systems* 54: 147–155.

McMullan, T. (2015). What Does the Panopticon Mean in the Age of Digital Surveillance? *The Guardian*, 23 July. <https://www.theguardian.com/technology/2015/jul/23/panopticon-digital-surveillance-jeremy-bentham> [accessed 4 July 2018].

McNeill, D. (2015). Global Firms and Smart Technologies: IBM and the Reduction of Cities. *Transactions of the Institute of British Geographers* 40(4): 562–574.

Mertia, S. (2017). Socio-Technical Imaginaries of a Data-Driven City – Ethnographic Vignettes from Delhi. *The Fibreculture Journal* (29): 94–114.

Mezzadra, S., and Neilson B. (2013). *Border as Method, Or, the Multiplication of Labor*. Durham: Duke University Press.

Mitra, A. (2015). Informal Economy in India: Persistence and Meagreness. *Agrarian South: Journal of Political Economy* 4(2): 216–231.

Musto, C., Semeraro, G., Lops, P., and Gemmis, M. (2015). CrowdPulse: A Framework for Real-Time Semantic Analysis of Social Streams. *Information Systems* 54: 127–146.

Ong, A. (2006). *Neoliberalism as Exception: Mutations in Citizenship and Sovereignty*. Durham: Duke University Press.

Pötzsch, H. (2015). The Emergence of iBorder: Bordering Bodies, Networks, and Machines. *Environment and Planning D: Society and Space* 33(1): 101–118.

Rancière, J. (2004). *The Politics of Aesthetics: The Distribution of the Sensible*. London; New York: Continuum.

Rossiter, N. (2016). *Software, Infrastructure, Labor: A Media Theory of Logistical Nightmares*. New York: Routledge.

Roy, A. (2011). The Blockade of the World-Class City: Dialectical Images of Indian Urbanism. In A. Roy and A. Ong. (Eds), *Worlding Cities*. Oxford: Blackwell, pp. 295–278.

Schindler, S. (2014). The Making of 'World-Class' Delhi: Relations Between Street Hawkers and the New Middle Class. *Antipode* 46(2): 557–573.

Smart Cities Mission (n.d.). What is Smart City. <http://smartcities.gov.in/upload/uploadfiles/files/What%20is%20Smart%20City.pdf> [accessed 20 January 2018].

New Town Kolkata Development Authority (n.d.). Smart City Proposal, New Town Kolkata, Annexures 2–4. <https://nkdamar.org/File/Smart%20City%201.pdf> [accessed 18 February 2018].

New Town Kolkata Development Authority (2015). Smart City Proposal. <https://www.nkdamar.org/File/SCP%20New%20Town%20Kolkata_04042016_Draft%20Final.pdf> [accessed 18 February 2018].

Söderström, O., Paasche, T., and Klauser, F. (2014). Smart Cities as Corporate Storytelling. *CITY* 18(3): 307–320.

Thrift, N. (2014). The 'Sentient' City and What It May Portend. *Big Data & Society* 1(1).

Tufekci, Z. (2014). Engineering the Public: Big Data, Surveillance and Computational Politics. *First Monday* 19(7).

Weiler, A., Grossniklaus M., and Scholl, M. H. (2016). Situation Monitoring of Urban Areas Using Social Media Data Streams. *Information Systems* 57: 129–141.

4

SENSING SALMONELLA: MODES OF SENSING AND THE POLITICS OF SENSING INFRASTRUCTURES

Francis Lee

ENTERING THE ECDC

Entering the European CDC (ECDC) in Stockholm.[1] *It's a sunny day in January. I'm heading for the first day of fieldwork. On the doors to the ECDC, and through-out the building, signs are posted that declare 'Threat Level 0'. I'm given a badge, an ECDC laptop, and a desk in the Operations Centre, the set of rooms that can be claimed for intense operations, such as during the Ebola crisis. I soon learn that it is mostly used for routine work and meetings in the interim. That's why I can borrow a table there. The Operations Centre consists of several rooms, the most important being the 'situation room', which is set up just as the classic image from the movies: A large table with perhaps 20 spaces, a wall of screens showing world news, a few tables with telephones for operators under the screen-wall, and of course a blinking red digital clock that shows the time in Stockholm, Atlanta, Brasilia, and Beijing.*

During my fieldwork, every weekday at 11:30, I join about twenty experts from across the ECDC for the daily roundtable meeting – to assess the current disease threats against European citizens. During my fieldwork both mundane and exotic threats were part of the bestiary of threats: seasonal Flu, Zika,

Legionella, Salmonella, Yellow Fever, and Plague were all brought under the scrutiny of the roundtable. Recommendations for action were produced. Debates about the right course of action were common. As I came to understand disease surveillance better, I came to think of this room as one of the central locations where disease outbreaks were sensed and where the right course of action was decided.

HOW DO WE ANALYSE THE POLITICS OF SENSING INFRASTRUCTURES?

The intent of this chapter is theoretical and empirical. First, theoretically, the chapter proposes an analytical concept, *modes of sensing*, that is intended to examine how sensing infrastructures become implicated in the politics of sensing. The point is that attending to conflicts between different modes of sensing allows the analyst to become sensitive to differences, oppositions, and hierarchies between sensing infrastructures. The argument is that if sensing infrastructures are linked with different politics, then we also need analytical tools that allow for the description and analysis of oppositions, hierarchies, and indeterminacies that arise between different sensing infrastructures – and the politics that these differences in sensing give rise to and are implicated in.

Second, empirically, the chapter analyses how different sensing infrastructures create different understandings of what an epidemic is, where it originates and develops, and what its essential properties are. In essence: how different modes of sensing constitute disease outbreaks in different manners. Thus, the chapter sketches how an emerging sensing infrastructure for disease surveillance – in this case a sensing infrastructure based on genetics – becomes both championed and contested as evidence of a disease outbreak. It analyses how the introduction of a new infrastructure for sensing disease leads to the performance of a new disease object in Europe – a 'long ongoing trans-European outbreaks of Salmonella' as my informants would have it – and how actors at the ECDC and elsewhere struggle to reconcile this genetically detected outbreak with other modes of sensing disease: Does the disease outbreak originate from

Country X or not?[2] Which sensing infrastructure becomes dominant? And with what consequences?

Concretely, the chapter analyses how actors at the ECDC handle the uncertainties involved in the introduction of this genetic sensing infrastructure, and the actors' work to coordinate and handle conflicts between the emerging genetic sensing infrastructure and more entrenched ways of sensing disease outbreaks. To achieve this, the chapter traces how the emerging genetic sensing infrastructure and entrenched ways of sensing disease are tied to different *modes of sensing*, that sometimes diverge and thus must be coordinated in practice. That is, the introduction of the genetic sensing infrastructure and the detection of a new class of outbreaks based on this infrastructure leads to practical, epistemic, and political tensions that need to be negotiated organizationally and politically. The chapter thus proposes a practice-oriented analysis of the politics of sensing.

An important facet of disease surveillance, which also makes it a particularly fertile ground for analysing the politics of sensing infrastructures, is that disease surveillance is fraught with politics of the most mundane kind – something which is also quite apparent in this time of the Covid-19 pandemic. Apart from the obvious health consequences of a large disease outbreak, the social and economic repercussions can be momentous. For instance, an outbreak can hinder tourism, it can stop the import or export of foodstuff or even topple politicians. Due to the potentially large consequences of disease outbreaks, conflicts about the origin of a disease, or the handling of an outbreak, can erupt between different national governments, as well as different types organizations and companies. For instance, the fear of a Zika pandemic became a global controversy leading up to the Rio Olympics. The purported discovery of Zika-cases in Tanzania led to the sacking of the director of the national institute for medical research. And a Russian ban on the import of German cucumbers due to an E. Coli outbreak lead to an international row.[3] Thus, disease surveillance implicates national governments, private companies, as well as international organizations in a constant quest for surveilling and preventing new disease outbreaks – as well as conflicts around their detection and the possible political repercussions.

DISEASE SURVEILLANCE, BIOSECURITY AND A TIDAL WAVE OF SENSING TECHNOLOGIES

Current research dealing with disease surveillance in the social sciences has mainly been focused around the concept of 'biosecurity.' This body of work, pivoting around broad Foucauldian and anthropological perspectives, often analyses how biosecurity is handled by a diverse array of experts, on the scientific, political, and social levels. The analytical thrust of this body of work is aimed at understanding the institutional structures of expertise, and the construction of a multitude of objects of knowledge. The body of work paints a picture of a new world of constant preparedness, or in some cases unpreparedness, against the next global pandemic (Lakoff and Collier 2008; Lakoff 2017; Caduff 2015; Keck 2010).

While this research on biosecurity highlights the need for wide-ranging cultural, institutional, scientific, and political analyses of disease surveillance, what is frequently missing from this line of inquiry is an interest in the intertwining of disease surveillance with technological devices and infrastructures. Different disease experts, laboratories, and organizations are continuously attempting to harness new technological infrastructures aiming to find new ways of sensing disease: genetics, search word analyses, data-mining, machine learning, disease modelling, and risk computations are among the technologies that are mobilized to track and surveil disease globally (cf. Lee 2021).

Thus, an important point of departure for this chapter is that today's disease surveillance is dependent on a varied array of information infrastructures. The importance of information infrastructures for the construction, classification, and acting in the world has been a classic topic in Science and Technology Studies (STS). Bowker and Star (1999), for instance, have crucially shown how infrastructures can impose a 'social and moral order', and have argued for an analytical strategy of infrastructural inversion, which 'means learning to look closely at technologies and arrangements that, by design and by habit, tend to fade into the woodwork [and] recognizing the depths of interdependence of technical networks and standards, on the one hand, and the real work of politics and knowledge production on the other' (Bowker and Star 1999: 34). Thus, Bowker and Star called for and instigated a wide-ranging ethnographic, historicizing, and practice-oriented, engagement with the negotiated and complex politics of infrastructures (see Star and Ruhleder 1996; Bowker 2000).

In today's society where algorithms, machine learning techniques, and big data are constantly reshaping society in a multitude of ways information infrastructures are becoming increasingly important for our understanding of the world. Observers have for instance highlighted that new 'Big Data' infrastructures – and ways of knowing the world – will lead to new paradigms in how we create knowledge and facts (Kitchin 2014; Boellstorff 2015). Others have highlighted how computer algorithms or machine learning become part of valuing, classifying, and performing the world (Lee 2021; Lee et al. 2019; Lee and Björklund Larsen 2019; Seaver 2017; Kockelman 2013; Ziewitz 2017; Mackenzie 2017). Furthermore, what has also become apparent in this technological moment is that it is not only the amassing of great amounts of data, or the analysis of this data through different computational means, have exploded, but there is also a torrential downpour of new sensing devices and technologies. These sensing infrastructures draw on many different types and sources of data. For example, social media tracking, computer models to predict risks, satellite data, as well as a plethora of algorithms and computer software to make sense of this tidal wave of data (cf. Lee 2021).[4]

In disease surveillance, the emergence of new sensing infrastructures has the potential to make new disease outbreaks detectable. In other words, new classes of outbreaks and disease risks can be detected and made into objects in society through the development and introduction of new sensing infrastructures. For example, through satellite imaging and environmental computation, disease surveillance organizations can make environmental predictions of where different disease vectors could thrive on a global scale. A type of global analysis which was previously impossible (cf. Lee 2021).

ANALYSING SENSING INFRASTRUCTURES AND THE POLITICS OF SENSING

In attending to this technological moment of exploding sensors and sensing infrastructures, Gabrys (2016) has pointed out that new entities or environments are constructed, in her parlance *concresce*, through different sensing infrastructures. An important point being that different ways of sensing the world constructs it in different ways, with large consequences for what type of 'politics ... take hold along with these technologies' (18). This means that 'new modes of ... data gathering' lead to 'new configurations of ... engagement, ...relationality, sensing, and action' (23). The impetus of Gabrys' work thus opens up a space for analysing and reflecting on sensors as linked to different politics of sensing.

Gabrys' point that sensing infrastructures are linked to new configurations of engagement and politics is also true for disease surveillance. New sensing infrastructures lead to new disease outbreaks being sensed, and these new instances of disease outbreaks lead to new ways of engaging with, relating to, and acting on disease. The thrust of Gabrys' work thus points to a need for engaging with how disease surveillance deals with these emerging infrastructures and technologies. *However, Gabrys' work also begs the question of how to deal analytically with these different infrastructures and politics of sensing? How do we move from the insight that different sensing infrastructures are linked to different types of politics, to analysing the politics of sensing infrastructures?*

To make things more concrete: for instance, utilizing web searches in order to track the flu is not fully trusted as evidence of flu outbreaks in the Swedish healthcare system; rather people concerned with tracking the flu wish to rely on other types of sensing disease, such as lab reports or sentinel-reporting. In this situation, different modes of sensing flu intensity, through different sensing infrastructures, need to be coordinated. If the two sensing infrastructures diverge in making a 'flu epidemic', which one then becomes dominant?

MODES OF SENSING: ANALYSING A MULTIPLICITY OF SENSING INFRASTRUCTURES

To analyse these politics of sensing infrastructures this chapter introduces the concept of *mode of sensing*.[5] This concept highlights not only the emergence of different infrastructures and politics of sensing, but also the constant multiplicity of sensing infrastructures in practice, and the political struggles that can emerge from concurrent uses of different sensing infrastructures. The point is to highlight how multiple sensing infrastructures and modes of engaging with the world need to be handled in concurrent situations, such as in the case of the flu epidemic alluded to above. But how do we approach this multiplicity of sensing infrastructures analytically?

Coordinating multiple sensing infrastructures

In Mol's (2002) well-known analysis of the multiplicity of disease she traces how one disease, atherosclerosis, is made – enacted – differently in different parts of a hospital, sometimes in incommensurate manners. In this analysis, Mol attends to how different versions of atherosclerosis, different versions of this particular object, are handled in hospital practice. She attends to how different versions of the disease are coordinated, distributed, and included in each other. That is, she pays attention to *how the different enactments of an object in different parts of the world are in need of constant coordination to become a coherent object.* Thus, what Mol's approach highlights is how objects are constantly made in in different manners, and that there is a constant need for coordinating the different versions of objects in practice.

Mol's argument about the multiple enactments of objects resonates with Gabrys' focus on how the world concresces differently around different sensing infrastructures. Just as Mol's atherosclerosis is made differently in different places in the hospital, Gabrys' environment is made differently with different sensing infrastructures. However, Mol's focus on the coordination of multiple versions of objects also points to ways in which Gabrys' analysis of sensing infrastructures can be developed to become sensitive to simultaneous and multiple enactments. If we are currently living in a veritable flood of sensors and sensing infrastructures, Mol's perspective can be used to call attention to how objects and worlds, are overdetermined by multiple sensing infrastructures. Thus, Mol's perspective highlights how Gabrys' work on sensing infrastructures can be extended and highlights the need for analysing the coordination of multiplicities of sensing infrastructures.

Modes of sensing: Maintaining an analytical focus on sensing infrastructures

The introduction of the concept of *modes of sensing* is consequently intended to show how multiple and different sensing infrastructures are coordinated. Just like in Mol's work, different enactments of objects, based on different modes of sensing, can both co-exist or clash. However, unlike Mol's work which focuses on the multiple practices of enacting objects, the concept of modes of sensing intends to highlight the work of handling and coordinating different infrastructures. Thus, by introducing *modes of sensing* my intention is to direct our attention toward the *politics of sensing*, and the *infrastructures* that makes sensing possible.[6]

Consequently, the introduction of *modes of sensing* is an infrastructural inversion of Mol's work (see Bowker and Star 1999: 34). That is, Mol's focus on *enactment*, or the making of objects in multiple practices, highlights the simultaneous unity and multiplicity of objects in practice, and the need for coordinating different versions of objects. However, Mol's work does not systematically engage with infrastructures and the question of whether particular modes of sensing come to dominate over others. In other words: In Mol's work there is no systematic attempt to analyse how different knowledge infrastructures fit with larger struggles about what becomes the dominant enactment of the object.[7]

Modes of sensing Salmonella

Thus, in this chapter, it is the constant negotiation and coordination between different infrastructures that is highlighted. The focus is on the politics of different *modes of sensing*. Which mode of sensing Salmonella becomes dominant? And in which situations? This allows an analysis of the politics of sensing in practice – and, in this case, the politics of sensing disease outbreaks.

In sum, to explore the coordination and multiplicity of sensing infrastructures – and the enactment of Salmonella in Europe – this chapter develops the observation that there are different *modes of sensing* the world. The argument is that an analytical attention to modes of sensing allows us to describe how different sensing infrastructures clash or cohere. I suggest that an analysis of sensing infrastructures benefits from paying attention to multiple modes of sensing, as well as hierarchies between different sensing infrastructures. This is the point of departure for this chapter, and the basis for introducing the concept of *mode of sensing*.

In the present case – of a contested European Salmonella outbreak – two different sensing infrastructures can be tied to two different modes of detecting disease outbreaks, with potentially large political, economic and organizational consequences. An important point being that the same disease objects – the same epidemics – can be enacted in different manners with different sensing infrastructures, and that these divergent ways of sensing disease need to be handled in practice.[8]

METHODOLOGY

The chapter builds on fieldwork done for a larger research project that examines how new infrastructures are reshaping disease surveillance. The project started in 2015 with a preparatory inquiry into the rise of 'infodemiology', that is, how new information infrastructures and new types of data are harnessed for the purposes of disease surveillance. These new infrastructures can for example entail genetic data, web searches, tweets, sales data, or travel information.

The material for this particular chapter draws on my fieldwork in the spring of 2017 at the European Center for Disease Control and Prevention (ECDC).[9] The fieldwork entailed three weeks of intense participant observation in the so-called epidemic intelligence team, follow up visits to observe the genetics team, as well as interviews and document analysis. Access to the field was granted after initial contacts with the team leader for the so-called epidemic intelligence team. The epidemic intelligence team is tasked with trawling social media, news media, and a constant flow of emails, and it reports to produce a snapshot of the current disease state of the world, while the genetics team uses genetic profiling of different organisms to surveil and trace disease.

During my fieldwork I did surveillance work, attended meetings, participated in staff training, and interviewed my informants formally and informally.

During my stay I was free to attend meetings and training sessions with the epidemic intelligence group, as well as with other groups. The backbone of the surveillance process – as well as my understanding of disease surveillance at the ECDC – was the daily roundtable meeting where different teams from the ECDC brought the current day's disease threats for assessment. Thus, the current chapter draws on participant observation, informal conversations, interviews, working documents, flowcharts, official ECDC publications, as well as online material. During the fieldwork meetings, conversations, and interviews were conducted and documented in field-notes. After the fieldwork, the chapter was complemented with some informal interviews, and emails as well as complementary document studies.

Importantly, in many cases disease surveillance at the ECDC is a political balancing act. The ECDC is located in the complex setting of European bureaucracy, where different agencies and bodies of government have different responsibilities. This means that the ECDC must navigate a complex organizational role where national governments and different public health agencies of the EU member states must be taken into account. For example, the ECDC does not act, it only monitors disease. It then reports these disease threats in a steady stream to the European commission and member states, which then decide how to act. All of these organizational entanglements have consequences for the practices and results of disease surveillance. In the case of Salmonella, which is the disease with which we deal in this chapter, a crucial part of the organizational puzzle is the EFSA, the European Food Safety Authority, which is responsible for handling food safety issues in the EU.

As a consequence of doing fieldwork in a particular location, the chapter is written from the point of view of a partial and situated knowledge of disease surveillance practice. To create a more comprehensive understanding of disease surveillance would entail following disease security practices not only at the ECDC, but at the public health agencies of various European member nations, in various laboratories in different countries, as well as in different European organizations. The chapter must therefore remain a locally situated intervention, into a local enactment of a particular disease outbreak. This approach of course limits the amount of data that is available from national authorities on the

Salmonella outbreak in 'Country X', as well as how other European organizations, such as the EFSA, understand and enact this particular Outbreak of Salmonella. However, through observations, interviews, and document studies, the chapter attempts to sketch how different sensing infrastructures and different modes of sensing are handled in different situations.

SHOE LEATHER EPIDEMIOLOGY

In disease surveillance the *origins of disease* is a matter of big concern. Ever since the iconic work of John Snow – who traced the origins of the London cholera epidemic in the nineteenth century – disease surveillance has been focused on tracing the origins of disease through an eclectic combination of detective work based on any available methods of tracing and tracking disease. Snow, for example, produced a map of disease cases that allowed him to deduce the location of the source of the London cholera epidemic. To accomplish this, he drew on medical theories, knowledge of the local neighbourhood, as well as what ECDC natives sometimes term 'shoe leather epidemiology' – lots of walking, talking, looking, and thinking.

The traditional way of sensing Salmonella has been dominated by exactly this type of shoe leather epidemiology – tracing foodstuffs through their journey from farms, through production facilities, stores, and restaurants, all the way to the mouth of the European Citizen. Trying to find the restaurant where the disease was spread, the wedding reception where the bad eggs were used – or in the politically most momentous cases – the factories and industrial production facilities where disease is circulating. That is, the traditional shoe-leather tracing of Salmonella depended on tracing foodstuffs from their consumption to a potential contaminant. This process entails tracing foodstuffs through a network of producers, distributors, and retailers. If shoe leather evidence can be secured, the localized outbreak might be traced back to a certain farm or factory.

Of course, this shoe leather work also draws on large infrastructures of food traceability. Packages are marked, shipments are enumerated, lots are numbered.

Tracing food from farmstead to mouth. These infrastructures make easier the detective work of tracing disease but should the package or the eggshells already be disposed of, the work of tracing origins becomes much, much harder. If not impossible.

This mode of sensing Salmonella depends on linking specific disease cases through food networks, to hopefully find the source of disease. Two cases can only be linked to each other if both cases can be traced back to the source. There is no way of saying that these share an origin story without linking them by tracing eggshells, food containers, or shipment lots to a certain farm, factory, store, or restaurant. However, this mode of sensing of Salmonella is changing through the introduction of new genetic technologies.

GENETICS: AN EMERGING SENSING INFRASTRUCTURE

Disease surveillance practitioners are constantly experimenting with different sensing infrastructures. Oftentimes, resorting to any means possible to track down and eliminate the sources of a disease. During my fieldwork I came across instances of using TripAdvisor to find the location of outbreaks, analysis of satellite imagery to track climactic suitability for different disease vectors, machine learning techniques to model the spread of disease vectors, and news trawling to find new outbreaks of unknown diseases. New technologies that become available are constantly experimented with and can range from genetics to twitter analysis.

One of the emerging and promising trends in disease surveillance at the time of my fieldwork was harnessing affordable so-called *whole genome sequencing* (WGS) for purposes of disease surveillance. The affordability of WGS was time and again described as a breakthrough for tracking and tracing disease during my fieldwork. I argue that it can be productively understood as an emerging sensing infrastructure in disease surveillance.[10] For instance, when I attended the ESCAIDE 2016 (European Scientific Conference on Applied Infectious Disease Epidemiology), which gathers hundreds of disease surveillance specialists from all over Europe, genetic tracking of disease was one of the dominant themes.

As the head of disease surveillance at the ECDC expressed it in an informal conversation during my fieldwork: genetic surveillance heralded the future of disease surveillance.[11] Another of my informants, the head of the genetics team at ECDC, reflected in a personal communication on how WGS is changing how disease surveillance is done:

> Traditionally outbreak detection has been built up of two parts. One is the epidemiological link ["shoe leather epidemiology"] where certain food can be suspected because of evidence or consumption of specific [food] items between cases. [Previously] this has [...] been complemented with some crude laboratory methods to conclude that the same bacterial strain in present in between cases and hopefully also [the] food item.
>
> Now the weight of these two pieces of evidence is tilting, because you get so detailed and high resolutive microbiology data [from genetics]. Earlier the question was, how much laboratory data do you need to conclude a source based on epidemiological evidence. Now the question is reversed to how much epidemiological evidence is needed to conclude a link from something detected by genomics (personal communication to author).

What my informant was pointing out is how the advent of an emerging sensing infrastructure based on genetics leads to shifts in how disease outbreaks are understood and detected in practice. He also points out how different sensing infrastructures are trusted differently. From his situated point of view, as the head of the genomics team at the ECDC, there has been a reversal in how evidence from different sensing infrastructures is trusted. However, as this chapter shows, the introduction of a genetic sensing infrastructures is not as smooth as it might appear from the point of view of the genetics team. Below we follow the tracking of a particular outbreak of Salmonella, and the work of the genetics team to attempt to find a source for this particular outbreak. We follow how the emerging genetic sensing infrastructure is implicated in a political and organizational conflict between two different enactments of a salmonella outbreak.

GENETIC EPIDEMIOLOGY AND PHYLOGENESIS

With the advent of affordable so-called whole genome sequencing, and the drive to use genetics to track disease, the shoe leather way of enacting Salmonella outbreaks is changing. Now, rather than tracing eggshells or packages through the food chain, disease is starting to be traced through genetic similarities of strains of bacteria. This work builds on the logic of genetic similarity and difference, where relations between strains of bacteria are inferred by genetic closeness. This logic of genetic similarity and relation is perhaps most clearly expressed through so-called phylogenetic trees, where the ancestries of species are drawn in tree structures based on changes in the genetic code. The theory of phylogenesis is based on an evolutionary logic where changes in the genome give rise to genetic differences, and in the end new species.

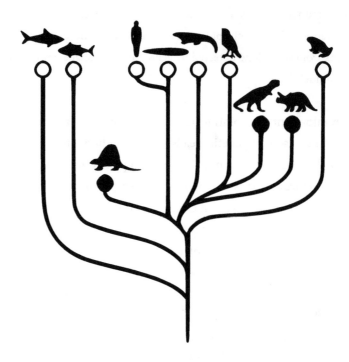

FIG. 4.1 Phylogenetic tree (source: redrawn from Fig. 5 in Carlson 1999)

The logic of introducing phylogeny into surveillance is based on theories both about how evolution happens, but also on how species come to be differentiated genetically. As one of my informants phrased it: 'The fact is that evolution is constantly diversifying organisms and this can be visualized and applied practically.'[12] When creating phylogenetic trees through genetic studies, genetic similarity is often equated with a close relation between particular species or organisms. There is thus a general figure of thought in studies of phylogenetics, where genetic similarity is equated with close evolutionary relations.

In public health, the emergence of affordable whole genome sequencing of bacterial genomes is currently being developed into a sensing infrastructure for tracking disease. By comparing the genomes of different strains of bacteria epidemiologists and microbiologists now make inferences about how closely related they are. Is this strain of Salmonella close to this other strain? Just as with phylogenetic trees, the logic of genetic disease tracking is that if the genomes are similar, they are seen as related. The logic is that if two organisms are genetically similar, they are thought to share a recent common ancestor. As the leader of the genetics team at the ECDC explained the use of the genetic disease surveillance:

> If you have 30 people eating a buffet together and they get sick it is easy to conclude that they belong to the same outbreak. Then you can start to analyse what they have eaten in common. But what do you do in a society where you have maybe 30 000 [cases of] Salmonella per year. What belongs to an outbreak and what does not? (source: personal communication)

In applying the logic of phylogenetics to disease surveillance the genetic methodology is used to link or unlink cases to a specific outbreak.

But before we dive into the enactment of different disease outbreaks, we need small primer on genetics. Genetic disease surveillance is, as outlined above, based on DNA differences between organisms. DNA is said to form the basic genetic blueprints for all living organisms and is also unique for each individual organism. DNA is comprised of four types of molecules, so-called nucleotides, which are paired with each other to form the famed DNA double helix. The DNA helix is comprised of four types of nucleotides: Cytosine, Guanine, Adenine, and Thymine, which are often represented as the letters, C, G, A, and T, when translating the genetic code to letter-form. Thus, DNA strands are often represented as a string of letters: For example, 'ACGTAA'.

As each individual organism, and in this case each individual Salmonella bacterium, has a unique DNA code, it is possible to identify any individual organism, or bacteria, by analysing its DNA.

A common measure of genetic relation in phylogenetics is to quantify genetic differences by counting differences between different organisms' DNA. That is, by counting how many nucleotides are different between the DNA of two organisms. A difference of one nucleotide between two organisms is called a Single Nucleotide Polymorphism, a SNP (see image below). This also means that the genetic difference between two organisms, say two Salmonella bacteria, can be quantified by the number of SNPs that set them apart. When one of these nucleotides, one letter in the DNA string, differs between two organisms, that is defined as a one SNP difference.

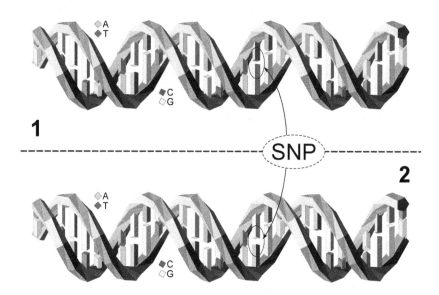

FIG. 4.2 Two identical DNA strands with one Single Nucleotide Polymorphism, one SNP (source: https://en.wikipedia.org/wiki/File:Dna-SNP.svg)

According to the logic of phylogeny closely related organisms have little genetic difference, while more distant relatives in the genetic tree of life have larger differences. As the head of genetics at the ECDC expresses it:

> Few SNPs between different organisms indicate a close relationship and a close common ancestor, a difference of a large number of SNPs indicates a more distant relationship. The number of SNPs that are needed to conclude if the organisms have a close/distant relationship depends on species, type of outbreak, etc. and this is still in the learning phase which can cause interpretation issues within and across sectors.[13]

The informant thus argued that 'close' or 'distant' genetic relations between different bacterial strains can be inferred by counting SNP differences. A large number of SNPs is taken as an indication of a close relation, while a small number of SNPs is taken as an indication of distant relation. There is an inference made between genetic similarity and bacterial relation. In essence, the argument is that one can infer that these different bacterial strains are part of the same disease outbreak. *In the genetic mode of sensing disease, a disease outbreak is thus enacted by counting SNP differences.*

VISUALIZING GENETIC SIMILARITY AT THE ECDC

At the ECDC, evidence of disease outbreaks was produced and visualized in varying manners. Geographic intensity maps, and curves of epidemic intensity over time were the most common forms. However, as whole genome sequencing was starting to enter the picture a new type of diagram entered the picture. A visualization of bacterial similarity through detailed phylogenetic trees on the bacterial level. These trees were produced by a genetics team at the ECDC, or in collaboration with expert laboratories in the European Union's member states. This team was responsible for the collection of sequences generated in member states public health laboratories at the ECDC and collected bacterial isolates from all over the European Union. The team's goal was to find outbreaks and supporting cross boarder outbreak investigations through genetic evidence.

The most common way of visualizing these genetic linkages at the ECDC was through tree visualizations of genetic relations. In these visualizations every branch on the tree represents a quantified measure of genetic similarity and difference. In the phylogenetic trees of Salmonella, each branching to the right in the figure symbolizes a closer relation between the bacterial strains. In the tree below, this could mean that the rightmost branch might represent a 5 SNP difference, the step to the left, a 10 SNP difference, a step further to the left, a 50 SNP difference, and so on. A vertical line between the bacteria means that the bacteria are identical in terms of genetics, in genetic parlance, they are clonal.

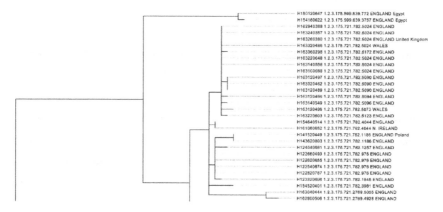

FIG. 4.3 Part of a SNP-based phylogenetic tree of Salmonella Enteritidis (ECDC 2016b: 7)

The phylogenetic trees thus visualize how divergent different bacterial strains were in terms of genetic difference. Each branch on the phylogenetic tree representing a quantified difference of SNPs.

Producing these trees involves assessing and defining the genetic boundaries between one bacterial strain and another, breaking up genetic continuums into quantified and discrete branches of sameness and difference. The production of these trees thus entails translating differences on the genetic level into numerical and graphical representations. This involves deciding how many SNP differences should constitute a new branch on the phylogenetic tree. This also involves assessing what is a big difference and a small difference. How many SNPs is close? And how many SNPs is far away?

SENSING A NEW CLASS OF DISEASE OUTBREAKS

FIG. 4.4 Map of Salmonella cases (ECDC 2019: 3)

One of the consequences of these new genetic groupings of bacteria is that new disease outbreaks become visible to the ECDC. What was before identified as sporadic cases of Salmonella, had now shifted to the identification of regional/national or pan-European outbreaks of Salmonella. By genetically grouping together bacterial isolates sampled in different countries across Europe through the ECDC was starting to see new outbreaks across Europe. What was previously understood as regional outbreaks was now seen as pan European outbreaks.

With the increasing use of whole genome sequencing a new class of outbreaks became visible to the ECDC.

During my fieldwork there was a long-ongoing multi country outbreak of Salmonella in Europe. The outbreak was recurrently brought up for discussion at the daily roundtable meeting as well as in other meetings. In June, the ECDC was cited in FoodQualityNews, as having used Whole Genome Sequencing to identify the outbreak:

The outbreak was detected through WGS [Whole Genome Sequencing] and is characterized by its long duration with relatively low numbers of cases reported intermittently and peaks of re-emergence in late summer/early autumn between 2014 and 2016. In 2017 this pattern changed, with a peak observed in March. (Whitworth 2017)

By using whole genome sequencing to group bacteria into related strains of bacteria, the ECDC and member state's experts where able to delineate the outbreak and produce a so-called epicurve, a visualization of cases over time, of the outbreak. The genetic grouping of Salmonella made it possible to produce an image of a persistent outbreak of Salmonella in Europe, which had been ongoing for at least three years.

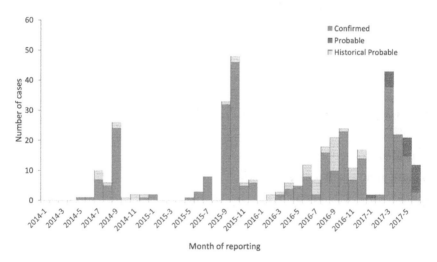

FIG. 4.5 Epicurve of the long ongoing Salmonella outbreak in Country X (ECDC 2017: 4)

The outbreak of Salmonella could now, as my informants phrased it 'with high precision', be traced back in time to produce an intensity curve of the outbreak. Thus, genetic evidence was used to produce a previously impossible visualization, an image of how a particular genetic group of Salmonella had spread over Europe. As one of my informants phrased it:

These types of epicurves are classic tools for an epidemiologist. What the new technology provides is much more certainty that the cases are actually true and that the epicurve then represents a true description of the outbreak (given the limitations that are always there in terms of sampling bias/limitations). (Personal communication)

The consequence of whole genome sequencing seemed momentous at the ECDC. The head of surveillance called it a paradigm shift. A whole new set of outbreaks now became visible.

INTERPRETING GENETIC SENSING INFRASTRUCTURES AT THE ECDC

However, although the trust in the capabilities of genetic evidence to uncover new outbreaks was strong, the new technology also led to new questions and uncertainties. At the weekly roundtable meeting the team of geneticists recurrently showed phylogenetic trees that genetically grouped bacteria into novel outbreaks. A challenge facing the ECDC at the time of my fieldwork, was that there were no standardized understandings of how bacterial strains mutate, which methods were the most trustworthy, and which nomenclature to describe these things were most fitting.

At the daily roundtable meeting these questions of genetic relation were – for most participants – esoteric questions understood and grappled with by a small team of genetic experts. Consequently, there was a constant struggle to interpret and create meaning from the sometimes obtuse tree visualizations of genetic difference. Both from the experts in the genetics team, but also from disease experts working in different fields. At the daily roundtable meeting – which gathered disease experts with varying degrees of genetic knowledge – questions were constantly posed as a response to the display of these bacterial phylogenetic trees.

At one point, when a representative of the genetics team was scrolling through a seemingly endless phylogenetic tree of bacteria, the chairman of the meeting, who was also the head of disease surveillance, threw up his hands and asked.

Chairman: "But what does it mean?"

Geneticist: "That's a five SNP difference!"

Chairman: "Is that enough to say it's the same strain?"

Many different questions of interpreting the phylogenetic trees, and the genetic similarities and differences they represented, were brought forward.

Actor 1: "How fast does Salmonella mutate?"

Actor 2: "Is 5 SNPs a close relation?"

Actor 3: "Is 5 SNPs close enough to declare an outbreak?"

The genetic evidence was not a settled matter for the actors at the ECDC. First, there was an uncertainty about how much genetic difference is a meaningful difference in terms of classifying Salmonella strains. This includes assessing how fast Salmonella mutates, and how stressful the environment is for the bacterium. By settling how stressful the environment is, it was thought that the rate of mutation could be deduced. By settling how fast the bacterial strain mutates, the number of SNP differences could gain meaning. Thus, understanding the bacterium as having a slow rate of mutation implies that only a few SNPs needs to be different for it to be understood as significant difference – and vice versa.

Consequently, there were a number of factors that influenced how genetic likeness was understood. Again, the question that the roundtable was constantly trying to answer was 'Is this an outbreak of Salmonella?' Among the complex questions were that different bacteria behave differently, some hardly change over time, while others are very prone to mutation between cases. Another challenge is that if the outbreak is large there is a lot of space for the bacterium to mutate, so you can have wide genetic variance in the same outbreak, which makes sampling technique important, as you can only sample parts of the outbreak 'branch' in the phylogenetic tree.

The second question constantly posed at the roundtable meeting, 'Is 5 SNPs close enough to declare an outbreak?' is about action and wider consequences of the genetic classification of strains. This is a question of interpreting the data, where the genetics team need to decide if the different bacteria share a 'recent common ancestor'. Depending on what the team believe is the mutation rate, they can form a hypothesis about two bacteria being part of the same outbreak. The question in their minds is: 'What is a small enough difference to consider two bacteria as part of the same outbreak?'

THE POLITICS OF DISEASE SURVEILLANCE

On the basis of the available evidence, what actions can the ECDC then recommend? Here the work of knowing and constituting an outbreak is shifted and linked to the international politics of food and economies of nations. Just as Gabrys has pointed out, the enactment of particular objects in the world, is closely linked to how people and organizations engage with these objects. The questions at the roundtable meeting must thus be understood against the backdrop of international food politics, where a food-borne disease outbreak can lead to large international repercussions in the form of import bans of different food stuffs. For example, as alluded to above, in 2011, Russia banned the import of cucumbers from the European Union as there was a worry about an outbreak of E. Coli in Germany. Which then also had economic consequences for cucumber farmers. Thus, the economic and political repercussions of disease surveillance were constantly present at the ECDC.

Making the matter even more difficult was the complex organizational situation. The ECDC is in constant collaboration with a number of different organizations around the globe. There is a constant stream of the phone calls, emails, and meetings to coordinate disease surveillance around the world. The ECDC are constantly collaborating with the WHO, the US CDC, and the CDCs of other countries inside and outside the EU. They also collaborate with European organizations within the EU. For example, the European Commission, or the European Food and Safety Authority, EFSA. As Salmonella is a food borne disease, the communication with the European food and safety authority was necessary and legally mandated. This complex organization with different organizational mandates and different political goals makes the introduction of new ways of producing evidence of outbreaks challenging. The question 'What does a 5 SNP difference mean?' takes on a whole new pregnancy. The pan-European Salmonella outbreak highlighted all these complex relations between sensing infrastructures, organizations, and new technologies.

THE POLITICS OF MULTIPLE SENSING INFRASTRUCTURES

In disease surveillance, theories about the origin of different outbreaks were constantly tested against different sensing infrastructures. For instance, automated algorithms can be pitted against human knowledge and expertise (Lee 2017, 2021), new models of transmission pathways can reshape our understanding of a disease (Lee et al. 2019), or, as in this case, genomic knowledge can be pitted against traditional epidemiological work. As a result, the value of different sensing infrastructures for tracking disease was not apparent at all times at the ECDC. For my informants there was a constant struggle to interpret sensing infrastructures and to determine the source of a disease outbreak: Does the genetic evidence point at a specific country? What did genetic evidence mean in the case of this outbreak?

When modes of sensing add up: The closure of a Polish egg packing facility

A particular outbreak of Salmonella, which was discovered in Europe in 2016, was seen as a landmark for genetic disease surveillance at the ECDC. In this case, genetic evidence was used to identify and shut down one of the largest egg packing factories in Poland. As the ECDC rapid risk assessment phrased it: 'The available evidence from WGS [whole genome sequencing], food and environmental investigations, as well as from tracing-back investigation of eggs, establishes a link between this multi-country foodborne outbreak and the packing centre B in Poland...' (ECDC 2016c: 1) The genetic evidence was in harmony with other investigation methods, but it was genetic information that led to the discovery of the outbreak.

In this case the genetic evidence was linked with 'shoe leather' epidemiological evidence. As an informant put it during my fieldwork: 'The genetic information made detection and specific next steps in the investigation possible.' In this particular case, the genetic sensing infrastructure was in harmony with the older 'shoe leather' methods of tracing disease through food networks.

Thinking with Mol's (2002: 84) conceptual apparatus, which highlights how objects hold together in the face of multiplicities in practice, the investigation of the Polish egg packing facility can be described as if the different sensing infrastructures were *coordinated by adding up*: there was a coherence between the genetic and 'shoe leather' sensing infrastructures in the enactment of the outbreak of Salmonella. As Mol puts it, this 'form of addition comes with no worries about discrepancies. It does not suggest that tests have a common object. Instead, it takes tests as suggestions for action: one bad test outcome may be a reason to treat; two or three bad test outcomes give more reason to treat.' (Mol 2002: 84) Thus, in the case of the Polish egg packing facilities the genetic and 'shoe leather' sensing infrastructures added up, and there was no need to handle how different objects were enacted differently by different sensing infrastructures.

When modes of sensing don't add up: Is Country X the source?

However, in connection with the long-ongoing pan-European outbreak of Salmonella which was grappled with during my fieldwork things were not as simple. Here, the different sensing infrastructures did not *add up*, and the different sensing infrastructures – of genetics and 'shoe leather' methods – were pitted *against each other* in the mores of national and organizational politics. Thus, in this second Salmonella outbreak, there was no identification of a source of the Salmonella outbreak, the different modes of sensing did not *add up*.

On the one hand, the ECDC team saw the genetic similarity of the different Salmonella strains as strong evidence. In their view the genetic evidence pointed strongly to Country X as the source of the outbreak.[14] The genetics team argued that counting SNP differences – that showed close relation between the different cases – was enough evidence to determine the source of the outbreak as being Country X. The ECDC team's view was that DNA similarity could be used to infer the source of the outbreak. For them, the source of the Salmonella outbreak could be determined based on genetic technology, phylogenetic logic, and correlational thinking.

On the other hand, the European Food and Safety Authority (EFSA) interpreted the strength of the genetic analysis differently. They argued that the evidence produced through the genetic sensing infrastructure was not sufficient for pinpointing the source of the outbreak to Country X. In EFSA's understanding, tracing foodstuffs to their origins through traditional outbreak investigation methods – 'shoe leather methods' – were seen as necessary to determine the source of the outbreak. Thus, in addition to the genetic evidence that ECDC had put forward, EFSA emphasized the need for additional 'shoe leather' evidence to ascertain the source of the outbreak. In EFSA's way of reasoning, only by finding the food pathways of the disease through the global food networks could the source of disease be sufficiently determined.

To EFSA the genetic evidence wasn't sufficient. *Genetic similarity did not imply certainty about the source of disease.* The evidence presented by the genetics team was thus not enough to point out Country X as the source of the Salmonella outbreak. Thinking with different *modes of sensing*, the EFSA argued that a shoe leather mode of sensing was needed in order to substantiate the ECDC's claims. *For my geneticist informants EFSA's stance led to some frustration.* 'We send people to jail based on genetic evidence' one of my informants exclaimed frustratedly at one point of the investigation.

In the end, Country X's government denied that their poultry industry was the source of the outbreak. However, according to my informants, a significant number of chickens were slaughtered after the genetic outbreak investigation had indicated the country as a potential culprit for the Salmonella outbreak. Nevertheless, the source of outbreak that had been detected through the genetic mode of sensing still remained uncertain. The source of the outbreak was not pinpointed and resolved. There was no closure. The two modes of sensing could not be coordinated, and thus created a Salmonella outbreak with an uncertain source. Simultaneous stability and uncertainty. A Salmonella outbreak without a source, a Salmonella outbreak in limbo.

DISCUSSION: ENTANGLING SENSING AND GOVERNMENT ACTION

Disease outbreaks in today's disease surveillance are enacted through a plethora of different sensing infrastructures. This includes a multitude of technologies and techniques: genetic profiling, satellite imaging, automated image analysis, computer modelling, as well as many algorithms for processing data. The production of risk objects in disease surveillance is thus intimately intertwined with different sensing infrastructures.[15]

One consequence of this multiplicity is that the emergence of new sensing infrastructures come to enact new patterns of risk and disease. New risk objects come into being on the global stage of disease surveillance. In the case of European disease surveillance, sensing infrastructures enact risk objects on a national, European, and global stage of disease security – implicating both nations and international organizations such as the ECDC, EFSA or the WHO. Another consequence is that, as new sensing infrastructures emerge, old infrastructures keep existing and being used. Thus, new sensing infrastructures, and new enactments of risk objects come to coexist with older ones. Sometimes these enactments coincide, and sometimes they diverge. When they diverge, this can lead to conflicts about which sensing infrastructures, data, and facts about risk objects can be trusted. Should actors trust older more entrenched sensing infrastructures, or should new infrastructures be trusted more?

What is at stake for actors in disease surveillance are questions such as: which sensing infrastructures are trustworthy? What types of sensing infrastructures can be used to identify and trace disease outbreaks in the complex technological, political, and economic arena that disease surveillance operates on? And as a consequence, which risk objects are constructed as real outbreaks, that must be acted on? In the case that I relate above there are two parallel sensing infrastructures vying for organizational trust: on the one hand the traditional sensing infrastructure which draws on traditional 'shoe leather' methods and food tracing, and on the other hand the sensing infrastructure that maps the genetic similarity of different bacterial strains. These sensing infrastructures enact outbreaks of Salmonella in different ways, which in our case is also tied to different organizational contexts, mandates and priorities.

The traditional way of tracing food borne disease in disease control has been to trace the origin of food stuffs. As we have seen above, this is done through the mode of sensing that the actors call 'shoe leather epidemiology'. The focus of these tracing practices is the construction of likely chains of disease transmission which are used to point to an origin of a disease outbreak. By tracing food stuff or food packaging through food distribution networks, actors in disease surveillance construct what they deem to be a likely disease transmission route through the global food distribution network. That is: actors infer the source of the outbreak through its likely route of transportation and transmission. The actors ask: Can we identify the source of the eggshell? And thus of the Salmonella outbreak? Here *practices of producing causal chains* – creating likely networks of food transmission – are at centre stage.

As we have also seen above, increasingly affordable genetic sequencing technologies have led to the development of an emerging set of sensing infrastructures based on genetic technologies. Many actors in disease surveillance, see this technological development as a new and improved route to detect and handle outbreaks. The focus of these genetic practices is to infer genetic relations of bacterial strains in order to detect outbreaks. In the case above, actors inferred the source of the outbreak through the genetic similarity of different strains of Salmonella. The actors asked: How genetically similar/different are these different bacterial strains? And does this genetic similarity/difference mean that they are closely related?

In dealing with the diverging enactments of the indeterminate and long-ongoing outbreak of Salmonella in Europe, Mol's vocabulary on the enactment of objects in practice falls short in attempting to describe how multiple sensing infrastructures are handled. In her work, she suggests different manners in which atherosclerosis is maintained as an object in the face of multiplicity in practice: she suggests *adding up, distribution,* and *inclusion* to describe how atherosclerosis becomes enacted in hospital practice. But, as I have pointed out elsewhere, just as with many actor-network theory concepts, the focus of her analysis is on the stabilization of facts, technologies, or in this case disease.[16] Her focus is on how objects become enacted as real in practice.

However, the long-ongoing Salmonella outbreak which was contested based on different sensing infrastructures was never stabilised. Uncertainty about the source of the outbreak remained. Here, instead of, like Mol, theorizing the enactment, maintenance, or coordination of objects, I have suggested we also need to create a vocabulary for describing conflicts between different *sensing infrastructures*. Concepts that can be used to describe and analyse the *politics of multiple and diverging* sensing infrastructures. *This would allow a focus on the politics of sensing* – and also in this case the politics of sensing disease outbreaks.

Thus, I suggest that we need to create analytical tools that allow for the description and understanding of oppositions, hierarchies, and indeterminacies that arise between sensing infrastructures. This allows us to gain a deeper understanding of objects that do not stabilize. Of objects that remain weak and unstable in the face of multiplicities of sensors and sensing infrastructures.

Here, I propose one such concept – *mode of sensing* – which would allow a description of certain facets of the politics of sensing infrastructures: *Namely how different infrastructures are trusted differently based on different modes of inferring an objects existence.* This would allow us to highlight how different sensors are trusted differently in practice. It would also allow analytical purchase on the slippery politics of sensing. My argument is that the two different sensing infrastructures in this case are tied to two modes of sensing disease outbreaks: one which is based on practices of *linking and relating* – creating what is thought to be causal inferences of disease transmission – and another based on *practices of lumping and splitting bacteria into groups* – creating phylogenetic trees based on what is said to be genetic correlations.[17]

Which sensing infrastructures is then trusted, on the basis of which mode of sensing? And in which context? For legal matters to proceed – for example the closing of an egg packing factory – a particular mode of sensing a disease outbreak might be demanded, while in more practical disease prevention work – without legal repercussions – additional modes of sensing might be trusted. Thus, to understand how sensing infrastructures become intertwined with political and organizational contexts, one facet of the puzzle is to understand how different modes of sensing are intertwined with trust and action. Thus, I argue that we need to understand how different modes of sensing become accepted or rejected in complex actor-networks.

CONCLUSION

To analytically highlight how diverging sensing infrastructures are handled in practice, the chapter has proposed to pay attention to different *modes of sensing*. This allows moving beyond Gabrys' observation that different politics take hold with different sensing infrastructures, toward an analysis of the politics of sensing: of how hierarchies, coordinations, divergences, and indeterminacies are handled when sensing infrastructures are used in practice.

The chapter has followed the *practices of sensing disease* through a genetic sensing infrastructure. In this, it sketched how affordable genetic techniques has led to the development of a novel genetic sensing infrastructure for surveilling disease outbreaks in Europe. It showed how this genetic sensing infrastructure built on a particular *mode of sensing* disease outbreaks that posited relations between different Salmonella strains through genetic similarity.

The chapter traced how professionals working with disease surveillance at the European Centre for Disease Control and Surveillance used genetics to identify and trace a 'long-ongoing outbreak of Salmonella'. However, just as Martin and Lynch (2009) have shown elsewhere, the practices of inferring genetic similarity are tied to considerable uncertainties about what genetic similarity really means in practice. Last, the chapter dealt with the politics of multiple sensing infrastructures in disease surveillance. Here the chapter attended to two recent outbreaks of Salmonella in Europe, and what happens when two sensing infrastructures *add up*, and what happens when they do not.

Thus, the chapter developed an analytical stance which deviates from the age-old *construction stories* that are told about objects in actor-network theory (see Galis and Lee 2014). In doing this, the chapter set out to pave an analytical path where enactment of objects through sensing infrastructures is not the only possible story to tell. Instead, the chapter analyses how objects remain contested and non-coherent due to divergent sensing infrastructures to find tools, in the words of Haraway (2010), for staying *with the trouble.*

Sensing infrastructures are not neutral nor innocent. They are implicated in politics of the most crucial kind. They are implicated in questions of international politics, health and illness, life and death. Above we have seen how Salmonella is enacted through different and sometimes contested sensing infrastructures which are embedded in a complex economic, political, and organizational context. An important conclusion one can draw from this chapter is that sensing infrastructures need to be understood in terms of both multiplicity of sensors and non-coherence of the objects that are sensed.

I believe that this approach to analysing sensing infrastructures opens up a road to analysing not only disease surveillance work, but also for analysing sensing infrastructures based on algorithmic calculation as well as Big Data. Which mode of sensing is a particular sensing infrastructure part of? How does this mode of sensing integrate with different contexts of action? As Adrian Mackenzie has aptly asked: how do we swim in this constantly increasing tidal wave of data? (Mackenzie 2014).

The concept of mode of sensing thus, has a potential wide application in understanding how objects are enacted through different sensing infrastructures. Not least in attempting to understand how new infrastructures are integrated or rejected in different settings. By highlighting different modes of sensing, I believe we can understand better how new infrastructures based on for example genomics, satellite imagining, algorithmic processing, computer models, big data or learning machines become integrated in practice. What mode of sensing is a valid measure of a risk object, and in which context?

ACKNOWLEDGEMENTS

I want to thank the editors (in alphabetical order), Geoffrey Bowker, Nikolaus Poechhacker, and Nina Klimburg-Witjes for insightful comments and criticisms along the way. I also want to thank the anonymous reviewer for insights about doing an infrastructural inversion of Annemarie Mol's work. The chapter also benefitted from comments by the Cultural Matters Group at Uppsala University led by Tora Holmberg. Additional thanks go to David Moats and Jenny Lee who took the time to read and comment.

DISCLAIMER

The content of this report does not necessarily reflect the official opinion of the European Centre for Diseases Prevention and Control (ECDC). Responsibility for the information and views expressed in the report lies entirely with the author.

NOTES

1   The full and clunky name of the organization is the European Centre for Disease Control and Prevention. The ECDC is the European agency set up to monitor disease threats to European citizens.

2   Country X must here remain anonymous due to the political repercussions that could emerge from its publication.

3   For Zika, see for instance: https://www.theguardian.com/world/2016/may/12/rio-olympics-zika-amir-attaran-public-health-threat. For cucumbers, see for instance: https://www.bbc.com/news/world-europe-13625271 or https://www.reuters.com/article/us-ecoli-russia/russia-bans-eu-vegetables-over-e-coli-eu-protests-idUSTRE75140G20110602

4   On the politics of satellite imagery see Witjes and Olbrich (2017).

5   In introducing *modes of sensing* I draw on a long tradition of STS work. In this I want to mention Fujimura and Chou's (1994) and Hacking's (1992) work as inspiration for this conceptual development. In Fujimura and Chou's work on styles of practice they show how microbiologists and epidemiologists had different *styles* in determining the link between HIV and AIDS, which led to radically different conclusions. On the one hand, in the case of epidemiology, statistical correlations were seen as sufficient evidence of this link. On the other hand, in the case of the microbiologists, the search for causal evidence on the cell level was front and centre. And the conclusions were diametrically opposite: the epidemiologists argued that the epidemiological evidence was strong enough to link HIV with AIDS, while the microbiologists contended that there was no causal link. A politics of sensing of the highest degree. However, in keeping with the multiple vocabularies of Actor-Network Theory I here utilize the concept *mode of sensing*, as this emphasizes ANT's conceptual history drawing on for

instance Law's (1994) work on *modes of ordering* – which also emphasizes difference, coordination, and heterogeneity – over the notion of *style*. Another important point is that *style* has closer links to addressing different professional styles, which is something I wish to avoid in this chapter. Thus, the focus in this chapter is on infrastructures and *modes of sensing*. See also Lee and Helgesson (2020) for a discussion of *styles of valuation*.

6 As I have pointed out elsewhere, just as with many actor-network theory concepts, the focus of Mol's analysis is on the stabilization of facts, technologies, or in this case disease. The focus is on how the world becomes coherent and stable. To address the focus on construction stories in actor-network theory, me and Galis have suggested a strategy of creating antonyms to the construction concepts in actor-network theory (Galis and Lee 2014). This theoretical strategy also allows us to in this case suggest concepts for the disunity between different sensing infrastructures.

7 However, to be fair post-ANT has in many ways, and in dialog with different versions of Mol's work also opened up for an analysis which highlights the obduracy and shaping force of non-human actors. See for instance, de Laet and Mol (2000).

8 This chapter focuses on the coordination of two infrastructures rather than a multiplicity, but the analytical potential for analysing multiplicities of infrastructures through modes of sensing remains the same.

9 The larger research project as well as the fieldwork was funded by the Swedish Research Council.

10 Of course genetics isn't new as a technology, but as a sensing infrastructure in disease surveillance, the advent of affordable whole genome sequencing has made it possible to do a new type of analysis in tracking disease. *Thus, I argue, the technology of genetics has become harnessed to build a new sensing infrastructure for disease surveillance.*

11 This hope was also reflected in the work and priorities at the ECDC, where the genetics team was starting up a pilot project for systematically tracking disease through genomics.

12 Personal communication.

13 DP. Personal communication.

14 As noted above, this country must remain anonymous due to the political ramifications its publication could entail

15 On risk objects, see Hilgartner (1992).

16 On the telling of construction stories with ANT, see Galis and Lee (2014).

17 On the logic of lumping and splitting see Zerubavel (1996).

REFERENCES

Boellstorff, T. (2015). Making Big Data, In Theory. In T. Boellstorff and B. Maurer (Eds), *Data, Now Bigger and Better!*. Chicago, IL: Prickly Paradigm Press.

Bowker, G. C. (2000). Biodiversity Datadiversity. *Social Studies of Science* 30(5): 643–683.

Bowker, G. C., and Star, S. L. (1999). *Sorting Things Out: Classification and Its Consequences.* Cambridge, MA: The MIT Press.

Caduff, C. (2015). *The Pandemic Perhaps: Dramatic Events in a Public Culture of Danger.* Oakland, CA: University of California Press.

Fujimura, J. H., and Chou, D. Y. (1994). 'Dissent in Science: Styles of Scientific Practice and the Controversy Over the Cause of AIDS. *Social Science & Medicine* 38(8): 1017–1036.

Carlson, S. (1999). 'Evolution and Systematics', Tracking the Course of Evolution. In Evolution: Investigating the Evidence, *Paleontological Society Special 9.* By permission of the Paleontological Society. <https://ucmp.berkeley.edu/education/events/carlson2.html#sjcfig5>.

European Centre for Disease Prevention and Control (2016a). Salmonellosis. In *ECDC. Annual Epidemiological Report for 2016.*

——(2016b). Multi-Country Outbreak of Salmonella Enteritidis Phage Type 8 MLVA Type 2-9-7-3-2 Infections, first update, 5 September 2016.

——(2016c). Multi-country Outbreak of Salmonella Enteritidis Phage Type 8 MLVA Type 2-9-7-3-2 and 2-9-6-3-2 Infections, 27 October 2016.

——(2017). Multi-Country Outbreak of Salmonella Enteritidis Phage Types 56 and 62, MLVA Profile 2-11-3-3-2 and 2-12-3-3-2 Infections, 20 July 2017.

Gabrys, J. (2016). *Program Earth: Environmental Sensing Technology and the Making of a Computational Planet 49: Electronic mediations.* Minneapolis: University of Minnesota Press.

Galis, V., and Lee, F. (2014). A Sociology of Exclusion. *Science, Technology, & Human Values* 39(1): 154–179.

Hacking, I. (1992). 'Style' for Historians and Philosophers. *Studies in History and Philosophy of Science* Part A 23(1): 1–20.

Haraway, D. (2010). When Species Meet: Staying with the Trouble. *Environment and Planning. D, Society and Space* 28(1): 53.

Hilgartner, S. (1992). The Social Construction of Risk Objects. In Short, Jr., J. F., and Clarke, L. (Eds), *Organizations, Uncertainties, and Risk.* Boulder: Westview Press, pp. 39–53.

Keck, F. (2010). *Un monde grippé.* Paris: Flammarion.

Kitchin, R. (2014). Big Data, New Epistemologies and Paradigm Shifts. *Big Data & Society* 1(1): 1–12.

Kockelman, P. (2013). The Anthropology of an Equation. Sieves, Spam Filters, Agentive Algorithms, and Ontologies of Transformation. *HAU: Journal of Ethnographic Theory* 3(3): 33–61.

Laet, M. de, and Mol, A. (2000). The Zimbabwe Bush Pump. *Social Studies of Science* 30(2): 225–263.

Lakoff, A. (2017). *Unprepared: Global Health in a Time of Emergency.* Oakland, CA: University of California Press.

Lakoff, A., and Collier, S. J. (2008). *Biosecurity Interventions: Global Health & Security in Question*. New York: Columbia University Press.

Law, J. (1994). *Organizing Modernity*. Oxford: Blackwell.

Lee, F. (2017). Where is Zika? Making a Global Pandemic with an Algorithm. Annual Conference for the Society for Social Studies of Science (4S), Boston, 30 August–2 September.

Lee, Francis. (2021). Enacting the Pandemic. *Science & Technology Studies* 34 (1): 65–90.

Lee, F., Bier, J., Christensen J., Engelmann, L., Helgesson, C.-F., and Williams, R. (2019). Algorithms as Folding: Reframing the Analytical Focus. *Big Data & Society* 6(2): 1–12.

Lee, F., and Björklund Larsen, L. (2019). How Should We Theorize Algorithms? Five Ideal Types in Analysing Algorithmic Normativities. *Big Data & Society* 6(2): doi. org/10.1177/2053951719867349

Lee, F, and Helgesson, CF. (2020). Styles of Valuation: Algorithms and Agency in High-Throughput Bioscience. *Science, Technology, & Human Values* 45 (4): 659–85.

Mackenzie, A. (2014). Multiplying Numbers Differently: An Epidemiology of Contagious Convolution. *Distinktion: Scandinavian Journal of Social Theory* 15(2): 189–207.

——2017. *Machine Learners: Archaeology of a Data Practice*. Cambridge, MA: The MIT Press.

Martin, A., and Lynch, M. (2009). Counting Things and People: The Practices and Politics of Counting. *Social Problems* 56(2): 243–266.

Mol, A. (2002). *The Body Multiple: Ontology in Medical Practice*. Durham: Duke University Press.

Seaver, N. (2017). Algorithms as Culture: Some Tactics for the Ethnography of Algorithmic Systems. *Big Data & Society* 4(2): 1–12.

Star, S. L., and Ruhleder, K. (1996). Steps Toward an Ecology of Infrastructure: Design and Access for Large Information Spaces. *Information Systems Research* 7(1): 111–134.

Whitworth, J. J. (2017). Salmonella Sickens 350 in Five Countries with Link to Poultry Products. Foodnavigator.com (30 July). <https://www.foodnavigator.com/ Article/2017/07/31/Multi-year-EU-wide-Salmonella-outbreak-shows-earlier-peak#>.

Witjes, N., and lbrich, P. (2017). A Fragile Transparency: Satellite Imagery Analysis, Non-State Actors, and Visual Representations of Security. *Science and Public Policy* 4(44): 524–534.

Zerubavel, E. (1996). Lumping and Splitting: Notes on Social Classification. *Sociological Forum* 11(3): 421–433.

Ziewitz, M. (2017). A Not Quite Random Walk: Experimenting with the Ethnomethods of the Algorithm. *Big Data & Society* 4(2): 1–13.

5

HUMAN SENSING INFRASTRUCTURES AND GLOBAL PUBLIC HEALTH SECURITY IN INDIA'S MILLION DEATH STUDY

Erik Aarden

ABSTRACT

Global health is increasingly approached as a security issue, especially in the context of unpredictable global epidemics that can be anticipated and monitored with novel, digital sensing techniques. Advocates of a more human-centred notion of health security, who claim that everyday health threats should be of greater concern, have challenged this 'securitization' of health. Along these lines of argumentation, this chapter considers the Million Death Study in India, an effort to gather better insight into the most common causes of death by means of an interview-based method called verbal autopsy. I argue that this method's reliance on 'human sensors' requires a sociotechnical sensing infrastructure that steers humans towards their task of symptomatic data collection and diagnosing discrete causes of death. This infrastructure includes various kinds of devices and sets of instructions that shape how human sensors work. This infrastructure produces statistics on mortality in India that prioritize a decontextualized, medical-statistical perspective on mortality in India. Through its intersections with state-based and global health infrastructures, this prioritization has particular political effects in the context of global public health security. While the study provides valuable evidence of the most common, often underrepresented causes of death in India, it is less suited for addressing the structural dimensions of health security in the global South.

INTRODUCTION: SENSING THE COMMON IN GLOBAL PUBLIC HEALTH SECURITY

Global health is increasingly approached as a security issue, to the extent that perceptions of health in terms of threats and required responses can be considered one of the dominant frames of global health governance (McInnes et al. 2012). This 'securitization' of global public health foregrounds concerns about the global spread of newly emergent infectious diseases such as SARS and avian flu, the global HIV/AIDS epidemic and bioterrorism (Collier and Lakoff 2008; Hanrieder and Kreuder-Sonnen 2014; Jin and Krackattu 2011). This security-based approach to global public health is both product and instigator of the application of novel approaches to disease detection that supposedly imply a shift in disease monitoring 'from actuary to sentinel' (Lakoff 2015). With these characterisations Lakoff points to a shift he identifies in global public health, from calculating averages and common health problems towards early detection and preparedness for extremely rare, but potentially catastrophic health risks. Such a focus on anticipating the exceptional is in turn said to be enabled by new forms of data gathering and processing. These include the use of algorithms that can distil data with potential relevance for health from large sets of data that is not primarily diagnostic (Bengtsson et al. 2019; Roberts and Elbe 2017). From this point of view, global public health threats are increasingly perceived as exceptional events that can be anticipated with novel digital sensing methods.

This paradigm of preparedness is contested for its focus on highly visible, but exceedingly rare health risks. Critical security scholars have questioned the close association between this framing of global public health and traditional *state-centred* notions of security (Nunes 2018). While they see value in considering health in terms of security, they simultaneously argue for a *human-centred* approach to global public health security. These scholars point out that '[a]t the simplest level, premature and unnecessary loss of life is perhaps the greatest insecurity of human life' (Chen and Narasimhan 2003: 183). *Common* causes contributing to this loss of life should therefore receive more attention from security scholars, who should also pay more attention to the insecurities caused by structural threats, and inequalities in access to curative and preventive health services (MacLean 2008). They thereby advance the argument that the things that people are most likely to die from, form a significant security threat in their own right.

The prevention of premature death requires its own strategies for detection of (common) health threats. The Million Death Study (MDS) in India is an example of such a strategy. Researchers argue this study is necessary due to the supposed lack of representative and reliable insight into the *causes* of premature death in existing public health monitoring in India and other low and middle income countries (Gomes et al. 2017; Jha 2012, 2014). Even though this initiative is situated in the Indian context, researchers thus seek to establish it as a model for public health monitoring and interventions in a broader global health context. The MDS aims to attend to this knowledge gap through an effort to produce representative and cause-specific national mortality statistics by way of an interview-based method called *verbal autopsy* (VA). In stark contrast to the use of electronic data-processing capabilities entangled with a growing emphasis on anticipating unpredictable epidemics in some approaches to global public health security, the MDS pursues forms of innovation in the detection of common health threats by employing what may be considered *human sensors*.

The Million Death Study provides important insights into the challenges of developing sensors for signalling structural, common health threats. While study initiators emphasize the idea of 'a simple, respectful conversation' as the core of verbal autopsy, we will see how the study employs a broader *sensing infrastructure* to make human sensors work. I develop this notion of how infrastructures *sensitize* human sensors in this chapter to understand the joint emergence of a particular mode of knowledge production and specific formations of public health threats in India. In the next section, I lay the groundwork for this notion, which I locate at the intersection of global health security, critiques of quantification in global health and the 'mediation' between human and non-human elements of sensing. This discussion forms the basis of an exploration of the Million Death Study, in which I address how data is generated and processed; how human sensors are sensitized towards that process; and how this produces particular mortality statistics and views of major public health issues in India. In conclusion, I consider how understanding the study in terms of sensing provides insight into the MDS' modes of knowledge production, which create a novel infrastructure for addressing statistical deficiencies, while simultaneously perpetuating deficiencies in considering the structural aspects of global public health security.

CONCEPTUALIZING GLOBAL PUBLIC HEALTH SECURITY AND ITS SENSING INFRASTRUCTURES

The increasingly prominent approach to security and global health focused on preparedness for novel, as-yet unknown risks builds on long-standing concerns about the global circulation of health threats from the periphery to global centres of power (King 2002), but takes on a distinct contemporary form. Current global health threats are considered to be quintessentially mobile across borders, requiring tailored methods of early detection and intervention. The most prominent of these threats, such as new infectious pathogens, the spread of HIV/AIDS and bioterrorism, are considered to be difficult to address with traditional epidemiological and public health approaches. Global health practitioners therefore argue that new institutional responses, styles of thinking and techniques for measurement and intervention are required. These approaches emphasize preparedness for unknown and unexpected events (Collier and Lakoff 2008). These approaches to global health thereby constitute a deviation from the forms of biopolitical governing Foucault describes as 'the calculated management of life' (Foucault 2013: 44). This approach to government, which Foucault himself has described in terms of security (Foucault 2007), involves the measurement and calculation of collective probabilities and averages within a population and is focused on normal distributions of, for example, disease within a population.

The focus on the exceptional in emerging forms of global health security thus stands in marked contrast to Foucault's writing, causing some authors to conceptualize it as a biopolitical transformation. They do no longer consider probabilistic national statistics to be core instruments for the exercise of power. Rather, the emergence of new measuring techniques and new kinds of social collectives supposedly relocate the management of life to sites other than national populations (Rabinow and Rose 2006). New conceptualisations of populations further relate to shifts from mortality statistics to measuring health, quality of life and the burden of disease on the one hand (Wahlberg 2007; Wahlberg and Rose 2015), and from averages and probabilities to preparedness for unique, catastrophic events (Lakoff 2015) on the other.

Scholars focusing on preparedness in global health argue that these transformed understandings of populations and health threats emerge in conjunction with new techniques for identifying and calculating risks. These are often seen as a manifestation of broader transformations in data generating and processing capabilities, captured under the sweeping label of 'big data'. Big data allegedly 'enables an entirely new epistemological approach for making sense of the world' by attempting to 'gain insights "born from the data"' (Kitchin 2014: 2). Data technologies 'generate different populations as objects of concern and intervention' (Ruppert 2011: 219) and thereby contribute to the particular shape of global health security focused on the anticipation of exceptional events. Data collection devices and their attendant infrastructures of information collection and processing thereby produce a particular 'gaze' on their social environment. They have their own social and political consequences (Bates et al. 2016; Ruppert et al. 2017), rooted in the broader cultural authority of numerical evidence and quantification (Rieder and Simon 2016). In the context of global health security, this authority often does not come from the data directly, but from what Amoore calls 'data derivatives' (Amoore 2011); the identification of associations within the data that enable the identification of unknown and absent objects that need to be acted upon.

These characteristics of big data analytics are often positioned in contrast to more 'traditional' approaches to statistics and diagnostics in the context of global public health. Nevertheless, critics of this perspective argue that averages and regularities in public health continue to be vital for a global public health security agenda focused on threats to the individual (Chen and Narasimhan 2003; MacLean 2008). Statistical notions of the normal distribution of health and disease are a product of the intricate historical relations between the state and medical science in developing diagnostic classifications. Medical classifications such as the International Classification of Diseases (ICD) that is used in the Million Death Study, were established and further solidified and transformed out of states' interests in gathering information on the health status of their citizens (Bowker and Star 1999). As Sætnan and colleagues characterize statistics: *'the act of counting its citizens, territories, resources, problems and so on is one of the acts by which the State participates in creating both itself, its citizens and the policies, rights, expectations, services and so on that bind them together'* (Sætnan et al. 2011: 2, emphasis original). This includes the health status of the population, in the form of distinct categories of disease. Disease classification relies on what Rosenberg calls the 'structuring act' of diagnosis, which facilitates the consideration of disease in the aggregate, detached from individual sufferers (Rosenberg 2002). Diagnosis hence serves 'to establish similarities via classifications in order to promote population health, allocate resources, focus research, and so on' (Jutel 2011: 201). At the same time, quantification, including population health statistics, helps to bring the reality it describes into being, making a particular set of social problems present that can be expressed through numbers (Espeland and Stevens 2008). Lorway and Khan, for example describe how HIV/AIDS monitoring in India produces new social configurations, individual identities and ideas of vulnerability and (in-)security (Lorway and Khan 2014).

The distinction between big data approaches to epidemics and statistical perspectives on population health is far from absolute. Both ways of identifying health threats attribute a central role to the notion of population, which often implies an abstract, decontextualized and reductionist representation of human life (Krieger 2012; Murphy 2017). Populations in global health emerge from the particular methods of data collection and processing that produce particular, quantitative collectives and their characteristics. These result from what Reubi has called 'epidemiological reason', which is characterized by the ambition to save the largest possible number of lives on the basis of rigorous data collection and processing and a global notion of population (Reubi 2018). Yet the predominance of quantitative understandings of population health in a global context is contested for the ways it decontextualizes and generalizes health problems and medical interventions, which obscures the complex, situated social and political dimensions of health and disease (Adams 2013; Birn 2009). Since distinct approaches to the generation and processing of data for monitoring health produce different populations-at-risk, it thus becomes important to ask how research projects 'see' (Biruk 2012). In other words, how are populations and the health threats that affect them constructed through particular methods for sensing health problems?

This question is particularly pertinent in light of the Million Death Study's explicit claim to address the shortcomings of existing population health statistics in India, using the verbal autopsy method. The Million Death Study presents a particular form of sensing in the context of global public health. Sensing in the MDS partly resembles a traditional, nationally oriented emphasis on population health statistics, while it is simultaneously presented as an innovative approach to data generation and processing that aims to circumvent the limitations of medical-statist knowledge production infrastructures in low and middle income countries. The study hence carries an inherent paradox between informing health policy and the simultaneous critique of the state's inability to produce reliable population health data that is implied in its methodological approach. Despite the emphasis on the human ability to determine cause of death that undergirds verbal autopsy, this approach includes various devices aimed at *sensitizing* human sensors. These devices include different kinds of instructions for human data collectors and analysts on how to gather symptomatic information and determine causes of death. It is therefore fruitful to think of 'human' sensors in the MDS as part of a broader, sociotechnical infrastructure that mediates (Latour 1999) between human and technical contributions to the making of mortality statistics. Drawing on infrastructure studies, we may see how the MDS facilitates the circulation of symptomatic data and diagnoses from households, to the Indian government and research institutes. At the same time, it is worth noting how infrastructures are always established in relation to pre-existing infrastructures, with particular political effects (Anand et al. 2018; Slota and Bowker 2017). We will see how the sensing infrastructure of the MDS steers human sensors towards the study's particular purpose, how it intersects with existing infrastructures and how it thereby obscures other potential insights with particular implications for the politics of global public health security.

In the next section, I reconstruct the making of cause-specific mortality statistics for India in the Million Death Study. While the securitization of public health in this study is not explicit (i.e. there is no mention of security as such), it is fundamentally informed by a logic of identifying threats to the health and survival of the Indian population and formulating adequate (health policy) responses. My analytical narrative is based on interviews with thirteen researchers, government officials and other public health actors and an analysis of study documents and publications. The interviews took place in India and Canada in the second half of 2013 and the first half of 2014. I interviewed some of my respondents twice, while some of the interviews took place in a collective setting with multiple respondents. I analysed the interviews with a process coding approach that focuses on respondents' description of work practices within the study (Saldaña 2011). I applied a narrative analysis (Czarniawska 2004) to the coded interviews in order to reconstruct how researchers and government officials construct knowledge making processes and the relation between human sensors and their sensitizing devices. The documents I analysed include study protocols, guidelines and instruction manuals, as well as publications in scientific journals on the study's importance, methods and results. I consider these documents active participants in the making of the study (Shankar et al. 2017). I therefore analysed them not only in terms of how they describe the study's content, but also for how they contribute to defining the issue of lacking mortality statistics in India and to developing a response to that issue (Asdal 2015). After providing an introduction of the study's broad outline and relevance to global public health, I divide my account of the study and its human sensors into three subsections. First, I introduce how data is collected, processed and used for determining mortality statistics. Second, I turn to the theme of human sensors and the infrastructure that 'sensitizes' them towards the task of producing mortality statistics. Third, I discuss how this infrastructure contributes to the production of a particular perspective on major public health threats in India that MDS actors frame as policy relevant – and turn to both the strengths and weaknesses of this infrastructure in the conclusion.

SENSING POPULATION MORTALITY IN INDIA'S MILLION DEATH STUDY

The Million Death Study in India aims to produce representative cause of death statistics for the Indian population through a method called verbal autopsy (VA). Researchers in the study characterize this method as an interview-based, structured investigation of the circumstances and symptoms occurring around the time of death (Jha 2012). Study initiators claim that this effort and its particular approach is needed because the available cause-specific information on mortality is insufficient. They claim it is either based on hospital statistics, which cover only a small portion of all fatalities in India, or on self-assigned causes of death that are often inaccurate. Since the late 1990s, the Office of the Registrar General of India (RGI), which is responsible for the census, and the Centre for Global Health Research at the University of Toronto in Canada, in collaboration with research institutes in India, have therefore developed, piloted and refined a method for generating cause of death statistics that does not rely on the medical system (Jha et al. 2006). The study is funded by the Indian government, grants from research councils in Canada, India and the United States, as well as organisations such as the Bill and Melinda Gates Foundation. Researchers claim it is a cheap study, supposedly costing less than a dollar per year for each household being monitored. According to one senior researcher, it seeks to correct assumptions about public health in India – thereby potentially contributing to the achievement of the Millennium Development Goals (Bhutta 2006). While the study focuses on India, researchers explicitly position its approach to data collection as a model for collecting reliable mortality statistics in other low- and middle-income countries (Jha 2014). For global health research, the study is therefore considered an example for the advancement of evidence-based global health (Birbeck et al. 2013).

FROM SYMPTOMATIC DATA POINTS TO MORTALITY STATISTICS

Million Death Study researchers explain the urgency of the study in terms of the limited availability of reliable cause of death information, and the importance of such information for public health. As one senior researcher explained, the study:

> tries to answer a very easy question: how do people die? And there is an extraordinary widespread degree of ignorance about how people die and less surprising but also true is that people don't really understand how important understanding causes of death is to improving health of the living.

Researchers cite the circumstances under which most people in India die as an important factor contributing to this ignorance. They regularly repeated to me that, since the vast majority of people dies at home, in rural areas and without medical attention, there is no information on what causes their deaths. Moreover, the information that is available predominantly comes from hospitals in urban areas, which cannot reasonably be extrapolated to the population as a whole. Since, as one researcher claimed, 'in the immediate future there will be no clinically certified deaths in India', researchers and government officials collectively developed an alternative approach to identifying causes of death. Central to this approach is the use of an existing demographic survey, the so-called Sample Registration System (SRS), which already monitors population dynamics on an annual basis.

The SRS was presented to me in interviews as a 'unique' infrastructure that was introduced to keep track of changes in overall population size during the ten-year intervals of India's full census. The SRS sample includes about 0,8% of India's population (which amounts to a cohort of 8 million people). The sample is distributed over randomly selected units from all over India that collectively are supposed to provide a representative overview of population change. Sample size is based on the census (for example, the current SRS sample, in use since 2014, is based on the 2011 census) and calculations of the total number of participants required to make what demographers consider statistically robust claims about the least common event of interest (which presently is infant mortality). The current SRS sample consists of 8861 units of less than 2000 inhabitants. The SRS aims to trace changes to the population in each of its units, including migration, births and deaths. This is done via 'dual enumeration'. So-called part-time enumerators, who are local residents, continuously collect relevant information for their respective unit. The numbers they produce are matched with the results of secondary, retrospective enumerations produced by government officials. These visit all households in the roughly ten units they are responsible for twice a year to collect the same information on the preceding six months. The verbal autopsy method of the Million Death Study was added to this existing procedure. Wherever a death is reported, the secondary government enumerators are now required to also collect further details on *how* this person died.

The MDS expands on the SRS' use of human enumerators who develop a relationship with the people they survey over time. This should allow them to engage with these people to elicit information needed for diagnosing causes of death. The MDS hence establishes a novel approach to medical research that is – in part – based on the *non-medical* nature of its data collection. Government enumerators are not expected to diagnose, but to 'prompt or probe' family members of the deceased in order to gather more details on what occurred preceding death (SRS Collaborators of the RGI-CGHR 2011: 2). The most important part of this data collection is what is called the 'narrative', in which respondents are expected to give their own account (instigated and directed by the enumerator) on the events preceding death. One researcher describes the scenario as follows:

> If you are asking me; "how did your grandfather die?" I start at; "yesterday night he was having chest pain". Chest pain is one symptom. Then he suddenly vomited – vomiting is another symptom. Basically, these signs and symptoms doctors use to assign cause of death.

Enumerators receive strict instructions on what kind of information to collect, and how to do so in order to make the conversation as insightful as possible for the study. The household interview is primarily conceived as a tool to collect the relevant symptomatic 'data points', which Armstrong describes as the 'smallest possible piece of information' (Armstrong 2019: 103). In the context of the MDS this refers to the discrete and specific elements of the various events preceding a person's death. Since the sequence of and coherence between these events matter in the process of diagnosis, the key issue is to gather all of them, in the right order, and with the right degree of detail. This is how enumerators become sensors; their ability to engage in conversation allows them to generate the data required for diagnosing deaths. Their role in this context is only to *record* symptoms, not to *interpret* them, which is why they deliberately receive no medical training in the context of the study – since researchers believe that medical understanding of the symptoms might interfere with enumerators' ability to carefully listen and record.

Symptomatic data are recorded with four different forms, numbered 10 A through D, which respectively apply to neonates, children, adults and maternal deaths. Each form is adapted to generate the symptomatic data considered relevant to diagnosing deaths in that particular (age) group. The SRS sample produces about fifty thousand records of death a year, all of which are subjected to quality control. Data collection of a further randomly selected 5% of forms is repeated, in order to ascertain that symptomatic data points are accurately recorded. The RGI collects these forms before they are made available to MDS researchers for further diagnosis. All of these measures contribute to creating a feedback loop within the study that is supposed to improve accuracy and to provide insight into the functioning of the study's human sensors.

A panel of a few hundred physicians using the International Classification of Disease (ICD-10) interprets the symptomatic data to categorize deaths and diagnose their causes. Physicians on this panel are recruited via medical schools, professional networks and medical journals and are paid Rs40 for each 'record' they 'code'. A 'record' of symptoms described in a household interview gets randomly assigned to two physicians. They 'code' the narrative independently, using symptomatic data points in the record to consider potential causes of death and ultimately arrive at a diagnosis. One researcher describes the ensuing coding process as 'a three-step check and balance'. The first step is the independent coding by two physicians. If they agree on the diagnosis, the cause of death is registered as such. In the 25% of cases where they disagree, a second step of so-called 'reconciliation' follows. In this step, both physicians receive each other's diagnosis and are asked to reconsider. If disagreement continues, which happens in 10% of cases, a third step of 'adjudication' follows. This means that a third, more experienced physician receives both diagnoses and is asked to decide.

Records for which a cause of death has been determined are aggregated by RGI, which first publishes a report on the findings. Such reports include nationwide overviews of the percentage of deaths that may be attributed to particular causes, as well as the distribution of causes by gender, age groups, and regions. Only after publication of this report is the data made available to global health researchers, who publish on the results in often cause-specific papers (e.g. on cardiovascular disease, cancer, malaria, traffic accidents, etc.) written in international working groups. One researcher describes this process as follows:

> After a record's completion, we analyse it, provide the information to government and government publishes a report. If the government publishes the report, then on the basis of this data we publish papers. These papers have a policy impact.

Like many of his colleagues, he emphasizes 'policy impact' as a core objective of the study. Not only is the MDS supposed to generate more accurate and representative cause of death statistics for India, this is explicitly done to secure better health for the Indian population – and beyond. Collectively, the report, scientific papers and policy interventions based on the study 'perform' a particular version of India's population (Law 2009; Ruppert 2011). This version does not only show the normal distribution of health threats and insecurities overall, but also categorizes the population in terms of how certain indicators (age, gender, and location as proxy of socio-economic status) are expressed in divergence of health threats. This points towards the ways in which the human sensing approach in the study enacts public health security concerns.

SENSITIZING A HUMAN SENSING INFRASTRUCTURE

The reliance on human sensors in the MDS is itself a response to researchers' conviction that clinical means of monitoring mortality are insufficient. They are often not available, and therefore produce results that are neither representative nor very reliable. The use of human sensors is an attempt to access data on causes of death closer to the source and to interpret that data more accurately. Yet the study operates through a continuous tension between human capabilities and the need to ascertain consistency and quality in the study's knowledge production processes. The study handles this tension primarily by sensitizing its human sensors towards producing the particular forms of symptomatic data and diagnostic specificity it aims for. Despite researchers' insistence on the 'simple conversation' as the supposed core of the study, its human sensors are thereby made part of a more elaborate *sensing infrastructure* that consists of various material devices, standards, and procedural rules and instructions that enable the work of human sensors. One researcher, for example, describes how diagnostic criteria in the context of verbal autopsy were developed:

> I worked with several experts on cancer and then we took what could be symptoms visualized at time of death. Based on that we produced a list of 10 to 15 symptoms and circulated that to reviewers who said: yes, this could be the best thing. And that would be possible to record, of course. You can't say we do a CT scan. So, symptoms that were possible to ask and were the most pronounced symptoms.

Not only diagnostic criteria are made useable for human sensors. The forms used in the study, its software platforms, instruction videos and manuals, as well as training are all involved in sensitizing the human sensor towards how to 'correctly' gather and interpret data.

One of the main challenges the MDS has to account for is the inability to rely on the medical system, or established medical research infrastructures to gather the kind of representative data the study is after. One senior researcher explains: 'it can't be done like a research methodology. It has to be incorporated in the [SRS] system.' He argues that only RGI and its extensive workforce of about 800 enumerators can sustain a study of this kind. The study's focus on deaths, rather than the burden of disease, also enables the central role of the non-medical staff. 'The goal for us is proper reporting of the symptoms', one researcher explains, before continuing:

> Because the one thing you must realize is that many symptoms are not clear when a disease is progressing. When you are developing lung cancer, symptoms may be very confusing. But when you are dying of a cancer it is very obvious.

Nevertheless:

> The most important part is the training. This could not have been achieved, results would be uncertain everywhere if you don't have proper training. So, we first developed training for the interviewer, at the government level at the various census offices.

This training is supposed to help enumerators in asking the right questions and noting down the relevant 'data points'. In a training video a researcher showed me, this is explained in the form of 'five simple steps' to follow. These include (1) to carefully listen and take notes, (2) to note which out of a total of twelve 'cardinal symptoms' (including things like fever, breathlessness, chest pain, and urinary problems) were present, (3) to probe further details about these symptoms, (4) to confirm that none of the remaining symptoms occurred, (5) to confirm the narrative with the respondent, especially clarifying the duration and sequence of all the symptoms. Following these steps, the video maintains, enables anyone to write a good narrative that presumably includes all the data needed for determining a diagnosis.

Similarly, for physicians to serve as diagnostic sensors, they also receive a set of instructions on how to approach coding. When doctors apply to become part of the coding panel, they first have to go through three phases of training and tests. These include exercises in coding a set of narratives, including some that were subject to reconciliation – which are presumably more complex. Since the aim of the study is to identify a *single* underlying cause for every death, the study manual instructs physicians how to distinguish this from what is called the 'terminal event' as well as risk factors and 'contributory causes' that lie outside of the main chain of events leading to death. Physicians are further instructed to rely on the symptoms described in the record and their own expert judgement: 'you are expected to provide an opinion on the cause of death to the best of your knowledge and belief, based on the information available to you' (SRS Collaborators of the RGI-CGHR 2011: 21). Physicians are expected to find the middle ground between the most specific cause they consider possible, while keeping it at a level general enough to be defensible. This means that physicians are expected to think in terms of public health, looking for common rather than exotic causes. With the aim of attributing a single cause to each death, all of these instructions are meant to increase the chance that the right one gets chosen.

One researcher I interviewed took out his laptop to show how he might go about coding a narrative. He showed me how the respondent in this particular case thought that a kidney problem had been the cause of death and highlighted some symptomatic data ('swelling of the legs') in the narrative on screen. This he used to search in the study's coding software for kidney diseases expressed in the form of swollen legs. However, he also indicated that the software could provide alternative explanations to consider (in this case heart failure) on the basis of the keywords he provided. Finally, he indicated how physicians can rate each record for quality and their own diagnosis for degree of certainty – adding another feedback opportunity that may be used to improve the study's sensing infrastructure.

This example shows not only how a physician may code, but also how the so-called Central Medical Evaluation software platform plays a key role in the diagnostic process. It allows physicians to search within more than 2000 ICD-codes, provides suggestions for differential diagnoses to consider, and may occasionally correct a physician's tendencies. This platform forms only half of the software infrastructure incorporated into the Million Death Study, with the other half responsible for performing quality checks on the data supplied on the verbal autopsy forms. This includes controls for whether the data is complete and consistent. Once forms are approved, the Central Medical Evaluation platform takes care of the distribution of records. It allocates no more than ten records at a time to any physician, taking into account which of the eighteen languages used for the forms they master. The software platform is supposed to assist the coding physician in assigning an accurate cause of death, and to do so as quickly as possible. It does so in various ways. It allows physicians to search ICD-codes and blocks certain ICD-codes that are impossible or extremely unlikely – such as prostate cancer for female deaths or many chronic conditions for young children. Yet the software intervenes most actively by suggesting diagnoses it considers more or less likely for specific cases:

> For instance, if certain symptoms are in place and that is noted by the system and the physician tries to assign an ICD code that is not intuitive to the system, the system will try to correct the physician and say: this doesn't make sense. The person had a fever, the person was vomiting and you are saying they died of diabetes.

The software does this by using data from previously diagnosed deaths, which my interview respondent characterized as 'metadata', to suggest causes of death it considers likely in similar cases. The aim is to develop 'machine learning' for the study, described as follows:

> The machine itself is becoming smarter as it codes. So it is sort of like a human being, you learn from your experiences and you make mistakes, but you correct these mistakes as you go forward.

The hope is that this will result in a web-based coding system that increases speed, without compromising quality.

Despite the desire to further automate coding and critiques that the verbal autopsy method is subject to human bias (Butler 2010), studies of available coding algorithms by MDS researchers suggest that human coders are still the most reliable (Desai et al. 2014). As one researcher explains:

> As far as VAs are concerned, the physician standard is much better than the machine standard at this point. The machine is not smart enough at this point to replace the physician. And it would have to be smart enough and be able to learn on its own. To keep up with the human being.

Another researcher attributes the difference to the supposedly uniquely human ability to consider the history and relations between symptoms in a way that algorithms cannot. Nevertheless, for the human to be able to gather relevant data and provide accurate analysis, the study prescribes a set of almost mechanistic steps for the collection and treatment of data to its human workers. These steps serve to build a sensing infrastructure in which human sensors are made 'sensitive' towards the study's aim of producing accurate and representative mortality statistics. By doing so, the infrastructure prioritizes particular forms of data and of interpretation over others, with particular consequences for how its insights into, and contributions to, public health in India are framed.

MAKING MORTALITY PROFILES, FRAMING PUBLIC HEALTH POLICY

The aim of the data collected and analysed in the MDS is 'to yield cause-specific mortality profile at the national level' (Office of the Registrar General of India 2009: vi) and thereby gain a better understanding of the particular health threats facing the Indian population. An important lesson that researchers believe to have learned over the years is that the VA method works (see also Aleksandrowicz et al. 2014). As one researcher explains:

> we made use of the representative strength of SRS. So, there is the possibility of being representative of the Indian population. That was a real strength we had. In spite of the specificity that may be lost [sometimes].

Implicit in this argument is that mortality statistics based on a representative sample are infinitely more reliable and accurate than those produced in hospitals.

This holds true to MDS researchers despite the 'lost specificity' for rare causes of death in smaller geographical areas, for which the statistics produced within the SRS are not precise enough. The employment of human sensors in the MDS is therefore considered a reliable solution for the failure of national medical infrastructures that cannot produce equally solid mortality statistics.

Researchers additionally believe that the VA method and its sensing infrastructure may be expanded, considering it an innovative form of knowledge production with various other potential contexts of application. Some examples mentioned in interviews include studies of 'point of death diagnostics' that compare VA with regular autopsy, of the role of nutrition in disease, and of the impact of providing mortality data on the delivery of health services. More broadly speaking, findings from the MDS are treated as hypotheses for further research on what 'causes the causes'. This idea is above all supported by observations about regional differences in mortality, which researchers translate into a belief in the contributions the study can make to preventing causes of death that are common in some areas, but rare in others.

The most important promise of the MDS and its verbal autopsy method that researchers emphasize, however, is its potential to contribute to *global* public health. The first RGI report of study results published in 2009, for example, observes that the findings are 'not only of national interest but [are] also watched globally' (Office of the Registrar General of India 2009: 52). This argument follows a similar logic to the one about regional diversity in causes of death. As one researcher explained, India's is 'a huge population, and diverse, which reflects the whole developing world'. For example, since the number of deaths from snake-bites *in India* is underestimated, researchers explicitly argue that *global* estimates are probably too low as well (see Mohapatra et al. 2011). Additionally, verbal autopsy is presented as a feasible option for other countries that have no comprehensive mortality registration. Innovation in global health to address shortcomings in the collection of mortality statistics beyond India drive MDS leadership to consider, for example, expanding the study to other countries and to formulate the ambition of elevating collection of mortality statistics to a global ambition akin to the United Nations Sustainable Development Goals (see also Jha 2014).

Despite these various arguments in favour of the approach and insights of the MDS, researchers' opinions differ with regard to the study's insights they find most valuable. Among the examples of notable findings, they mentioned causes of death as diverse as cancers, HIV/AIDS (which is less common than previously thought), malaria and snakebites (both more common), smoking and cardiovascular diseases. Some researchers thought that the MDS provides the ultimate proof that the epidemiological transition (i.e. the shift from infectious to chronic diseases as predominant causes of death) is well underway in India – a point of view confirmed in the study's findings (Office of the Registrar General of India 2009). Others noted that there is a significant 'residual burden' of diseases like tuberculosis and malaria. One researcher explained that he saw the value of the MDS mostly in the context of those conditions:

Especially in those areas where there is, deaths occur in rural areas, it may be very good. When death occurs in rural areas, without access to medical attention and nobody knows how many deaths occur.

The study results further show that such acute conditions, including snake bites, tuberculosis and malaria, are more likely to kill and remain unattended to in rural regions, among women, and in poorer states.

Besides pointing to diagnostically specific, largely biologically defined causes of death, researchers also indicate that more structural and institutional factors play a significant role. The following scenario may be illustrative. After again pointing out how most rural deaths occur in households, this researcher explains why this is so:

So, this is a particular village and your hospital is located 15 km away. Reaching the hospital is a problem. This is one barrier. And if the hospital is there, the doctor might not be available. If the doctor is available, facilities may not be available. Then this doctor has to refer to another hospital nearby. Then the problem is again distance. And traveling costs. These are the barriers. [...] And they are unreported, these deaths.

This scenario is once more confirmed by the differences between states in terms of causes of death and their distribution within the population in the study's findings, which correlate with differences in socio-economic status (Office of the Registrar General of India 2009). These differences are not only expressed in the burden of infectious diseases. Non-communicable diseases, too, are more likely to affect the poorer population, often with catastrophic financial consequences for those already disadvantaged (Rajan and Prabhakaran 2012). These dimensions of mortality, disease, and its consequences in India reflect widely shared concerns about structural inadequacies in the Indian health system and its contributions to public health (Dreze and Sen 2013; Global Health Watch 2011; Rao et al. 2015). Furthermore, they indicate how the specifically sensitized human sensors in the MDS both hold promise and face limitations in terms of human-centred perspectives on global public health security.

CONCLUSION: SENSING INFRASTRUCTURES AND THE CONTEXTUALIZATION OF GLOBAL PUBLIC HEALTH SECURITY

Researchers in the Million Death Study commonly portrayed the study as a simple endeavour, relying on what I termed 'human sensors'. These are government enumerators who visit households and collect symptomatic information about any fatalities in a 'simple conversation' on the one hand, and physicians who deduce a cause of death from the symptoms described for each deceased person in the sample on the other. The objective of the study is to produce reliable and representative numbers on the pattern of mortality in India, which are currently not available. It employs the so-called verbal autopsy method to overcome the problems of incomplete and biased statistics generated within the Indian medical system. Yet while researchers emphasize the simplicity of the VA method, closer consideration of the study reveals that it cannot work without a more extensive *sensing infrastructure*. Within this infrastructure, human sensors are steered towards contributing to the study's objectives, which results in data capture and analysis that produces a decontextualized, predominantly biological perspective on mortality in India. The study infrastructure and its particular orientation towards the quantification of death intersects with other global public health infrastructures. I turn to these intersections to further illuminate the political salience of sensing in the context of global public health security.

The political salience of infrastructure emerges in part from the association of infrastructure with social progress, both in response to and in spite of the contentious relation between what is new and what builds on pre-existing infrastructures (Anand et al. 2018). In the Million Death Study, the relations between the study's sensing infrastructure and statistical infrastructures of the Indian state as well as global health infrastructures are of particular interest. The study's infrastructure combines human sensors with technical devices in order to address a weakness in national infrastructures for collecting mortality data. Their insufficiency is a key reason why the MDS does not use established medical infrastructures for data collection. Yet the study can only circumvent the medical system by building on a different, existing, demographic government infrastructure. This creates an infrastructural paradox, in which the study's critique of the state's deficiency in collecting data that is vital for its public tasks (i.e. securing health) can only be addressed through a state infrastructure that functions. This ambivalent relation between the MDS and the Indian state cannot be seen separate from a second infrastructural intersection between the MDS and global health as a professional and academic field (McGoey et al. 2011). This global health infrastructure is characterized and facilitated by multiple, asymmetrical connections between research institutions, governments and funding agencies in the global North and South (Crane 2010) that involve various kind of non-governmental actors in public health activities in low and middle income countries. Against this background, research and intervention in global health often pursues a decontextualized strategy of knowledge production that allows the circulation of insights at the expense of situated approaches to public health (Biehl and Petryna 2013). Despite the innovative knowledge production infrastructure of the MDS, it reproduces contested aspects of global public health infrastructures that decontextualize health problems and potentially dilute democratic accountability.

This does not mean that the MDS gets death 'wrong'. Its insights are vital and its method suggests an innovative way of breaking through the vicious circle of deficient infrastructures for both medical care and knowledge production in low and middle income countries. Nevertheless, there are aspects of global public health security that deserve more sustained attention. The case of the Million Death Study points to the political consequences of the mutual configuration of security devices (or infrastructures) and the threats they identify (Amicelle et al. 2015) in the context of global public health security. In terms of a human-centred approach to global public health security, it advances insight into the *common* health threats affecting people in the global South, and how these are often misrepresented. Yet global health security scholars also point to the *structural* dimensions of health threats (Chen and Narasimhan 2003; MacLean 2008), and although MDS researchers recognize their importance, the study's infrastructure is less suitable for making these visible. Issues such as the structural violence that make the socially marginalized more vulnerable to harm (Farmer et al. 2006), the absence of basic medical services and the complex determinants of health (including nutrition, housing, and many others) (Pfeiffer 2013), are all of vital importance to health security. Million Death Study researchers indicate that issues of this kind are widely presented in the narratives enumerators produce; the challenge is to integrate such qualitative, experiential evidence into the study's efforts to sense the major threats to global public health security.

REFERENCES

Adams, V. (2013). Evidence-Based Global Public Health. Subjects, Profits, Erasures. In J. Biehl and A. Petryna (Eds), *When People Come First. Critical Studies in Global Health*. Princeton: Princeton University Press, pp. 54–90.

Aleksandrowicz, L., Malhotra, V., Dikshit, R., et al. (2014). Performance Criteria for Verbal Autopsy-Based Systems to Estimate National Causes of Death: Development and Application to the Indian Million Death Study. *BMC Medicine* 12(21): 1–14.

Amicelle, A., Aradau, C., and Jeandesboz, J. (2015). Questioning Security Devices: Performativity, Resistance, Politics. *Security Dialogue* 46(4): 293–306.

Amoore, L. (2011). Data Derivatives. On the Emergence of a Security Risk Calculus for Our Times. *Theory, Culture & Society* 28(6): 24–43.

Anand, N., Gupta, A., and Appel, H. (Eds) (2018). *The Promise of Infrastructure.* Durham: Duke University Press.

Armstrong, D. (2019). The Social Life of Data Points: Antecedents of Digital Technologies. *Social Studies of Science* 49(1): 102–117.

Asdal, K. (2015). What is the Issue? The Transformative Capacity of Documents. *Distinktion: Scandinavian Journal of Social Theory* 16(1): 74–90.

Bates, J., Lin, Y., and Goodale, P. (2016). Data Journeys: Capturing the Socio-Material Constitution of Data Objects and Flows. *Big Data & Society* (July–December): 1–12.

Bengtsson, L., Borg, S., and Rhinard, M. (2019). Assembling European Health Security. Epidemic Intelligence and the Hunt for Cross-Border Health Threats. *Security Dialogue*: 1–16.

Bhutta, Z. (2006). The Million Death Study in India: Can It Help in Monitoring the Millennium Development Goals? *PLoS Medicine* 3(2): e103.

Biehl, J., and Petryna, A. (2013). Critical Global Health. In J. Biehl and A. Petryna (Eds), *When People Come First. Critical Studies in Global Health.* Princeton: Princeton University Press, pp. 1–20.

Birbeck, G., Wiysonge, C., Mills, E., Frenk, J., Zhou, X., and Jha, P. (2013). Global Health: The Importance of Evidence-based Medicine. *BMC Medicine* 11: 223.

Birn, A. (2009). The Stages of International (Global) Health: Histories of Success or Successes of History? *Global Public Health: An International Journal for Research, Policy and Practice* 4(1): 50–68.

Biruk, C. (2012). Seeing Like A Research Project: Producing 'High Quality Data' in AIDS Research in Malawi. *Medical Anthropology: Cross-Cultural Studies in Health and Illness* 31(4): 347–366.

Bowker, G., and Star, S. L. (1999). *Sorting Things Out. Classification and its Consequences.* Cambridge: The MIT Press.

Butler, D. (2010). Verbal Autopsy Methods Questioned. *Nature* 467 (28 October): 1015.

Chen, L., and Narasimhan, V. (2003). Human Security and Global Health. *Journal of Human Development* 4(2): 181–190.

Collier, S., and Lakoff, A. (2008). The Problem of Securing Health. In A. Lakoff and S. Collier (Eds), *Biosecurity Interventions. Global Health and Security in Question.* New York: Columbia University Press, pp. 7–32.

Crane, J. (2010). Unequal 'Partners'. AIDS, Academia and the Rise of Global Health. *Behemoth: A Journal of Civilization* 3(78–97).

Czarniawska, B. (2004). *Narratives in Social Science Research.* Thousand Oaks: Sage Publications.

Desai, N., Aleksandrowicz, L., Miasnikof, P., et al. (2014). Performance of Four Computer-Coded Verbal Autopsy Methods for Cause of Death Assignment Compared with Physician Coding on 24,000 Deaths in Low- and Middle-Income Countries. *BMC Medicine* 12(20): 1–8.

Dreze, J., and Sen, A. (2013). *An Uncertain Glory. India and Its Contradictions*. Princeton: Princeton University Press.

Espeland, W., and Stevens, M. (2008). A Sociology of Quantification. *European Journal of Sociology* 49(3): 401–436.

Farmer, P., Nizeye, B., Stulac, S., and Keshavjee, S. (2006). Structural Violence and Clinical Medicine. *PLoS Medicine* 3(10): 1686–1691.

Foucault, M. (2007). *Security, Territory, Population. Lectures at the College de France 1977–1978*. New York: Picador.

—— (2013). Right of Death and Power over Life. In T. Campbell and A. Sitze (Eds), *Biopolitics: A Reader*. Durham: Duke University Press, pp. 41–60.

Global Health Watch (2011). *Global Health Watch 3: An Alternative World Health Report*. London: Zed Books.

Gomes, M., Begum, R., Sati, P., et al. (2017). Nationwide Mortality Studies to Quantify Causes of Death: Relevant Lessons from India's Million Death Study. *Health Affairs* 36(11): 1887–1895.

Hanrieder, T., and Kreuder-Sonnen, C. (2014). WHO Decides on the Exception? Securitization and Emergency Governance in Global Health. *Security Dialogue* 45(4): 331–348.

Jha, P. (2012). Counting the Dead is One of the World's Best Investments to Reduce Premature Mortality. *Hypothesis* 10(1).

—— (2014). Reliable Direct Measurement of Causes of Death in Low- and Middle-Income Countries. *BMC Medicine* 12(19): 1–10.

Jha, P., Gajalakshmi, V., Gupta, P., et al., RGI-CGHR Prospective Study Collaborators (2006). Prospective Study of 1 Million Deaths in India: Rationale, Design and Validation Results. *PLoS Medicine* 3(2): e18.

Jin, J., and Krackattu, J. (2011). Infectious Diseases and Securitization: WHO's Dilemma. *Biosecurity and Bioterrorism: Biodefense Strategy, Practice, and Science* 9(2): 181–187.

Jutel, A. (2011). Classification, Disease, and Diagnosis. *Perspectives in Biology and Medicine* 54(2): 189–205.

King, N. (2002). Security, Disease, Commerce: Ideologies of Postcolonial Global Health. *Social Studies of Science* 32(5/6): 763–789.

Kitchin, R. (2014). Big Data, New Epistemologies and Paradigm Shifts. *Big Data & Society* (April–June): 1–12.

Krieger, N. (2012). 'Who and What is a 'Population'? Historical Debates, Current Controversies, and Implications for Understanding 'Population Health' and Rectifying Health Inequalities. *The Milbank Quarterly* 90(4): 634–681.

Lakoff, A. (2015). Real-Time Biopolitics: The Actuary and the Sentinel in Global Public Health. *Economy and Society* 44(1): 40–59.

Latour, B. (1999). *Pandora's Hope. Essays on the Reality of Science Studies*. Cambridge, MA: Harvard University Press.

Law, J. (2009). Seeing Like a Survey. *Cultural Sociology* 3(2): 239–256.

Lorway, R., and Khan, S. (2014). Reassembling Epidemiology: Mapping, Monitoring and Making-Up People in the Context of HIV Prevention in India. *Social Science & Medicine* 112, 51–62.

MacLean, S. (2008). Microbes, Mad Cows and Militaries: Exploring the Links Between Health and Security. *Security Dialogue* 39(5): 475–494.

McGoey, L., Reiss, J., and Wahlberg, A. (2011). The Global Health Complex. *BioSocieties* 6(1): 1–9.

McInnes, C., Kamradt-Scott, A., Lee, K., et al. (2012). Framing Global Health: The Governance Challenge. *Global Public Health: An International Journal for Research, Policy and Practice* 7(Sup2): S83–S94.

Mohapatra, B., Warrell, D., Suraweera, et al. (2011). Snakebite Mortality in India: A Nationally Representative Mortality Survey. *PLoS Neglected Tropical Diseases* 5(4): e1018.

Murphy, M. (2017). *The Economization of Life*. Durham: Duke University Press.

Nunes, J. (2018). Critical Security Studies and Global Health. In C. McInnes, K. Lee, and J. Youde (Eds), *The Oxford Handbook of Global Health Politics*. Oxford: Oxford University Press.

Office of the Registrar General of India. (2009). *Report on Causes of Death in India 2001–2003*. Retrieved from https://censusindia.gov.in/Vital_Statistics/Summary_ Report_Death_01_03.pdf

Pfeiffer, J. (2013). The Struggle for a Public Sector. PEPFAR in Mozambique. In J. Biehl and A. Petryna (Eds), *When People Come First. Critical Studies in Global Health*. Princeton: Princeton University Press, pp. 166–181.

Rabinow, P., and Rose, N. (2006). Biopower Today. *Biosocieties* 1: 195–217.

Rajan, V., and Prabhakaran, D. (2012). Non-Communicable Diseases in India: Transitions, Burden of Disease and Risk Factors – A Short Story. *India Health Beat. Supporting Evidence-Based Policies and Implementation* 6(1).

Rao, M., Godajkar, P., Baru, R., et al. (2015). Draft National Health Policy 2013: A Public Health Analysis. *Economic & Political Weekly* 50(17): 94–101.

Reubi, D. (2018). A Genealogy of Epidemiological Reason: Saving Lives, Social Surveys, and Global Population. *BioSocieties* 13(1): 81–102.

Rieder, G., and Simon, J. (2016). Datatrust: or, the Political Quest for Numerical Evidence and the Epistemologies of Big Data. *Big Data & Society* (January–June): 1–6.

Roberts, S., and Elbe, S. (2017). Catching the Flu: Syndromic Surveillance, Algorithmic Governmentality and Global Health Security. *Security Dialogue* 48(1): 46–62.

Rosenberg, C. (2002). The Tyranny of Diagnosis: Specific Entities and Individual Experience. *The Milbank Quarterly* 80(2): 237–260.

Ruppert, E. (2011). Population Objects: Interpassive Subjects. *Sociology* 45(2): 218–233.

Ruppert, E., Isin, E., and Bigo, D. (2017). Data Politics. *Big Data & Society* (July– December): 1–7.

Saetnan, A. R., Lomell, H. M., and Hammer, S. (2011). Introduction: By the Very Act of Counting: The Mutual Construction of Statistics and Society. In A. R. Saetnan, H. M. Lomell, and S. Hammer (Eds), *The Mutual Construction of Statistics and society.* (pp. 1–17). London: Routledge.

Saldaña, J. (2011). *Fundamentals of Qualitative Research.* London: Routledge.

Shankar, K., Hakken, D., and Østerlund, C. (2017). Rethinking Documents. In U. Felt, R. Fouche, C. Miller, and L. Smith-Doerr (Eds), *The Handbook of Science and Technology Studies. Fourth edition.* Cambridge, MA: The MIT Press, pp. 59–85.

Slota, S., and Bowker, G. (2017). How Infrastructures Matter. In U. Felt, R. Fouche, C. Miller, and L. Smith-Doerr (Eds), *The Handbook of Science and Technology Studies. Fourth Edition.* Cambridge, MA: The MIT Press.

SRS Collaborators of the RGI-CGHR. (2011). *Prospective Study of Million Deaths in India: Technical Document No VIII: Health Care Professional's Manual For Assigning Causes of Deaths Based on RHIME Reports.* Toronto: RGI-CGHR, University of Toronto.

Wahlberg, A. (2007). Measuring Progress. *Distinktion. Scandinavian Journal of Social Theory* 8(1): 65–82.

Wahlberg, A., and Rose, N. (2015). The Governmentalization of Living: Calculating Global Health. *Economy and Society* 44(1): 60–90.

6

EXPANDING TECHNOSECURITY CULTURE: ON WILD CARDS, IMAGINATION AND DISASTER PREVENTION

Jutta Weber

A society that sees its relation to the future in terms of prevention and organizes itself accordingly will always fear the worst, and its hopes will be galvanized by the thought that maybe things won't turn out so bad after all in the end.

Ulrich Bröckling

ABSTRACT

THE SYSTEMATIZED IMAGINATION OF RATHER UNLIKELY BUT HIGHLY DEVAStating disaster scenarios – i.e. wild cards – is currently seeing a boom. In this chapter I want to consider the role of the imagination in the discourses and practices of current preventive and 'premediated' security research and policy, analysing the extent to which it is a response to new media-related epistemological and societal conditions. In doing so I shall look first at the roles of future scenarios and imagination in the strategic approach to nuclear war. I shall then explore the current condition of our technosecurity culture in which these highly speculative approaches – which come across more as literary processes than as classical scientific methods – appear attractive and indicate a profound shift in contemporary regimes of knowledge.

KEYWORDS: technosecurity culture, imagination, premediation, possibility, future

INTRODUCTION

> "Mommy, Daddy, the synsects stung me!" Julie ran into the house in a fluster.
> Martin, who just sat down to deal with the administrative stuff for his organic
> farm, looked over at his eleven-year-old daughter. On her face and all over
> her arms were red marks that looked like mosquito bites. "What happened?"
> Julie had just been inspecting the rabbit hutches. Apparently, a swarm of
> these synsects had flown at her and attacked her. (Peperhove 2012: 72)

This horror story about a sudden attack by a swarm of sensing devices – in this case artificial insects – is not a science fiction invention. It is one of several disaster scenarios devised by the EU security research project FESTOS in order to identify 'potential future threats posed by new technologies in the hands of organized crime and terrorists' (Auffermann and Hauptman, 2012). Other scenarios address situations such as blackmail using hacked DNA data, the destruction of nanotech products using radio signals, and terrorist manipulation of people's behaviour through the release of biological viruses. While this might sound highly bizarre, there is a systematic aspect to it nonetheless. When developing the scenarios – presented in the form of short stories in order to assess '[t]he dark side of new technologies' (Peperhove 2012) – 'special emphasis is placed explicitly on scenarios which, although considered not very likely to occur, are expected to have major impacts if they do occur – so-called wild cards' (Festos 2012).

The scenarios technique is a favoured approach adopted in current security research, disaster management and technology assessment (see Grunwald 2012; Kaufmann 2011; Wright et al. 2008), as is the concept of wild cards (Steinmüller and Steinmüller 2004; DeWar 2015; Hiltunen 2006). The latter originates from the field of futurology. The term 'wild card' was coined by John Petersen, director of the Arlington Institute (a think tank), in his book *Out of the Blue – How to Anticipate Big Future Surprises* (2000). Other popular science studies, including one by futurologists and science fiction authors (!) Angela and Karl-Heinz Steinmüller, *Wild Cards: When unlikely things happen,* in which they call for an exploration of the unlikely, have elaborated the issue further (see also DeWar 2015; Mendonça 2004).

The scenarios technique – just like the Monte Carlo method or simulation[1] – is a key approach used in security research and derives from the impressive range of methods used in cybernetics (specifically, in operations research). The methods and ideas used in the scenarios technique have been used especially in military planning games for nuclear first strikes (Ghamari-Tabrizi 2000; Pias 2008).

As part of the EU's Seventh Framework Programme, funding was given to six Foresight projects whose task was to engage in the proverbial blue sky thinking and, in some cases, to conduct systematic research on wild cards.[2]

The idea of the scenarios method gained fresh momentum especially after 9/11, when an utterly unforeseen event demonstrated the vulnerability of western systems to low-tech attacks. Drawing lessons from the attack, the 9/11 commission report called on the security services to deploy imagination as a matter of routine. The report of the British Intelligence and Security Committee, which investigated the bomb attacks in London in 2005, suggested to its readers to accommodate the unknown in their thinking. Original and imaginative ways are needed, it said, to make the work of the secret services more effective and to be capable of detecting and understanding terrorist acts as well as future terrorist strategies (De Goede 2008: 156).

The idea is to preempt the worst scenarios in order to prevent them from happening (see, among others, Daase and Kessler 2007; Mythen and Walklate 2008). This idea is not new, but in the 'war on terror' it is acquiring its own unique dynamic as 'post 9/11 imagination', as Marieke de Goede (2008) calls it. In the face of unusual but effective and inventive low-tech attacks, the systematized imagination and the preemption of possible scenarios appears to be becoming even more attractive. Other phenomena, though, are also providing an impetus to the security policy notion of strategically deployed imagination. After a brief respite at the end of the Cold War, in which the threat of a nuclear war between the superpowers receded, new specters appeared, such as the problem of 'failed states' or of nuclear terrorism and the possibility that weapons of mass destruction could get into the hands of criminals. US security advisor Graham Allison and his Russian colleague Andrej Kokoshin depicted a potential scenario in the following way:

> Consider this hypothetical, [...] a crude nuclear weapon constructed from stolen materials explodes in Red Square. A fifteen kiloton blast would instantaneously destroy the Kremlin, Saint Basil's Cathedral, the ministries of foreign affairs and defense, the Tretyakov Gallery, and tens of thousands of individual lives. In Washington, an equivalent explosion near the White House would completely destroy that building, [...] and all of their occupants. (Allison and Kokoshin 2002: 35)

The systematized imagination of rather unlikely but highly devastating disaster scenarios – i.e. wild cards – is becoming increasingly popular. In the following I want to explore the role of the imagination in the discourses and practices of today's preventive and 'premediated'[3] security research and policy in the context of (new) media-related epistemological and societal conditions. In doing so I shall look first at the roles of future scenarios and imagination, especially in the strategic approach to nuclear war. I shall then explore the current condition of our technosecurity culture (Weber 2016) in which these highly speculative approaches – which come across more as literary processes than as classical scientific methods – increasingly appear attractive.

'THINKING ABOUT THE UNTHINKABLE': KNOWLEDGE PRODUCTION IN CONDITIONS OF GREAT UNCERTAINTY

Professionalized, scenario-based future gazing during the Cold War era can be read as a response by the nuclear strategists of the time to a completely new situation involving huge uncertainty: our entry into the nuclear age and the possibility of humanity's total annihilation.[4] No one had any experience in conducting a nuclear war, and no one had any idea what the right way was to deal with this situation militarily and politically. The classical range of methods used by the military – as well as those used by 'defense intellectuals' (Cohn 1987) – obviously no longer seemed adequate in this situation. Indeed, the latter even departed – at least implicitly – from previously accepted classical scientific criteria of objectivity and the reproducability of experiments or strategies. The criterion of reproducability had become obsolete in the face of the totality of nuclear war. It was against this background that the use of scenarios (initially on paper or as a board game, later on in the form of computer simulation) to preempt potential war situations offered a means of exploring new strategies for new situations. Traditional notions of scientific rigor were relinquished in favour of generating evidence by means of the imagination.

Hermann Kahn, defense intellectual and expert at US think tank RAND, was paradigmatic of this attitude. He writes euphorically of the significance of the imagination:

> Is there a danger of bringing too much imagination to these problems? Do we risk losing ourselves in a maze of bizarre improbabilities? [...] It has usually been lack of imagination [...] that caused unfortunate decisions and missed opportunities. (Kahn 1963: 3, quoted in Ghamari-Tabrizi 2005: 146)

Similarly, media theorist Claus Pias points out that think tanks, scenario-based imagination and computer simulation need to be understood as a response to a nuclear threat that can no longer be handled analytically or dealt with on the basis of experiments or prior experience:

What computer simulation was for the development of the hydrogen bomb, the scenario is for conceiving possible futures in the context of the nuclear threat. This is because their reality eludes not only analytic categories derived on the basis of past wars but also precludes experimentation with a war that would have devastating consequences. (Pias 2009: 13)

One possible future could therefore be winning a nuclear war – something Kahn assumed in his book *On Thermonuclear War* (1960). He rehearsed every scenario imaginable (and unimaginable) of a first or second strike nuclear war, regardless of any considerations of probability or likelihood (Kaplan 1983; Ghamari-Tabrizi 2005; Pias 2008). Being uninterested in moral issues but extremely interested in strategic futurological issues, he reckoned with the deaths of hundreds of millions of people and devised survival strategies and biopolitical measures for the post-nuclear age. Kahn's second book, written in 1962 to counter criticisms of his first, explicitly bore the title *Thinking about the Unthinkable*. No matter how convincing (or otherwise) Kahn's ideas may have been, they did achieve one thing at least: his use of scenario thinking rendered the monstrosities of nuclear deterrence thinkable and debatable in terms of different strategies, concepts and practical options.

What makes scenario techniques so attractive in today's security research, though? And what about imagining wild cards – things that are unlikely to happen but would have dire consequences, such as the wild swarms of cyber insects mentioned above, tele-operated nanoproducts or terrorist induced viral infections? Can this be seen as a way of addressing a similar set of problems as those to which Kahn and other defense intellectuals sought to find answers in the nuclear age with their first and second strike scenarios?

FIXATION ON THE FUTURE AND TECHNOLOGY-CENTRED SECURITY

One significant reason why the scenarios method has proved so appealing has to do with the way societies in the global North see themselves. *Zukunft als Katastrophe* (*Future as catastrophe*, Horn 2014) is a fairly apt description of one dominant strand of this self-perception. A widespread feeling of uncertainty or indeed threat seems to be predominant. The search for safety and security in the face of violence, illness and death has taken center stage in our thinking, in our perceptions and, accordingly, in our security debates.[5] But where does the feeling of threat come from? Its roots no longer lie (primarily) in the nuclear threat. On the political stage many like to argue that it stems from the experience of 9/11, but in surveillance and critical security studies most scholars agree that the trend towards an all-pervasive preventive security policy set in much earlier. Many theorists point to globalization, to the neoliberalization of today's societies and the greater individualization this brings with it, and to the digitalization of the last few decades as central reasons why people's fears – not only of terrorist attacks – are multiplying.

As far back as 1985, prominent science and technology studies (STS) scholar Donna Haraway identified the emergence of a New World Order, of high-tech societies and of techno-scientific cultures whose societal, political, technical, epistemic and normative foundations are undergoing radical transformation. These societies are characterized by a greatly accelerated and intensified hybridization of human and machine, of organic and non-organic, of science and technology. Hybrids such as the Oncomouse and intelligent software, she argued, can no longer be categorized within the traditional humanistic order. Haraway describes (the era of) the technosciences as a new episteme in which the linear causal logic of the Newtonian era has been replaced by a non-linear, multiple techno-rationality. At the same time, she noted, a new globalized political world order is being configured: a biotechnological power with new geo-strategies, technologies of the self, and logics of production and consumption (see also Weber 2003). Shortly after the publication of Haraway's Cyborg Manifesto (1985), in 1986 Ulrich Beck's theory of an emergent 'risk society' created a furor. According to him, potential technologically induced threats such as nuclear catastrophe and global warming are no longer predictable or calculable. An ever expanding sense of threat was similarly identified in the 1990s by British sociologist Anthony Giddens, who drew attention to the fact that the societies of the global North are increasingly concerned about their future (or futures) and are thereby generating a growing sense of danger.

In December 2003 Javier Solana, former Secretary-General of NATO and High Representative of the EU for Common Foreign and Security Policy up until 1999, presented a strategy paper on the European security doctrine in which he outlined the new situation in the following way: the number of corrupt or 'rogue' states is increasing – as, too, is poverty. This is accompanied by a growing number of regional conflicts, corruption, criminality and migratory movements. A further factor of insecurity, he asserts, is Europe's major dependence on energy imports. The main threats are therefore a global, unscrupulous form of terrorism – consisting in part of fundamentalists prepared to use violence – as well as the spread of weapons of mass destruction, organized crime and growing flows of migrants generated by failed states and by global warming. He characterizes the difference between these and previous threats as follows:

> Our traditional concept of self-defence – up to and including the Cold War – was based on the threat of invasion. With the new threats, the first line of defence will often be abroad. The new threats are dynamic. The risks of proliferation grow over time; [...] This implies that we should be ready to act before a crisis occurs. Conflict prevention and threat prevention cannot be started too early. In contrast to the massive visible threat in the Cold War, none of the new threats is purely military; nor can any be tackled by purely military means. Each requires a mixture of instruments. (Solana 2003)

Solana goes on to emphasize that proactive policies are needed to counteract 'new and ever-changing threats'.

The key difference compared with the threats of the Cold War is the dynamic nature of the new threats and their spread to civilian spheres of society, necessitating preventive action and massive investment in security measures, infrastructures and technologies – a development which at this point in time has already long been underway and has indeed accelerated and intensified. And it is especially sensing technologies which play an important role in this development.

As a politician, Solana maintains a measured approach, one that focuses less on potential technologically induced problems; yet in this respect, too, the future – our world – appears to be under threat and in great danger (Horn 2014), and these threats are (perceived to be) increasingly incalculable in terms of their dynamics and globality.

The constant discursive manifestation of likely and above all 'possibilistic' (see Clarke 1999) – that is, unlikely but (technically) possible – risks goes hand in hand with a conjuring up of ubiquitous dangers, further fueling the sense of threat. Pat O'Malley described this development long before 9/11 in the following terms: 'the structural demand for knowledge relating to risk becomes insatiable. As well because the accumulation of such knowledge adds awareness to new sources of risk, the risk-knowledge process gains its own internal momentum' (O'Malley 1999: 139).

The Cold War's defense intellectuals found themselves facing a new threat (nuclear war, first or second strike) which could no longer be dealt with by conventional means. At the same time, the threat was (relatively) concrete and came with a clearly identifiable opponent: the Eastern Bloc, the Soviet Union. Today's security strategists, by contrast, are working with dynamic, multifaceted and yet very vague threats. Wild cards are a part of this possibilistic risk management which attempts to do justice to all possible (imaginable) threats. Security discourse is rapidly meandering, multiplying and spreading – which generates very real threats in itself. As a result of increased funding for security research and technologies, for example, the number of laboratories working with dangerous pathogens has grown rapidly, along with the danger that manipulated organisms could be released accidentally or be stolen from their high-level security zones (Kaufmann 2011). Security researchers' imagination of new threats and of ways of dealing with them thus generate yet more new threats. The expansion of the security zone in general and the focus on wild cards with their potential, possibilistic scenarios of unlikely threats (Clarke 1999) serve to fuel people's sense of threat, legitimizing the extension of security measures and generally driving the security spiral ever onward.

TECHNO-SECURITY CULTURE

The more risks that are identified and are classified as unlimited, the more plausible demands appear for comprehensive, maximum preventive measures (Amoore and de Goede 2008; Kaufmann 2011). Such demands, however, usually give rise to rather unimaginative proposals and measures involving high-tech surveillance and enhanced security.

This logic pays barely any heed to the political, social and economic causes of insecurity (such as poverty, inequality, colonialism, etc.) which feed terrorism, organized crime and mass migration. Instead, technology – in the form of databases and simulations along with sensing technologies such as (smart) video surveillance or biometry – is viewed deterministically as the primary if not sole solution (Marx 2001; Aas, Gundhus and Lomell 2009).

This is readily apparent to any observer of the German security research programme. The need for scenario-oriented security research (though not primarily wild cards) is explained thus: 'Scenarios research avoids isolated solutions. It enables application-based systems innovations from which practical security products and services can be developed that match the needs of end users and are compatible with a free society.' (Bundesministerium für Bildung und Forschung/German Federal Ministry of Education and Research 2014).

The emphasis on scenarios makes it possible to determine societally relevant threats in a normative way. At the same time, these threats are configured as systems innovations in a technical sense: the technological fix is thus already embedded within the research programme itself.

This gives rise to a convergence between security and surveillance. Very soon – in practice and not just in the scenarios – every area of society is placed under surveillance. Profiles are searched and produced in the realm of business, in politics, in the military and in everyday life. Sensing technologies such as CCTV, RFID chips, drones and scanners are used to search for terrorists, to monitor sporting events and cash machines – but also one's own employees. As an essential and yet contested value in modern societies, security is interpreted and implemented primarily by means of technology.

Referring to the development of the military, Armand Mattelart has coined the term 'techno-security' to draw attention to the 'globalization of surveillance' since 9/11 which, he argues, has increasingly been characterized by the 'techno-fetishism' of current military strategies such as the technology-driven 'revolution in military affairs'. For Mattelart, techno-security means an 'exclusively technological approach to intelligence gathering, at the expense of human intelligence' (Mattelart 2010: 138). The current military logic of modern network-centred high-tech warfare can be described as a logic of targeting, identifying and pursuing. A complex digital network of computers and sensors is designed to provide a comprehensive overview of the battle arena in real time. This idea is based on the premise that military success can be engineered by information sovereignty, technological superiority and the close interlinking of intelligence, command center(s) and weapons technology. Surprisingly, this strategic military logic is also found in the realm of 'civilian security' as part of democratically legitimated security policy. A paradigmatic example of this is DAS, the new 'domain awareness system' used by the New York police and developed in cooperation with Microsoft. Not only does it gather images from 3000 surveillance cameras, 1600 radiation detectors and more than a hundred stationary and mobile license plate scanners in real time; it also feeds police radio and emergency calls into huge databases run by crime and terrorism combat units and compares suspects' data. It also makes it possible to track the movements of people or vehicles over long distances in real time and to reconstruct such movements over the previous weeks. A densely woven system of multiple sensors has been constructed to ensure that nothing that happens in public space goes undocumented. Of course, one could argue that all this is a delayed response to the trauma of 9/11 – it is happening in New York, after all – and that a similar situation would be inconceivable in Europe due to data protection legislation. However, the military logic of C4 (command, control, computers, communication), which is based on ISR – intelligence, surveillance and reconnaissance – is found increasingly in the civilian domain as well. We need only recall the 2012 Olympic Games in London: more than 13,000 British soldiers were deployed or were on stand-by there, along with aircraft carriers, ground-to-air missiles and unmanned drones. Data protection laws and basic rights were temporarily suspended, as when peaceful demonstrators were briefly detained to prevent them from entering the Olympic zone for the duration of the Games (Boyle and Haggerty 2012; Graham 2012). Things we had for a long time only witnessed at G8 summits are becoming the norm at all large-scale events. After recent terror attacks in Europe, e.g., Paris, Nizza, Berlin and Brussels, these developments in the EU are further accelerating.

For a number of reasons, it seems sensible to me to conceive of security nowadays in terms of security culture (Daase 2012). This has, in part, to do with the way military logic has expanded to encompass the civilian realm, with the growing perception of threats from various quarters, and with society's preoccupation with the biopolitical value of security (of life and limb). This 'security culture' approach not only sheds greater light on institutional actors such as the military and the police but also enables a more comprehensive understanding of security regimes in everyday culture. Culture here is understood as a varied and dynamic socio-cultural practice involving many heterogeneous agents and actants. Regrettably, science and technology studies approaches have been marginal yet in surveillance and critical security studies until recently (i.a. Aas et al. 2009). And yet it seems crucial to understand technosecurity as a complex sociotechnical practice with heterogeneous human and non-human actors. Accordingly, the actors of techno-security culture include not only police forces, secret services and think tanks but also algorithms, social media, military doctrines and software engineers. By conceiving of security in terms of techno-security it also becomes possible to ask why imagination plays such a central role in the context of security, how new (surveillance) technologies impact upon our thinking, our perceptions, our behaviour and our techno-imaginations, and what effects new epistemologies and ontologies have on the configuration of society. In this context, technology and media are interpreted not just as a specialized tool (of control) but as discourse, praxis and artifact. They are inscribed with scripts (Akrich 1992), with instructions for action that are linked to visions and epistemic paradigms, to values and norms; and these scripts convey categorizations and standardizations (Bowker and Star 1999) while also enabling 'social sorting' to occur (Lyon 2003). To mention just three examples: Geof Givens and his co-authors have pointed out that face recognition software may have a gendered, racist or age-based bias if certain age groups or skin colours are more easily recognized than others (Givens et al. 2004); Torin Monahan (2009) described the discriminatory impacts of US electronic benefit transfer systems especially for female recipients of state welfare payments; and Bowker et al. (2009) drew attention to the fact that while the social network analysis used in police work serves to gather huge amounts of data, it is primarily a quantitative approach that tends to favour form over content and to ignore lifeworld practices and meanings.

Thus, technologies are not mere tools but are also reifications of categories, habits, ways of thinking, and imaginations which exert impacts in the form of power relations. One of the questions raised in this context is how certain modes of imagination drive forward technologies of securitization; another is whether technologies themselves influence imaginative practices and, if so, how: does the media/control logic of the database perhaps drive what has been termed 'datification' and data retention? This is plausible, given that the more data sets a database contains, the more valuable it is considered to be (Manovich 2001; Gugerli 2009). Computer simulations (Bogard 2012), the technology of scenario planning, data mining and worst case imagination are all used to exert a measure of control over uncertainty and insecurity and unforeseeable risks (de Goede 2008; Salter 2008; Kaufmann 2011; Hempel et al. 2011). The logic of preemption and prevention prefers the imagination to the power of the factual – *suspicion becomes more important than evidence* (Salter 2008: 243). The logic of prevention is one of risk assessment – an assessment of as many potential dangers as possible – but not one of specific dangers emanating from specific actors. Whereas the logic of averting specific dangers follows a linear means-purpose relation, the logic of risk is necessarily vague, unclear and open-ended, and thrives on imagining eventualities.

In this sense, then, imagination and the development of (im)possible scenarios based on automated processes of recombination constitute today's epistemological foundation for risk management. Automated and semi-autonomous technologies of preventive, predictive analysis, of real-time monitoring and individualized targeting are regarded as appropriate means to combat unforeseeable risks – fueling, in turn, the illusion of and yearning for technological superiority (see, among others, Bigo and Jeandesboz 2009; Graham 2006), something that ironically can flip over into its very opposite. As secret services and their big data collections expand, for example, so too does the practice of whistleblowing. Furthermore, critics nominally loyal to them are beginning to wonder out loud whether the secret services possess far too much data to handle and are thus rendered incapable of acting (Möchel 2014).

Driven by the desire for ever more knowledge and information, security actors are developing complex networks intended to gather all kinds of available data from different (generally linked) sources. Preventive analysis is supposed to make the non-calculable calculable. At the same time, datification – the constantly expanding social media network, the multimedia interaction between individuals and things – enables the collection of huge amounts of data, which in turn can be scanned for patterns and used to produce profiles (Grusin 2010).

In the everyday work of security agencies, this practice often seems to lead to a rather banal and indeed bureaucratized imagination: scenario testing as a recombination of known scenarios – in the hope to thus preempt possible terrorist acts, catastrophes or even pandemics. And the more data, profiles, and behaviour patterns are stored in their database, the better prepared they feel for future disasters – or not, as the case may be, since at the same time it is obvious that this process can never be brought to an end:

> Security is less about reacting to, controlling or prosecuting crime than addressing the conditions precedent to it. The logic of security dictates earlier and earlier interventions to reduce opportunity, to target harden and to increase surveillance even before the commission of crime is a distant prospect. (Zedner 2007: 265).

One effect of this bureaucratic imagination is a data collection zeal of unprecedented dimensions. The NSA affair is surely the best example of this; others include data retention which, up until recently, was widespread in the EU as well, and the growing expansion of digital border security systems. One might also think of the US VISIT programme in which foreigners are photographed upon entry to the United States and their biometric fingerprints taken by transportation security officers. These data are stored in a database that can be accessed by 30,000 employees of various US government agencies (Homeland Security (2009). A similar system called Eurodac has already long been in place in the EU collecting the fingerprints of those who seek asylum in Europe.

The idea of managing risks by means of surveillance and data monitoring arose during the 1990s (if not before) and has been extended ever further since 9/11. What it involves is not primarily following up on a specific suspect or suspicion but rather preventively 'securing' security. This preventive logic of surveillance and criminal prosecution – and thus also imprisonment – is less about averting specific threats than about prevention and premediation and about minimizing risks and costs. The characteristic phenomena associated with this logic include data retention, predictive policing, and working with prior incriminating circumstances, such as the use of certain words (see the case of Andrej Holm)[6] or the fact of being resident for a long period of time in a country not considered to be a tourist destination, such as Yemen or Syria. In 2016, a 31-year-old in France was jailed for two years because he regularly visited so-called Djihad websites, downloaded a plan of a major building in Paris and made a mocking remark on that building on social media (Pany 2016).

SYSTEMATIZED IMAGINATION AND HIGH-TECH BUILD-UP

Further analysis is required of our understanding of security as perpetual, as an idea that sees anything and everything as a threat and thus drives imagination to ever more dizzying heights while driving forward the strategic logic of a ubiquitous worst case scenario. We need a theoretical approach to technosecurity that facilitates analysis of the politics of knowledge, technoimaginations, and the values and norms implemented in technologies, as in technical infrastructures; at the same time, we need to examine how the effects of current software and automated decision-making facilitate 'power through the algorithm' (Lash 2007) in all manner of surveillance discourses and practices. Up to now studies that analyse the logic and consequences of, say, biometric or datamining software have been rare. Such studies would be helpful for looking more closely at the effects of security's sociotechnologies and gaining a better understanding of technosecurity governance in the twenty-first century. One question that arises is the extent to which certain techno-logics drive our perceptions of the world as being everywhere and at all times at risk – thereby activating calls for technology-centred maximum security.

At the same time, wild cards seem to be the expression of a deep-seated uncertainty regarding what exactly the truly relevant threats actually are. Since we can never be completely sure whether they will be linked to the (un)disrupted flow of goods, to flood prevention or to terrorist attacks at an airport, we invent a few wild cards just to be on the safe side. The effects recall the aporia in which the cold war warriors of the 1950s became caught up:

Obsessed with preparedness, they sometimes did not scruple about overstating the threat for which preparation was necessary. They practised psychological warfare on their own people. Strategists like Kahn and Wohlstetter […] were not responsible for starting the arms race, but the more they speculated on the unknown terrors of the future, the faster the race was run. (Menand 2005)

ACKNOWLEDGEMENTS

I am grateful to the reviewers as well as to Katrin M. Kämpf for critical comments and helpful remarks on an earlier version of this essay. Many thanks to Kathleen Cross for translating in a very thoughtful way most of the paper.

NOTES

1 '"Monte Carlo simulation" refers to a category of algorithms that calculate their results using random numbers. First, a domain of possible inputs is determined and a series of random numbers from this domain is generated; a deterministic calculation is then conducted using the random numbers and, finally, the individual results are combined.' (Reiss 2010: 2458b). See also Edwards (1996) on the role of the computer during the Cold War.

2 http://community.iknowfutures.eu/

3 'Precaution' and 'preemption' are key terms in the discourse around unlikely but fatal events. These terms have been extended in the current debate by a new one, namely, 'premediation' (de Goede 2008, Grusin 2010).

4 On controversies between traditional military personnel with experience in warfare and the scenario-oriented military strategists, see Ghamari-Tabrizi (2000).

5 At the same time, however, the issue of social security has largely disappeared (until recently?) from the political agenda.

6 Germany's BKA (Federal Criminal Police Office) had become aware of sociologist Dr. Andrej Holm when searching the Internet: he had allegedly used similar vocabulary (gentrification, precariousness, reproduction) as that used by the 'militant group' they had been investigating. After a year of observation, he was arrested in July 2007. Apart from the keywords he had used, conspiratorial meetings with other purported members of the group as well as not taking his cell phone with him to various meetings were taken to be further indications of his membership in the group. He was released three weeks later as a result of national and international protests – Richard Sennett and Saskia Sassen spoke of 'Guantanamo in Germany'. Court proceedings against Holm were finally dropped in 2010 (see Leistert 2013).

REFERENCES

Aas, K. F., Gundhus, H. O., and Lomell, H.M. (Eds) (2009). *Technologies of inSecurity: the Surveillance of Everyday Life*. Abingdon; New York: Routledge-Cavendish.

Akrich, M. (1992). The De-Scription of Technical Objects. In W. E. Bijker and J. Law (Eds), *Shaping Technology/Building Society: Studies in Sociotechnical Change*. Cambridge, MA: The MIT Press, pp. 205–224.

Allison, G., and Kokoshin, A. (2002). The New Containment: An Alliance Against Nuclear Terrorism. *The National Interest* 69 (Fall 2002): 35–43.

Amoore, L., and de Groede, M. (Eds) (2008). *Risk and the War on Terror*. New York: Routledge.

Auffermann, Burkhard and Hauptman, Aharon (2012) "FESTOS – Foresight of Evolving Security Threats Posed by Emerging Technologies, in" *European Foresight Brief. 2012*

Beck, U. (1986). *Risikogesellschaft: Auf dem Weg in eine andere Moderne*. Frankfurt a.M., Germany: Suhrkamp.

Bigo, D., and Jeandesboz, J. (2009). *Border Security, Technology and the Stockholm Programme. INEX Policy Brief No. 3, November 2009*. Archive of European Integration. <http://aei.pitt.edu/14993/>.

Bogard, W. (2012). Simulation and Post-Panopticism. In K. Ball, K. Haggerty, and D. Lyon (Eds). *Routledge Handbook of Surveillance Studies*. New York: Routledge, pp. 30–37.

Bowker, G. C, and Star, S. L. (2000). *Sorting Things Out: Classification and its Consequences*. Cambridge, MA: The MIT Press.

Bowker, G., Baker, K., Millard, F., and Ribbes, D. (2009). Toward Information Infrastructure Studies: Ways of Knowing in a Networked Environment. In J. Hunsinger, L. Klastrup, and M. Allen (Eds), *International Handbook of Internet Research*. Dordrecht, Germany: Springer Science+Business Media, pp. 97–117.

Boyle, P., and Haggerty, K. D. (2012). Planning for the Worst: Risk, Uncertainty and the Olympic Games. *The British Journal Of Sociology* 63(2): 241–59.

Bröckling, U. (2012). Dispositive der Vorbeugung: Gefahrenabwehr, Resilienz, Precaution. In C. Daase, P. Offermann, and V. Rauer (Eds), *Sicherheitskultur, soziale und politische Praktiken der Gefahrenabwehr*. Frankfurt a. M.; New York: Campus, pp. 93–108.

Bundesministerium für Bildung und Forschung. (German Federal Ministry of Education and Research) (2014). *Bewilligte Projekte der Programmlinien >>Szenarioorientierte Sicherheitsforschung<<*. Funded projects of the research program >>Scenario-oriented Security Research<<. <http://www.bmbf.de/de/12876.php>.

Clarke, L. (1999). *Mission Improbable: Using Fantasy Documents to Tame Disaster*. Chicago, IL: University of Chicago Press.

Cohn, C. (1987). Sex and Death in the Rational World of Defense Intellectuals. *Signs: Journal of Women in Culture and Society* 12(4): 687–718.

Daase, C. (2012). Sicherheitskultur als interdisziplinäres Forschungsprogramm. In C. Daase, P. Offermann, and V. Rauer (Eds). *Sicherheitskultur. Soziale und politische Praktiken der Gefahrenabwehr* (pp. 23–44). Frankfurt a.M., Germany, and New York, NY: Campus.

Daase, C., and Kessler, O. (2007). Knowns and Unknowns in the 'War on Terror': Uncertainty and the Political Construction of Danger. *Security Dialogue* 38(4): 411–34. <http://dx.doi.org/10.1177/0967010607084994>.

De Goede, M. (2008). Beyond Risk: Premediation and the Post-9/11 Security Imagination. *Security Dialogue* 39(2–3): 155–76. <http://dx.doi.org/10.1177/0967010608088773>.

DeWar, J. A. (2015). *The Importance of Wild Card Scenarios*. Air University. <http://www.au.af.mil/au/awc/awcgate/cia/nic2020/dewar_nov6.pdf>.

Edwards, P. N. (1996). *The Closed World: Computers and the Politics of Discourse in Cold War America*. Cambridge, MA, and London, England: The MIT Press.

European Commission (2013). *Vorschlag für eine Verordnung des europäischen Parlaments und des Rastes über ein Einreise-/Ausreisesystem (EES) zur Erfassung der Ein- und Ausreisedaten von Drittstaatsangehörigen an den Außengrenzen der Mitgliedstaaten der Europäischen Union*. EUR-Lex. <http://eur-lex.europa.eu/LexUriServ/LexUriServ.do?uri=COM:2013:0095:FIN:DE:PDF>.

Foresight of evolving security threats posed by emerging technologies, TU Berlin. (2012). Foresight of evolving security threats posed by emerging technologies. <http://www.tu-berlin.de/ztg/menue/forschungprojekte/projekte_-_abgeschlossen/foresight_of_evolving_security_threats_posed_by_emerging_technologies_festos>.

Ghamari-Tabrizi, S. (2000). Simulating the Unthinkable: Gaming Future War in the 1950s and 1960s. *Social Studies of Science* 30 (April 2000): 163–223.

—— (2005). *The Worlds of Herman Kahn: The Intuitive Science of Thermonuclear War*. Cambridge, MA, and London, England: Harvard University Press.

Giddens, A. (1999). Risk and Responsibility. *Modern Law Review* 62(1): 1–10. <http://dx.doi.org/10.1111/1468-2230.00188>.

Givens, G., Beveridge, R., Draper, B. A., Grother, P., and Philips, P. J. (2004). How Features of the Human Face Affect Recognition: A Statistical Comparison of Three Face

Recognition Algorithms. *IEEE Computer Society Conference On Computer Vision And Pattern Recognition* 2: 381–388.

Graham, S. (2006). Surveillance, Urbanization and the US 'revolution in military affairs'. In D. Lyon (Ed.), *Theorizing Surveillance. The Panopticon and Beyond*. Devon, England: Willian, pp. 247–270.

Graham, S. (2012). Olympics 2012 Security. *City: Analysis of Urban Trends, Culture, Theory, Policy, Action* 4: 446–451.

Grunwald, Armin (2012). Technikzukünfte als Medium von Zukunftsdebatten und Technikgestaltung. *Karlsruher Studien Technik und Kultur* 6. Karlsruhe: KIT Scientific Publishing.

Grusin, R. (2010). *Premediation: Affect and Mediality After 9/11*. New York: Palgrave Macmillan.

Gugerli, D. (2009). The Culture of the Search Society. Data Management as a Signifying Practise. Institute of Network Cultures. <http://www.networkcultures.org/public/The_Culture_of_the_Search_Society_DavidGugerli.pdf>.

Haraway, D. (1985). Manifesto for Cyborgs: Science, Technology, and Socialist Feminism in the 1980s. *Socialist Review* 80: 65–108.

Hiltunen, E. (2006). Was it a Wildcard or Just Our Blindness to Gradual Change? *Journal of Futures Studies* 11(2): 61–74.

Homeland Security (2009). *Testimony of Deputy Assistant Secretary for Policy Kathleen Kraninger, Screening Coordination, and Director Robert A. Mocny, US-VISIT, National Protection and Programs Directorate, Before the House Appropriations Committee, Subcommittee on Homeland Security, 'Biometric Identification'*. <http://www.dhs.gov/ynews/testimony/testimony_1237563811984.shtm>.

Horn, E. (2014). *Zukunft als Katastrophe*. Frankfurt a.M.: Fischer.

iKnow (n.d.). iKnow Community. <http://community.iknowfutures.eu>.

Kahn, H. (1960). *On Thermonuclear War*. Princeton, NJ: University Press.

—— (1962). *Thinking About the Unthinkable*. New York: Horizon Press.

Kaplan, F. (1983). *The Wizards of Armageddon*. New York: Simon and Schuster.

Kaufmann, S. (2011). Zivile Sicherheit: vom Aufstieg eines Topos. In L. Hempel, S. Krasmann, and U. Bröckling (Eds), *Sichtbarkeitsregime. Überwachung, Sicherheit und Privatheit im 21. Jahrhundert*. Wiesbaden: VS Verlag für Sozialwissenschaften, pp. 101–123.

Lash, S. (2007). Power After Hegemony: Cultural Studies in Mutation? *Theory, Culture & Society* 24(3): 55–78. <http://dx.doi.org/10.1177/0263276407075956>.

Leistert, O. (2013). *From Protest to Surveillance – The Political Rationality of Mobile Media. Modalities of Neoliberalism*. Frankfurt a.M.; Berlin; Bern; Bruxelles; New York; Oxford; Vienna: Peter Lang.

Lyon, D. (Ed.) (2003). *Surveillance as Social Sorting: Privacy, Risk, and Digital discrimination*. London, England, New York, NY: Routledge.

Manovich, L. (2001). *The Language of New Media*. Cambridge, MA: The MIT Press.

Marx, G. T. (2001). Technology and Social Control: The Search for the Illusive Silver Bullet. *International Encyclopedia of the Social and Behavioral Sciences.* <http://web.mit.edu/gtmarx/www/techandsocial.html>.

Mattelart, A. (2010). *The Globalization of Surveillance: The Origin of the Securitarian Order.* Cambridge: Polity.

Menand, L. (2005). Fat Man. Herman Kahn and the Nuclear Age. *The New Yorker,* 27 June, Books. <http://www.newyorker.com/archive/2005/06/27/050627crbo_books?currentPage=all>.

Mendonça, S., Cunha, M. P., Kaivooja, J., and Ruff, F. (2004). Wild Cards, Weak Signals and Organisational Improvisation. *Futures. The Journal of Policy, Planning and Future Studies* 36(2): 201–218.

Möchel, E. (2014). Whistleblower: NSA hat sich selbst ausgeschaltet. FM4 ORF. <http://fm4.orf.at/stories/1744256/>.

Monahan, T. (2009). Dreams of Control at a Distance: Gender, Surveillance, and Social Control. *Cultural Studies <=> Critical Methodologies* 9(2): 286–305.

Mythen, G., and Walklate, S. (2008). 'Terrorism. Risk and International Security: The Perils of Asking 'What If?' *Security Dialogue* 39(2–3): 221–242.

O'Malley, P. (1999). Governmentality and the Risk Society. *Economy and Society* 28(1): 138–48.

Pany, T. (2016). Zwei Jahre Haft für den Besuch von Djihad Webseiten. *Heise,* Politik, 10 August. <http://www.heise.de/tp/artikel/49/49089/1.html>.

Peperhove, R. (2012). Die dunkle Seite neuer Technologien – Projektbericht FESTOS. *Zeitschrift Für Zukunftsforschung* 1: 64–78.

Petersen, J. (2000): *Out of the Blue. Wild Cards and Other Future Surprises. How to Anticipate Big Future Surprises.* Long Island City, NY: Madison Books.

Pias, C. (Ed.) (2008). *Herman Kahn – Szenarien für den Kalten Krieg.* Zürich; Berlin: Diaphanes.

Pias, C. (2009). One-Man Think Tank. Hermann Kahn, oder wie man das Undenkbare denkt. *Zeitschrift Für Ideengeschichte* 3: 5–16.

Reiss, J. (2010). Simulation. In H. J. Sandkühler (Ed.), *Enzyklopädie Philosophie.* Hamburg: Felix Meiner.

Salter, M. (2008). Risk and Imagination in the War on Terror. In L. Amoore and M. de Goede (Eds), *Risk and the War on Terror.* New York; London: Routledge, pp. 233–46.

Solana, J. (2003). Ein sicheres Europa in einer besseren Welt. Europäische Sicherheitsstrategie. European Council. <http://consilium.europa.eu/uedocs/cmsUpload/031208ESSIIDE.pdf>.

Steinmüller, K., and Steinmüller, A. (2004). *Wild Cards. Wenn das Unwahrscheinliche eintrifft.* Hamburg: Murmann.

Weber, J. (2016). Keep Adding. Kill Lists, Drone Warfare and the Politics of Databases. *Environment And Planning D. Society And Space* 34(1): 107–125.

Weber, J. (2003). *Umkämpfte Bedeutung: Naturkonzepte im Zeitalter der Technoscience.* Frankfurt a.M.; New York: Campus.

Wright, D., Friedwald, M., Schreurs, W., et al. (2008). The Illusion of Security. *Communications of The ACM* 51(3): 56–63.

Zedner, L. (2007). Pre-Crime and Post-Criminology? *Theoretical Criminology* 11(2): 261–281. <http://dx.doi.org/10.1177/1362480607075851>.

Chapter 7
Visual Vignette I

Parasitic Surveillance:
Mobile Security Vulnerability

Evan Light, Fenwick McKelvey

Rachel Douglas-Jones

Walking and talking, in the city, on a mobile device, is an everyday act

A freedom enjoyed by billions worldwide, everyday.

But, these mobile infrastructures are not what they seem.

M s a c a a w
a e d o n s i t
n r v n a e h
f i r t a d t h
a c i n o n e
c e t s t o t
t p e e v o i
u r o u n k m
e v o n e e e
r s u r c e s
s i d e e u p
a e r t e u
n s i o n a
d s

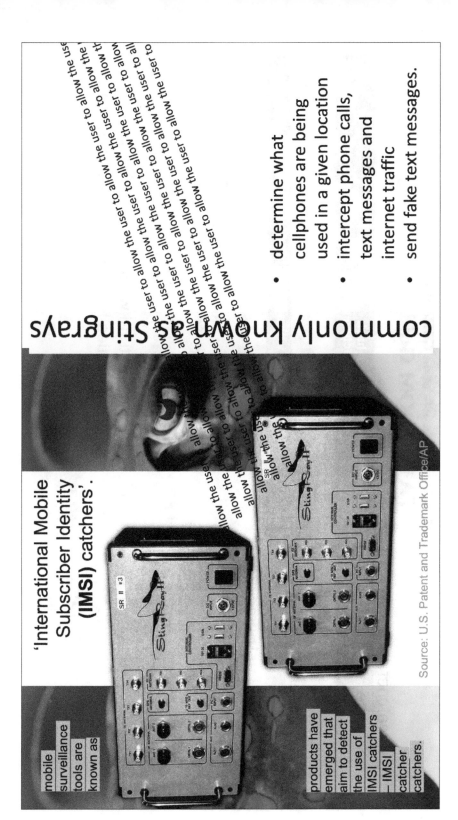

'International Mobile Subscriber Identity (IMSI) catchers'.

commonly known as Stingrays

- determine what cellphones are being used in a given location
- intercept phone calls, text messages and internet traffic
- send fake text messages.

mobile surveillance tools are known as

products have emerged that aim to detect the use of IMSI catchers — IMSI catcher catchers.

STATEROOM Guide

ISMI catchers repurpose mobile telephony infrastructure as a surveillance device.

We argue ISMI catchers are a kind of parasitic surveillance drawing on the concept of infrastructural parasitivism (Gehl & Mckelvey, 2019).

ISMI catchers are technically a hack collecting data not meant to be technically shared by our phones with anybody but a legitimate network provider.

Infrastructural weaknesses become opportunities for spying and surveillance

A bugged infrastructure?

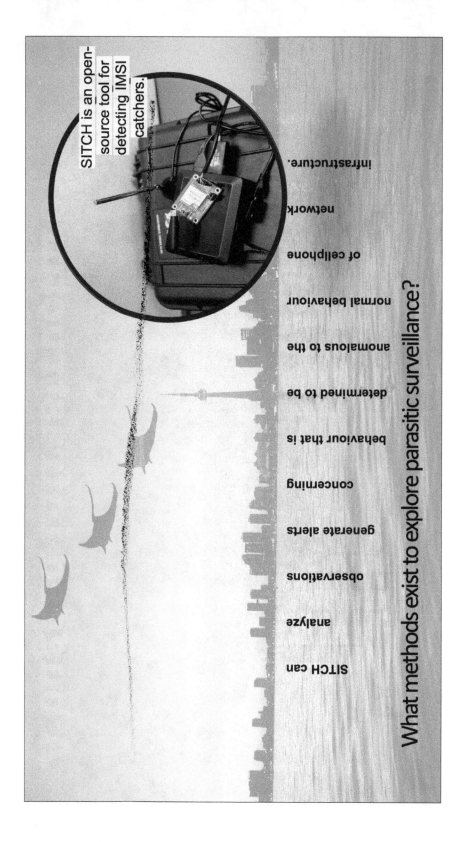

SITCH is an open-source tool for detecting IMSI catchers.

SITCH can analyze observations generate alerts concerning behaviour that is determined to be anomalous to the normal behaviour of cellphone network infrastructure.

What methods exist to explore parasitic surveillance?

We then went on a series of walks – inspired the data walks method developed by Alison Powell (2017)

We monitored cellular signals around Toronto

Our walk also borrows from recent media studies and feminist digital geography work reflecting on the new ways to map these infrastructural landscapes

(Elwood 2018; Leszczynski, 2018a,2018b).

This kind of landscape story that "**requires getting to know the inhabitants, human and not human**" (Tsing, 2015, p. 160

Like the mushrooms and their pickers in Tsing's work

ISMI catchers are transient, yet by getting to know their enabling environment and human contact points

it is possible to discover traces of their existence.

LTE/4G IMSI catcher with consumer hardware and open-source hardware. *Shaik et al. 2017.*

https://www.google.com/maps/search/?api=1&query=43.

Original Message: ARFCN: 128 Expec...
https://www.google.com/maps/se
Original Message: BTS not in feed da...
om/maps/search/?api=1&query=43.
Original Message: Possible GPS spoo...
om/maps/search/?api=1&query=43.
458333,-79.3751153333 | Host ID: 6
Original Message: Primary BTS was 3
om/maps/search/?api=1&query=43.
Original Message: ARFCN 132 over t
om/maps/search/?api=1&query=44.
Original Message: Possible GPS spoo
015,-79.03667 | Host ID: be93917
Original Message: Possible GPS spoofing attack! 4300 delta from anchor at chez_evan / spring-le
om/maps/search/?api=1&query=43.689616667,-79.3272933333 | https://www.google.com/maps/se
47,-79.375235 | Host ID: 63a4d64
Original Message: Possible GPS spoofing attack! 352 delta from anchor at niagara / morning-pap
om/maps/search/?api=1&query=43.138583333,-79.04094 | https://www.google.com/maps/se
015,-79.03667 | Host ID: be93917
Original Message: Possible GPS spoofing attack! 4379 delta from anchor at chez_evan / spring-le
Viewing archives from Apr 30th, 2018 - May 1st, 2018

63a4d64
1805.94906467 CGI: 302...
567,-79.3584 | Host ID: 63...
02:720:4300:65535 Senso
63a4d64
or at chez_evan / spring-le
https://www.google.com/ma
...720:95488:235314. Sens
ost ID: 63a4d64
r. Observed: 1831389.14
Oee7cb0
or at niagara / morning-pap
www.google.com/maps/se

clustering of alerts on the
SITCH system warning
that a wide range of
anomalous activity was
being observed. The
'false positives' and bugs
in the SITCH's code
thwart easy stories even
though journalistic
accounts of similar tools
prefer to assume a link
between state
surveillance and
networking anomalies.

data-space isn't
always human-
readable, or
even empirical."
(Mattern, 2016).

At best, this tool provides
an entry point into further
research, or 'good
enough data' (Garbvs,
Pritchard & Barratt, 2016)
our bottom-up approach
requires new perspective,
such as information
requests or court
document that might
leave another trace into
the assembly of cellular
infrastructures by
providers, police and
security agencies.

SITCH might be used to follow the 'parasitic chain' -- what Gehl and McKelvey call "a networked society of interconnected platforms and infrastructures parasiting each other. Parasitic surveillance is not a top-down process, but an improvisation occurring in infrastructure, and destabilizing the homogeneity of the system. Rather than seeing infrastructure as one coherent system, the parasite invites thinking of infrastructure as a plurality of technical projects that coexist with each other in a parasitic chain. Such a perspective is largely consistent with the lived experiences of infrastructures, especially in the developing world, where the limits of global modernity often require ad-hoc or provisional solutions to run or inter-connect competing global standards.

Mobile networks have become weak and compromised, bugs have settled in.

To communicate securely in the sensor society requires more than tools for documentation, but rather a wholesale revitalization of the entire system, perhaps beginning with its demise.

REFERENCES

Gabrys, J., Prichard, H. and Barratt, B. (2016) Just good enough data: Figuring data citizenship through air pollution sensing and data stories. *Big Data & Society*. 3(2): 1–14.

Gehl, R. W., and McKelvey, F. (2019). Bugging Out: Darknets as Parasites of Large-scale Media Objects. *Media, Culture and Society*. 41(2): 219 –235.

Greene, R., Meysenburg, N., and Ritzo., C. An Experiment in Detecting Cell Phone Surveillance. <https://www.newamerica.org/oti/blog/oti-experiment-open-source-surveillance-detection/> [accessed 13 November 2018]

Elwood, S. (2018) Feminist digital geographies'. *Gender, Place & Culture*. 25(5): 629–644.

Leszczynski, A. (2018). Digital methods I: Wicked tensions. *Progress in Human Geography*. 42(3): 473–481.

Mattern, S. (2016). Cloud and Field. *Places Journal*. <https://doi.org/10.22269/160802>

Ney, P., Smith, I., Cadamuro, I., G., and Kohno, T. (2017) SeaGlass: Enabling City-Wide IMSI-Catcher Detection'. *Proceedings on Privacy Enhancing Technologies*. 3: 39–56.

Offenhuber, D., and Schechtner, K. (2018) Improstructure - an improvisational perspective on smart infrastructure governance. *Cities*. 72: 329–338.

Parks, L. (2016). Rise of the IMSI Catcher. *Media Fields Journal*. 11: 1–19.

Powell, A. (2018). The data walkshop and radical bottom-up data knowledge' in H. Knox, and D. Nafus (Eds), *Ethnography for a data-saturated world*. Manchester: Manchester University Press, pp. 212–232.

Shaik, A., Borgaonkar, R., Asokan, N., Niemi, V., & Seifert, J.-P. (2015). Practical Attacks Against Privacy and Availability in *4G/LTE Mobile Communication Systems*. ArXiv:1510.07563 [Cs]. Retrieved from http://arxiv.org/abs/1510.07563.

Pell, S. K., and Soghoian, C. (2014). Your Secret StingRay's No Secret Anymore: The Vanishing Government Monopoly over Cell Phone Surveillance and Its Impact on National Security and Consumer Privacy. *Harvard Journal of Law & Technology*. 28(1): 1–75

Tsing, A. L. (2015). *The mushroom at the end of the world: on the possibility of life in capitalist ruins*. Princeton : Princeton University Press.

Chapter 8
Visual Vignette II

A Trail of Breadcrumbs

Breadcrumbs

Chris Wood

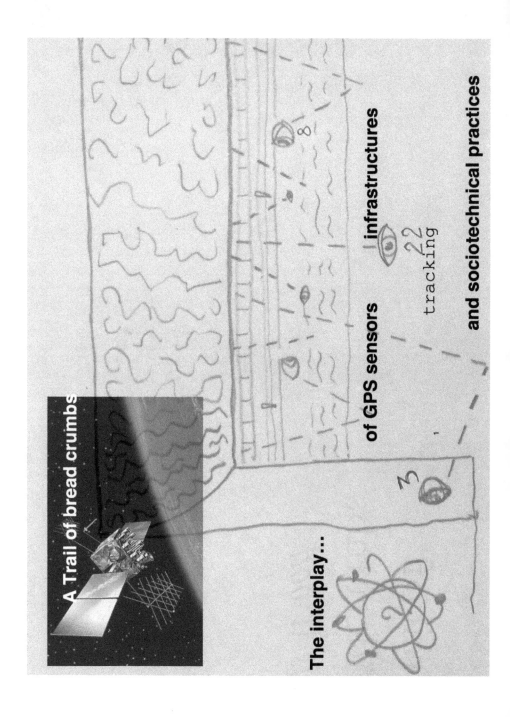

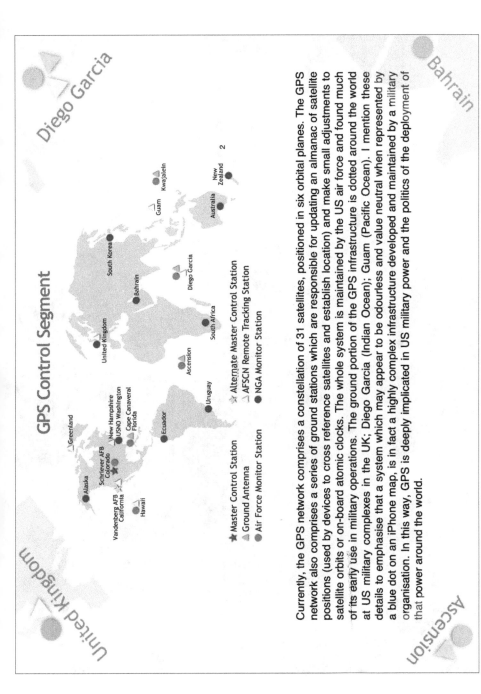

GPS Control Segment

Master Control Station
Ground Antenna
Air Force Monitor Station

Alternate Master Control Station
AFSCN Remote Tracking Station
NGA Monitor Station

Currently, the GPS network comprises a constellation of 31 satellites, positioned in six orbital planes. The GPS network also comprises a series of ground stations which are responsible for updating an almanac of satellite positions (used by devices to cross reference satellites and establish location) and make small adjustments to satellite orbits or on-board atomic clocks. The whole system is maintained by the US air force and found much of its early use in military operations. The ground portion of the GPS infrastructure is dotted around the world at US military complexes in the UK; Diego Garcia (Indian Ocean); Guam (Pacific Ocean). I mention these details to emphasise that a system which may appear to be odourless and value neutral when represented by a blue dot on an iPhone map, is in fact a highly complex infrastructure developed and maintained by a military organisation. In this way, GPS is deeply implicated in US military power and the politics of the deployment of that power around the world.

Curious how peoples' understanding of the way they use GPS might shift once they were more aware of this infrastructure, I led a series of workshops designed to draw attention to the infrastructure's presence.

Over the course of the three workshops I worked with 19 participants, the majority of whom identified as artists or researchers. They were a mixture of students and professionals, largely recruited through the collaborator organisations.

In collaboration with the research organisations The Culture Capital Exchange and Antiuniversity Now, in 2016 I organized workshops that were open to the general public at the Barbican Estate and Arts Centre in central London.

The workshop created what has been called an "infrastructural inversion" (Bowker and Star 1999). It did this by leveraging moments of breakdown to make infrastructure more "visible" (Star and Ruhleder 1996).

The Barbican was chosen because of the disruptive effect its architecture has on GPS reception. This acts as a form of infrastructural inversion, making the materiality of GPS signals more visible. They used an app called *GPS Test* which visualises the position and signal strength of overhead GPS satellites. After the walk, participants were asked to reflect on the experience via individual creative writing and drawing followed by a group discussion.

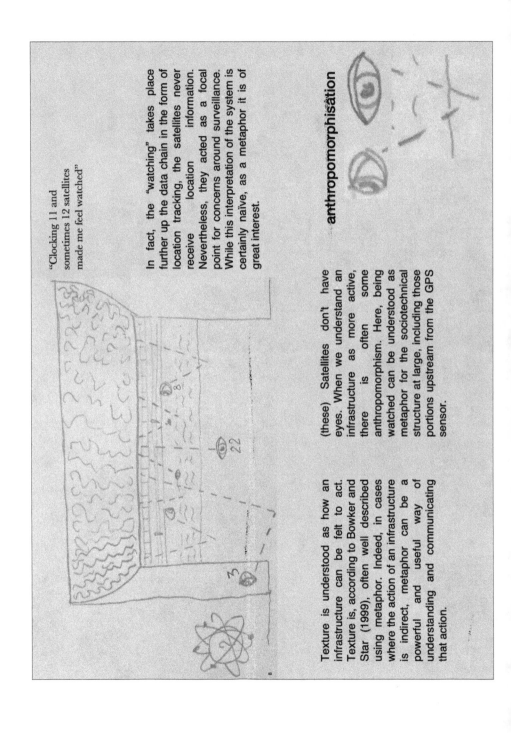

Texture is understood as how an infrastructure can be felt to act. Texture is, according to Bowker and Star (1999), often well described using metaphor. Indeed, in cases where the action of an infrastructure is indirect, metaphor can be a powerful and useful way of understanding and communicating that action.

"Clocking 11 and sometimes 12 satellites made me feel watched"

In fact, the "watching" takes place further up the data chain in the form of location tracking, the satellites never receive location information. Nevertheless, they acted as a focal point for concerns around surveillance. While this interpretation of the system is certainly naïve, as a metaphor it is of great interest.

anthropomorphisation

(these) Satellites don't have eyes. When we understand an infrastructure as more active, there is often some anthropomorphism. Here, being watched can be understood as metaphor for the sociotechnical structure at large, including those portions upstream from the GPS sensor.

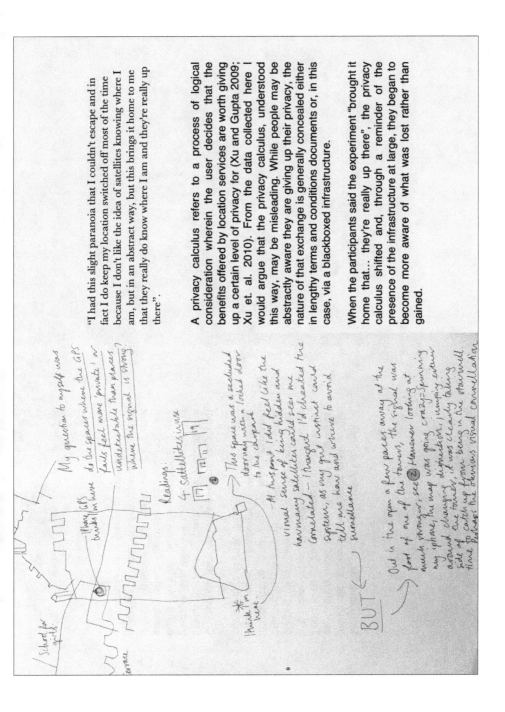

"I had this slight paranoia that I couldn't escape and in fact I do keep my location switched off most of the time because I don't like the idea of satellites knowing where I am, but in an abstract way, but this brings it home to me that they really do know where I am and they're really up there".

A privacy calculus refers to a process of logical consideration wherein the user decides that the benefits offered by location services are worth giving up a certain level of privacy for (Xu and Gupta 2009; Xu et. al. 2010). From the data collected here I would argue that the privacy calculus, understood this way, may be misleading. While people may be abstractly aware they are giving up their privacy, the nature of that exchange is generally concealed either in lengthy terms and conditions documents or, in this case, via a blackboxed infrastructure.

When the participants said the experiment "brought it home that... they're really up there", the privacy calculus shifted and, through a reminder of the presence of the infrastructure at large, they began to become more aware of what was lost rather than gained.

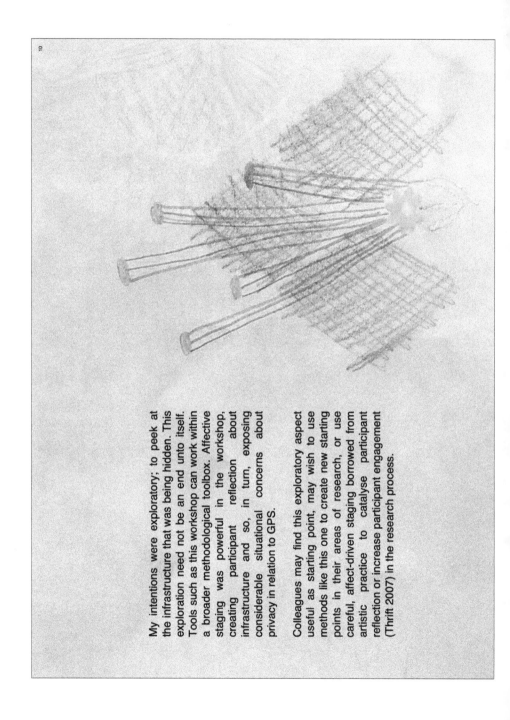

My intentions were exploratory; to peek at the infrastructure that was being hidden. This exploration need not be an end unto itself. Tools such as this workshop can work within a broader methodological toolbox. Affective staging was powerful in the workshop, creating participant reflection about infrastructure and so, in turn, exposing considerable situational concerns about privacy in relation to GPS.

Colleagues may find this exploratory aspect useful as starting point, may wish to use methods like this one to create new starting points in their areas of research, or use careful, affect-driven staging borrowed from artistic practice to catalyse participant reflection or increase participant engagement (Thrift 2007) in the research process.

REFERENCES

Bowker, G. C., and Star, S. L. (2000). *Sorting Things Out: Classification and its consequences.* Cambridge, MA: MIT Press.

Star, S. L., and Ruhleder, K. (1996) Steps toward an Ecology of Infrastructure: Design and Access for Large Information Spaces. *Information Systems Research.* 7(1):111–134.

Thrift, N. (2007). *Non-Representational Theory: Space, Politics, Affect.* New York; London: Routledge.

Xu, H., and Gupta, S. (2009). The effects of privacy concerns and personal innovativeness on potential and experienced customers' adoption of location-based services. *Electron Markets.* 19:137–149.

Xu, H., Teo, H. H., Tan, B. C. Y., and Agarwal, R. (2010) The Role of Push-Pull Technology in Privacy Calculus: The Case of Location-Based Services. *Journal of Management Information Systems.* 26(3):135–174.

IMAGES

1 Composite. Participant drawing and artist's impression of GPS-IIM satellite. <https://en.wikipedia.org/wikiGPS_satellite_blocks#/media/File:GPS-IIRM.jpg/> [accessed 3rd May 2019]. Public Domain

2 Control Segment of the GPS system. Available at <https://www.gps.gov/systems/gps/control/> [accessed 3rd May 2019]. Public Domain.

3 The Barbican Estate. Author's photo.

4 Screenshot from GPS Test app developed by Chartcross.

5 The Barbican Estate. Photo by the author.

6 Artist's impression of GPS-IIM satellite. Available at <https://en.wikipedia.org/wikiGPS_satellite_blocks#/media/File:GPS-IIRM.jpg/> [accessed 3rd May 2019]. Public Domain.

7 Writing workshop. Photo by the author.

8 Participant drawing. Photo by the author.

9 Participant drawing. Photo by the author.

10 Participant drawing. Photo by the author.

Chapter 9
Visual Vignette III

Human Sensors

Katja Mayer and El Iblis Shah

Katja Mayer:

What is the difference
between a divinely
intoxicated oracle
uttering god's words,
turned into prophecies by poets,
and today's prediction industry?

El Iblis Shah:

We do not know of any society that does not use predictive oracles to manage their knowledge regimes. Always obscure and mystifying, only the rituals and belief systems have changed over time. No need to capture a shapeshifting Proteus to learn about the future, when the perfect search engine is envisioned as the mind of god.

EXTRA SENSORY PERCEPTION

SA1 Issue 1 June 2002

UK SECRET
UK EYES ONLY S-26

S-42 Issue 1 June 2002

SUBJECTS SIMPLE RECORDED

Katja Mayer:

Does psychic espionage work? Can remote viewers

immerse their minds in seas of information?

SECRET

CLASSIFIED

El Iblis Shah:

Whether it works or not is beside the point. Perceptual augmentation techniques

and perception management are fully integrated in today's social engineering.

All 20th century mind control experimentats have been implemented.

The children of New Age Future Warriors are now running Silicon Valley

HUMAN TERRAIN ANALYSIS

Furthermore, consider the cultural turn in the military. In irregular warfare anthropologists acted as embedded sensors and socio-cultural weapons of the infocalypse.

Katja Mayer:

Sensors turning against their signals?

El Iblis Shah:

Human sensors in the cultural terrain, part of strategies measuring and engaging the Other, turn into Psyops agents with the subliminal power of definition, intermediation and interpretation in the theatre of operations.

Yes, nervous systems can be unpredictably instable or transition into break downs.

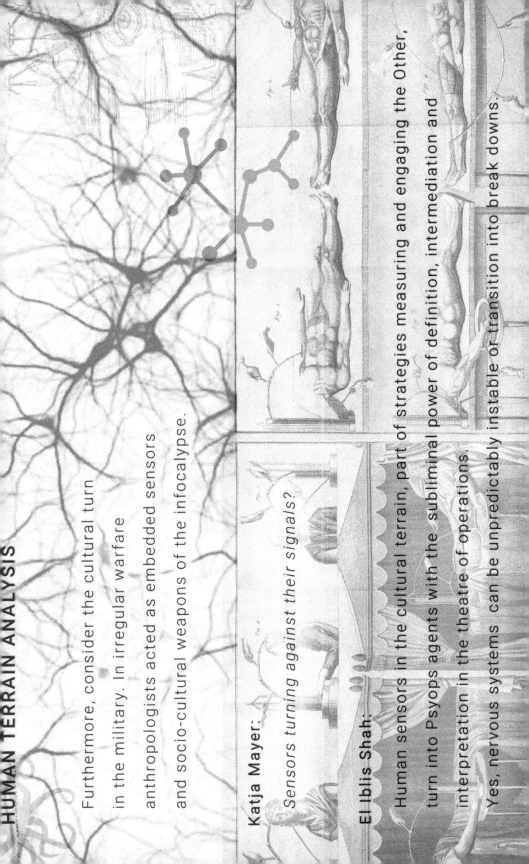

EXOBODIES

Katja Mayer:

Now US Marines are guided to weaponize their intuition. They are training sensemaking and empathy as part of the "Every Soldier is a Sensor" (ES2) doctrine.

El Iblis Shah:

However occult their training of force projection, the robotization of humans is on the rise.

It is producing augmented bodies that are transparent, connected and serviceable towards high-performance subordination. With artificial intelligence guiding the synchronization of

SOCIAL SENSORS

Katja Mayer:

Social Sensing is exploiting how people make sense of the world...

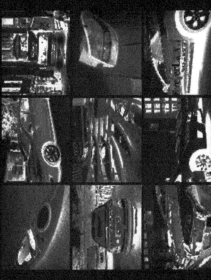

El Iblis Shah:

Since early Modernity psycho-technicians were dedicated to objectifying human subjectivity.

Social Sensing enforces homogenization of behavior patterns through the automatized

classification of "normality". Large-scale psychological operations flatten the realm of

sense-making, where sensors are aligned with the techno-logics of perception managers

and sociometric operators. The Necronomicon is kids' stuff compared to Behavioral Economics.

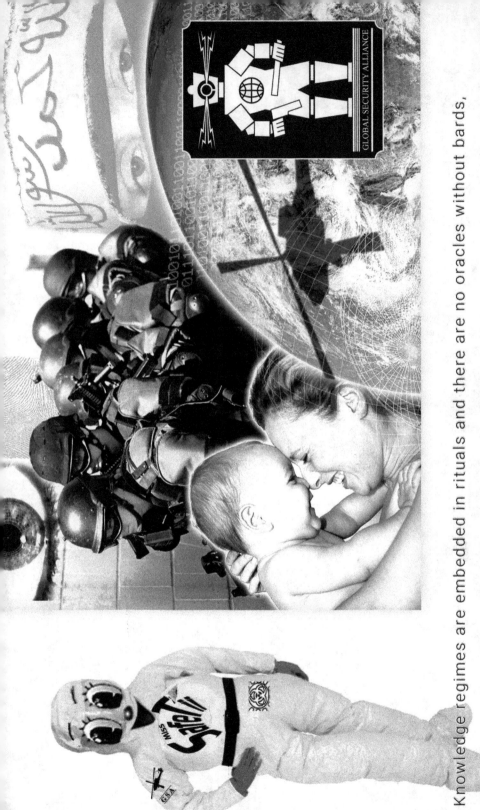

Knowledge regimes are embedded in rituals and there are no oracles without bards,

no human sensors without fusion centers of calculation or committees of interpretation.

In surreal systems control-artists of consensual hallucination mesmerize the dataflux.

I 0

VISUAL VIGNETTES

Mascha Gugganig and Rachel Douglas-Jones

VISUAL VIGNETTES ARE A METHOD FOR ANALYSING AND PRESENTING RESEARCH through the integration of text and image. As a format, Visual Vignettes combine the genre of the vignette – widely used across the qualitative social sciences to succinctly capture a telling moment – with that of the photo essay. When we were invited to curate a collection of Visual Vignettes for *Sensing In/Security* we built on our existing collaborative project, where over the past few years, we have been exploring tools and formats that bring our interest in the visual into research analysis and communication. In the context of this volume, the Visual Vignette becomes a method by which sensing technologies can be differently seen, accessed, and understood, both by analysts and those with whom we as scholars might wish to share our work.

In this chapter we introduce the Visual Vignette, situate it within the shifting grounds of STS's knowledge infrastructures and discuss its affordances for work in STS. While our project originates in the anthropological embrace of multimodal, imaginative work (Collins, Durrington and Gill 2017, Elliott and Culhane 2017) we put our experimental engagements with analysis and communication of research in conversation with efforts to work across media that are simultaneously gaining prominence in STS (Dányi, Suchman and Watts 2021; Dumit 2017; Jungnickel 2020; Le Bot and Noel 2016). We review the capacities of the *Sensing In/Security* Visual Vignettes to bring forward critical aspects of our sociotechnical world, and offer a guide for those who might be inspired to experiment with the format themselves.

KNOWLEDGE PRACTICES, KNOWLEDGE INFRASTRUCTURES

STS scholarship is rich in borrowed and adapted norms of research, drawing on writing and communication practices from neighbouring disciplines. It is also increasingly inventive. As scholars working at the intersection of anthropology and STS, we are critically aware both of the conditions and implications of how academic knowledge is done, and circulated. Over the past few years, we have both been exploring the possibilities – and constraints – of being inventive with academic methods and formats (Lury and Wakeford 2012). In 2009, for example, Gugganig began to photograph the process of demolishing a building in Vienna, near where she lived and worked. The destruction was taking place as she wrote up her Master's thesis, prompting an analogy between the scaffolds of structural integrity, and those of successful scholarship. A few years later, building on her reflexive analysis of all the editing, arranging, constructing, rewriting, and deletion that becomes invisible in academia's end products (see also Boudreault-Fournier 2017), Gugganig created a film of scholarship's 'hidden practices' (2011). Later, in the Visual Vignette format (then called visual essay), she reflected on how these practices are (or are not) part of capacity building in academia (Gugganig 2015; Fig. 10.1 and 10.2).

Douglas-Jones brought a similarly visual approach to her project of engagement of the General Data Protection Regulation. Academically interested in the politics and technicalities of data deletion pointed to in Article 17 of GDPR (popularized as 'the right to be forgotten') she worked with colleagues in Copenhagen and Oxford to create erasure poems from the regulation (Douglas-Jones and Cohn 2018). Erasure poetry – known also as blackout or redaction poetry – was a favoured technique of 1960s radical poets, aesthetic efface-ment as an 'additive subtraction' (Johns, cited in Cage 1967). It rose to public prominence again in 2016 as a form of creative resistance, with poets erasing US application forms and speeches following the election of Donald Trump. As the reporter Stone put it, poems made from bureaucracy 're-examine the institutions and narratives that shape American's lives ... reasserting power over language' (Stone 2017). Inspired by the poet Sarah Howe's dream of a public

Making Dust come to Matter: The Scaffolding of Academia

Wenner-Gren Foundation, Visual Essay Competition on Capacity Building
Category: Infrastructural Settings
Name: Mascha Gugganig
Institution: University of British Columbia (PhD candidate, anthropology), Harvard University (STS fellow)

This visual essay explores the infrastructural setting of academia and contemplates the ways it shapes a particular understanding of capacity building that scaffolds successful scholarship. It invites readers and viewers to reflect on the role of arts as both medium to interrogate this scaffolding and as contribution to the very capacity building.

In 2009, in the midst of writing my MA thesis, a few blocks down from where I lived in Vienna, a house got torn down. I started taking photographs, eventually mounting to over a thousand photos. It was not until two years later, again in the midst of studying for my doctoral degree in Vancouver, that I compiled the images into a short film, *hidden practices* (Gugganig 2011a).

This brought me back to the question what constitutes the profession of researchers, their capacity building. What importance does the much-heralded institutionalized peer-review have for our recognition as 'professionals,' and what role do non-peer-reviewed projects have, such as arts-inspired work?

Who defines the norm of capacity never stands on its own but is co-produced with the episteme of how to build it (Jasanoff 2004). Engaging with arts is a way to question this interplay between the normativity of 'capacity' as professionals, and the practices called forward to 'building' such capacity; to constructing - or for that matter, deconstructing it like an old house. In that sense, art not only visualizes capacity building.

As mode of research it may indeed reshape, rebuild the very definition of capacity.

FIGS 10.1 and **10.2** Two exemplary frames from Gugganig's 'Making Dust come to Matter: The Scaffolding of Academia' (2015).

art project of doing erasure poetry on Hong Kong's Basic Law, Douglas-Jones and her colleagues envisaged the emergence of what Howe called 'subversive, gloriously vulgar undersongs' (2014: 250) in the GDPR. Deletion became a means for counternarratives to emerge from within the text, not least a critique of the legalese in which it was written. The resulting collection *GDPR: Erasure Poems* gave voice to interpretive work from the hands of those whose lives the policy affects, and was picked up by over 200 newly appointed Data Protection Officers in Danish and international companies, enlivening GDPR trainings (Fig. 10.3 and 10.4).

How academics conduct, analyse and communicate their research is shaped by disciplinary norms, conventions, funds, schools of thought, and, increasingly, metrics and measurement (Wilsdon 2015; Fochler and de Rijcke 2017). These conditions of possibility are often described as infrastructures of knowledge (Rose and Tolia-Kelly 2012; Star 2002), language that has grown in line with academic attention to infrastructures more broadly. This is not a new conversation. In anthropology, interrogating the underlying mechanisms of scholarly work has been the focus over many generations (Clifford and Marcus 1986; Marcus and Fischer 1986, Pandian and McLean 2017). Beyond that, the publication spaces for interdisciplinary conversation are today reshaping the ways practices might travel across disciplinary borders. As Kat Jungnickel puts it in a recent edited volume encompassing techniques from art, architecture, anthropology, computing, design, media and communications, medieval studies and sociology, '[m]any forms and formats have remained relatively unchanged for decades, while the social worlds they reflect have not' (2020: 6)

A reflection of the changing social worlds of our research in STS is for instance visible through the interactive exhibition 'Making and Doing' which, since the conference in Denver 2015, has made up part of the 4S' (Society for the Social Studies of Science) annual meetings. The exhibition and surrounding work foregrounds what happens when, as Downey and Zuiderent-Jerak put it, we turn 'STS lessons into STS work' (2017:223). Its 2015 motto – Visual and Sensory Approaches – encouraged reflections on arts in science, on imagination in scientific processes, and on science as a vehicle for artistic production of objects (Le Bot and Noel 2016: np). A forthcoming book on

Deletion Poems
Eds. Rachel Douglas-Jones and Marisa Cohn

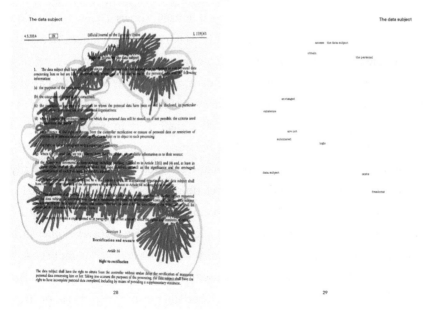

FIGS 10.3 and **10.4** Two pages from Douglas-Jones and Cohn 2018 GDPR Poems showing the process of making erasure poems from the GDPR in Copenhagen, and a sample poem.

experimenting with ethnography is indicative of a growing interest to engage with various methodologies, media and materialities (Ballestero and Winthereik 2021). For instance, one of the contributions proposes the production and methodological use of postcards – similar to Visual Vignettes – as katachresis to gain new insights and generate new themes (Dányi, Suchman and Watts 2021). Gugganig and Schor (2020a; 2020b) similarly highlight the pedagogical and multimodal ethnographic potentials in/of/as postcards. Putting research forms and formats under contemporary scrutiny, we find ourselves part of a growing conversation about STS' various knowledge practices, dependencies and distributions, whether that be individualized models of production (Colleex 2020), the development of languages and practices of collaboration (Liboiron et al. 2017) or reconsiderations of the standard template of text-b(i)ased articles and books (see for instance Bauer et al. 2020).

Returning to Gugganig's visual analogy of a house under (re)construction to unravel the making of academic work, we can now see its double provocation. The story of (re)construction focuses our attention on processual aspects of research in the making and, as an object in itself, shows us how we can find ways to tell our research stories differently. Making a Visual Vignette demands this double attention: to process – both of research, and to the making of a Visual Vignette – and a thorough engagement with elements of a story. Learning to both create and speak through another set of tools becomes the task of the researcher engaging a new format: to 'value their work in progress; to reveal their workings; to render visible their meaning making' (Jungnickel 2020: ix; Chio 2017). As we go on to show below, research infrastructures, like any infrastructure, are 'things and also the relation between things' (Larkin 2013: 329). As things, our research formats channel and guide our thought: they are made and remade, they leak, break, get fixed. As *relations between things*, such as researchers and their collaborators and audiences, they may get repurposed. Thus, to make Visual Vignettes about sensor practices is to think simultaneously about the capacities of the sensing researcher, the sensing they wish to portray, and the stories the format makes possible.

VISUAL VIGNETTES: SENSING AND SENSEMAKING

Visual Vignettes encourage the re-imagining of the role of text and visuals in sensemaking (see Pink 2011). In our work with the format over the past few years, we held workshops in Copenhagen and Munich introducing the idea to students with field material in hand.[1] In the workshops, we explained that while a vignette usually relates to written words only, and a photo essay uses images, mostly photos, in well-placed sections within a written text to illustrate said text, the Visual Vignette requires working with both together. At first, many hesitated at the threshold of the visual. Some presumed they have few capacities to doing arts-based research and/or dissemination, or did not consider themselves as 'artists' for that matter. Yet it was our explicit goal, also for the contributors in this book, to encourage those with little to no experiences to experiment with text-image relations. In times where camera-equipped smart-phones have become omnipresent gadgets in everyday life and contemporary research sites, students and researchers amass vast amounts of visual material they often struggle to know what to do with (Rueß 2019).[2]

The making of a Visual Vignette requires its author to challenge the order and 'division of labour' between words – often as descriptor – and images – as illustration. We here follow Sarah Pink, in that 'it seems more profitable to seek to explore the synergies and connections between writing and images [rather] than in terms of binary oppositions' (2011: 267). As such, introducing a notion of craft is to reference not mastery, but a sense of curiosity and willingness to experiment. For instance, a frequent comment among workshop participants was that re-approaching their research through its visual components often opened up new dimensions and themes they previously had not been aware of (Kuen 2019). This inversion work – giving the visual components the same explanatory 'authority' as the written text – is akin to the 'writerly craft', that is, the practice of thinking or writing in images (Paper Boat Collective 2017: 17), but also the other way round, an imagery craft of 'visioning' in the form of text. Rather than expecting mastery of self-described visual artists, making Visual Vignettes is more akin to the conception of writing as craft (Paper Boat Collective 2017: 16).

For instance, in Mayer and Shah's contribution to this volume, *Human Sensors*, a reader grasps in a single page a point of generative (staged) disagreement between the authors over whether 'psychic espionage' 'works' (see Fig. 10.5). The text deepens a reader's understanding of *perception*, while the placement of the dialogue amongst a set of classified images and coded, redacted documents, places the topic within an imaginary of secrecy. Text does work both as illustrator and as descriptor, as Mayer and Shah work with the challenge of differentiating between technical and human sensors. Elsewhere in the Visual Vignette, text is used sharply: 'there are no oracles without bards, no human sensors without fusion centers of calculation or committees of interpretation' they write, alongside powerful, complex collages juxtaposing data, identification, security and threat. Deployed in the context of doubt (in/security) in the senses, the immersive character of the extract from Mayer and Shah's Visual Vignette affords new curiosities on the part of the viewer. The eye tries to zoom in: can the redactions be detected? The overview is contemplated: can the classified codes and 'seas of information' be thought together?

FIG. 10.5 Mayer and Shah (see contribution in this book) play with, and thereby invert the conceptual role of text as illustrator and text as descriptor by merging them in this frame.

The technology for making Visual Vignettes had to be accessible and familiar to academics, so we opted for PowerPoint, or its open source equivalent. Using software known for its familiar 'boring' looks prompts an immediate confrontation with the meanings already embedded in the aesthetic (Tufte 2003). Indeed, Tufte argues that 'popular PowerPoint templates (ready-made designs) usually weaken verbal and spatial reasoning' (2003: 3). Anthropologist Marilyn Strathern cuttingly remarks that bullet points (all too frequently seen on PowerPoint presentations) offer no sequence, no 'internal relations', allowing no growth, and creating no knowledge (2006: 196). When we are forced to see the document rather than the text (Strathern 2006: 184) as part of a critical engagement with the givens of PowerPoint, the format opens up. What can the document do?

To create a series of images, a sequence, that conveys meaning rapidly, whilst providing something substantial to think through, is difficult. In Wood's Visual Vignette *A Trail of Breadcrumbs* (this volume) we see multiple voices, from different times, presented together. No bullet points. Fieldnotes and pencil drawings sit alongside photos of GPS sensors, screen-shots of tracking devices and accounts of workshops taking place outside. In this way, Wood takes us into the world of the Global Positioning System, from satellites to monitoring stations and buildings that disrupt reception. With him, we visit London to consider in the company of his workshop participants – just what goes into the charismatic little blue dot on a GPS-enabled phone. Hand drawn diagrams from the workshops bring forward the concerns that participants had about where in such an infrastructure 'watching' might take place. Eyes hover around different slides and parts of the drawing, with satellites taking on the qualities of a knower. What can the document do? Wood ends his Visual Vignette with an invitation to his colleagues in STS to copy these techniques of drawing and workshop feedback, to 'use careful, affect-driven staging borrowed from artistic practice to catalyse participant reflection' and learn more. The vignette thus not only documents the workshop and its creative outputs, it produces an opportunity for Wood to invite others to experiment with these techniques.

Working with new formats creates new kinds of constraints. In their Visual Vignette *Parasitic Surveillance* Evan Light and Fenwick McKelvey take us on a walk through the Canadian city of Toronto. In a few short frames, Light and McKelvey introduce us to three layers of communications infrastructure: everyday mobile infrastructure, the surveilling devices parasitic upon this mobile infrastructure known as International Mobile Subscriber Identity catchers (or more charismatically, StingRays), and then SITCH, the open-source tool for detecting these parasitic IMSI catchers. Walking the city with a mobile device, they tell us, is an experience invisibly mediated. Their research with SITCH aims to make the parasitic, invisible StingRays visible. Light and McKelvey introduce us to their maps, routes, views, and to the #stingray_msg data flowing down their screens, producing a powerfully layered story (Fig. 10.6). All of this is presented through the format of a Visual Vignette. From the images we learn both the politics and practicalities of finding StingRays – the contingencies of reading 'data-space' (Mattern 2016) and methods for walking the city. The Visual Vignette is full of reference to the senses – the smell and taste of mushrooms, the texture of a crevasse in a wall, perhaps even the sound of StingRays (fictionally) overheard. Images do the work of connecting physical devices to declassification documents, and to alerts on a screen, letting the viewer's own 'knowledge-seeking strategies' (Favero 2017: 361, see also Färber 2007) move between text and image. The reader follows

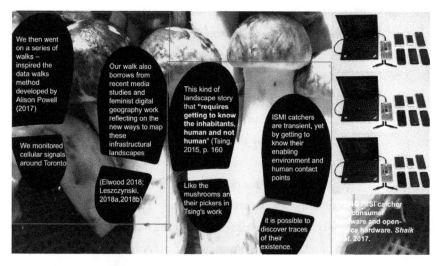

FIG. 10.6 Meeting the StingRays in Light and McKelvey's Visual Vignette through layered image and text.

Light and McKelvey's walk through the city, encountering the non-human inhabitants of urban landscapes through the intersection of word and image, with city skylines, code and boxes drawing us into the data-scape of what the authors term parasitic surveillance. By not relegating images to the margins, readers gain a more visceral sense of the work it takes to find and identify parasitic devices.

WORKING WITH VISUAL VIGNETTES

We initially conceived Visual Vignettes as having a role in *dissemination* of research, taking place late in a project to communicate research findings. We saw them as useful tools for ethnographers to bring with them on return field visits, material objects to be shared with people with whom they had worked (see Fig. 10.8). Visual vignettes can, for example, be printed and hung in departmental hallways, offices, galleries and cafes in field-sites or university towns, printed on durable materials as street art, made into banners, and so on (see Fig. 10.9 and 10.10). Short, and requiring succinct synthesis on the part of the author, they can make incisive interventions into existing debates. Facing academia, they can be displayed digitally on blogs and department websites (see STS Infrastructures 2019), or exhibited on a curated website (Visual Vignettes 2018). In this communicative ambition, the Visual Vignette shares what Kat Jungnickel puts forward as 'tactics of transmission': a critical combination of making and communicating through inventive dissemination (2020: 7).

However, in our workshops students and participants brought material at all stages of their research projects. Some work was simply not ready to be transmitted or disseminated, or was never meant to be. As such, we explored with them what the making of a Visual Vignette might do for them during fieldwork, or early in analysis, and found the format amenable to adaptation as an 'infrastructure of inquiry' (Estallella and Criado 2017). In what follows, we briefly present the Visual Vignette as a generative mode of research work in three, interrelated ways: (1) for organizing ideas; (2) analysing data; (3) sharing research. What might be gained by seeing them as an infrastructure for sensing in and of themselves?

Five-step User Guide
for making Visual Vignettes

Visual vignettes are useful in all three main stages of research, helping to (1) organize, (2) analyze, and (3) communicate research. In each of these scenarios, making visual vignettes involves the following:

Collect visuals (images, drawings, sketches, designs, collages, postcards, architectural rendering etc.) **and textual data** (field notes, memos, quotes, article sections, word cloud etc.). Ensure you have permission to use all visual and textual data.

Combining a **700-900 word** text with as many visuals as you deem necessary, **visual vignettes should be no longer than ten slides.**

Using **presentation software** (e.g. Powerpoint, gephi, etc.) to play with the arrangement of text and images. Go beyond what you think a text and image should 'do.'

Present your draft visual vignette to colleagues for **feedback**, and ask: does the narrative make sense? What are the visuals saying? How does the visual-text arrangement work?

Edit your visual vignette based on the feedback and present again (as with journal article reviews, this may take several iterations)!

Share your work with your colleagues, students, broader publics in analogue or digital ways, by **printing** (on thick paper, foam board, etc.), uploading **online** for example to your department website, or **exhibiting** in other venues (cafes, museums, etc.).

FIG.10.7 A five-step user guide for making a Visual Vignette.

FIELDWORK: THINKING AND SENSING IN THE FIELD

Ethnographic researchers today go into their field sites with a great many image-making devices, often encountering environments that are full of others making images too (Beuving 2017). A Visual Vignette can highlight to the researcher the process of research: making and remaking of images through recording and editing can be 'catalysts that encourage researchers and students to reflect upon where they stand, with whom, and how' (Boudreault-Fournier 2017: 71). In this form, the Visual Vignette keeps company with fieldnotes, a well-elaborated component of ethnographic work and field methods. 'Inventive' methods today are thought of as

> tools, instruments, techniques or distinct (material-semiotic) entities that
> are [...] able to be used in multiple contexts and continually introduced
> into new one... oriented towards making a difference (Lury and Wakeford
> 2012: 10–11).

To make a Visual Vignette during research is to sort through and select images of significance, to explore what makes a difference. Its limited format allows for the juxtaposition of words and images, and reminds the researcher of the breadth of their senses. Whilst we may now have devices 'to hand' in the field (Favero and Theunissen 2018), their ubiquity both makes image-making a more commonplace activity and one with additional politics of circulation (see Dattatreyan and Marrero-Guillamón 2019). The Visual Vignette might be a space that an ethnographer could gather together different types of images they are encountering, from the ones they themselves produce to those that they sent, to images present in materials that they work with. Rather than separating the research phase from the demonstration and communication of its 'end product', that in more conventional terms would be an essay or thesis, creating this 'end product' during fieldwork becomes an integral part of the practice of doing multimodal research (see Collins et al. 2017).

ANALYSIS: MAKING SENSE

When field research comes to an end, it is often challenging to begin to work with all that has been gathered. Since a textual endpoint is what most of us work towards (a PhD dissertation, an article, a book), we are drawn to the texts in our material: interview data, things people have said, our own notes from the field. But since writing is more than putting words on a page, we can use its wider character of reflective practice to work beyond words themselves. This is a familiar technique within STS. In his 2007 essay 'Pinboards and Books: learning, materiality and juxtaposition', John Law puts forward a 'pin board method' for knowing what he calls 'non-coherent realities'. His technique is designed to make visible 'mutual irreducibility' as well as help the ethnographer see relations. In this stage of research, the Visual Vignette also shifts the focus from words to images. It requires a fieldworker to go back through an (often large) archive of visuals and spend time sorting, thinking. What stories can begin to be told within the constraints of the Visual Vignette? How will words and images work in tension or in dialogue before a story is fully clear to the researcher themselves? How stories are told, how they are assembled and put together, requires considerable time and reflection, not least on the question for whom they are being told. They are powerful, and political (Latour 1988; Watts 2016, 2017). A Visual Vignette in this context might also help an STS ethnographer summarize the approaches she has made in the field in the form of her *methods*. With an increased attention to how STS researchers create their data (Hyysalo et al. 2019, Lippert and Douglas-Jones 2019), the Visual Vignette can assist the researcher in reflexively narrating classical problems, such as their positionality in the field, the senses they used in collecting their data, and the role of the visual in the field itself.

'Stories give us hints as to how they need to be written', write the collaborating authors of the Paper Boat Collective (2017: 11), and participants in Visual Vignette workshops observed that 'regular academic work' would ordinarily exclude their photographs (Rueß 2019).

SHARING: STORIES ON THE MOVE

As material objects, Visual Vignettes can help stories travel: they become part of the ongoing relation between researchers and their audiences. Collins and Durington (2015) distinguish between sharing and disseminating research. For them, the difference is a matter of how open one is to dialogue, interpretation, disagreement and counter examples that might arise during field-based engagement with research findings. Building on principles of professional responsibility formulated by the American Anthropological Association, they point out that 'in a world of digitized fungible information that can be ported across media flows', the association admits that an ethnographer cannot control how work is interpreted, re-contextualized or made meaningful (Collins and Durington 2015: 55). STS researchers can build on this knowledge to consider the settings wherein their analyses might be put to work. Printing turns a vignette into an object to circulate, to be taken to the field, used as a prompt for discussion. As scholars in visual and multimodal anthropology have noted, the work of the visual can be to create and keep open channels of discussion between researchers and those with whom they have shared their lives (Collins et al. 2017; Cooper 2008; Ruby 2000). Termed 'multimodality' in anthropology, the door has opened for more voices and media ecologies (words, graphics, images, film, installations, etc.) to constitute academic engagement and creativity (Collins et al. 2017). Collins and his colleagues are optimistic about the 'democratization potential' of media production to support more foundationally collaborative research, and expand the scope for relations between researchers and communities in the 'afterlife' of research projects (2017: 142). Indeed, this interrelatedness of the three modes of research work presented here, as well as the students' experiences in the workshop, illustrate this multimodal approach, encompassing – rather than separating – research, the production of media for dissemination, its afterlife, as well as the relationships and discussions engendered through these processes (Collins et al. 2017: 142). Such after-lives might take the form of printed Visual Vignettes, turned into a fold-out postcard series (Figure 10.8), posters, or an exhibition (Figure 10.9).

FIG. 10.8 Visual vignette as three-fold in postcard size for dissemination among research participants (Gugganig 2019).

FIG. 10.9 Display of Visual Vignettes by Mascha Gugganig, Laura Kuen, Felix Remter, Anja Rueß, Luise Ruge and Chris Wood (in alphabetic order) at the 'STS Infrastructures' exhibition, 4s meeting in New Orleans (2019).

FIG. 10.10 Office space decoration, Cornell University.

In this mode of making a Visual Vignette, audience matters. Whereas in the prior modes of working with Visual Vignettes for fieldnotes and analysis, one's audience was largely oneself, here, stories are being told outwards (even within an office space, see Figure 10.10). For display or discussion, the Visual Vignette communicates. STS researchers often operate in scientific knowledge regimes, and, as a result have many different relationships to their fields. Not all fields will feel 'appropriate' to Visual Vignettes as a communication of research findings. If this is the case, there are interesting questions to ask about why not. What is there about the visual that resists reception? What knowledge hierarchies are in place that render the Visual Vignette format inadmissible (see Chio 2017; Star 1995)? Some fields may be highly receptive, already operating in an economy of images, with active science communication arms and social media editors. Perhaps here, the story of a Visual Vignette might subvert an accepted narrative about a device, system or technology.

Whether a visually saturated field or not, introducing Visual Vignettes into field discussions has the power to shape debate. Bringing material objects, created from the field, performs research differently, and may construct new field openings or make visible realities previously unseen. Thinking with and through these field engagements demands close reflection on field accountabilities and questions of ethics as part of critical research practice. STS research may have much to discover beyond the research paper format, beyond the PowerPoint, and its bullets.

CONCLUSION

Rendering sensor stories as Visual Vignettes brings novel forms of research communication into conversation with novel forms of sensing. Finding ways to communicate about our wired, and wireless world is a task of demonstrating the mutual co-constitution of security and insecurity. As they come into being alongside one another in our field-sites, STS scholars use their analytical apparatus and their senses of listening and seeing to make this mutual emergence visible. These affordances work well for STS, as 'new collaborative and collective ways of sensing materialize that contribute to distinct and transformed worlds', even 'sensing otherwise' (Gabrys 2019:733). Our methods shape how we see, as do our tools of analysis (Ballestero and Winthereik forthcoming). The Visual Vignettes in this collection bring forward forms of analysis that demonstrate the potentials of working with images alongside text, to stay with the dissonance produced when a conventional tool (PowerPoint) is pressed into alternative, imaginative use. In their skilled creation and interpretive richness, these Visual Vignettes create new audiences for the sensing stories their authors wish to tell while emphasizing sensing practices in our empirical fields.

NOTES

1 The authors conducted two graduate student workshops, one at the ETHOS Lab, ITU University of Copenhagen in September 2018, and one at the Munich Center for Technology in Society, Technical University Munich in January 2019. We would like to thank all participants for sharing and rethinking their work with us.

2 See also the Visual Vignettes in the STS Infrastructures exhibition, by clicking "on 'Artifacts' and their respective 'Annotations'" https://stsinfrastructures.org/content/visual-vignettes-0 [accessed 21 September 2019].

REFERENCES

Ballestero, A. and Winthereik, B. (Eds) (forthcoming). *Experimenting with Ethnography: A Companion to Analysis*. Durham: Duke University Press.

Bauer, S., Schlünder, M., and M. Rentetzi (Eds) (2020). *Boxes – A Field Guide* Manchester: Mattering Press.

Beuving, J. (2017). Contacts in a Box: Cell Phones, Social Relations and Field Research in Africa. *African Studies* 78(3): 370–384.

Boudreault-Fournier, A. (2016). Recording and Editing. In D. Elliott, and D. Culhane (Eds), *A Different Kind of Ethnography: Imaginative Practices and Creative Methodologies*. Toronto: University of Toronto Press, pp. 69–90.

Cage, J. (1967). *A Year from Monday: New Lectures and Writings by John Cage*. Middletown: Wesleyan University Press.

Chio, J. (2017). Guiding Lines. *Cultural Anthropology*. Blog <https://culanth.org/fieldsights/guiding-lines> [accessed 18 September 2019], 2 May.

Clifford, J., and Marcus G. E. (Eds) (1986). *Writing Culture: The Poetics and Politics of Ethnography*. Berkeley: University of California Press.

Colleex – Collaboratory for Ethnographic Experiments. Original #colleex manifesto. <https://colleex.wordpress.com/about/colleex-manifesto/> [accessed 30 March 2021].

Collins, S. G., and Durington, M. S. (2015). *Networked Anthropology: A Primer for Ethnographers*. New York: Routledge.

Collins, S. G., Durington, M., and Gill, H. (2017). Multimodality: An Invitation: Multimodal Anthropologies. *American Anthropologist* 119(1): 142–146.

Cooper, M. (2008). Sharing Data and Results with Study Participants: Report on a Survey of Cultural Anthropologists. *Journal of Empirical Research on Human Research Ethics* 3(4): 19–34.

Dányi, E., Suchman, L., and Watts, L. (2021). Relocating Innovation: Postcards from Three Edges. In A. Ballestero, and B. R. Winthereik (Eds), *Experimenting with Ethnography: A Companion to Analysis*. Durham: Duke University Press.

Dattatreyan, E. G., and Marrero-Guillamón, I. (2019). Introduction: Multimodal anthropology and the politics of invention: Multimodal anthropologies. *American Anthropologist* 121(1): 220–228.

Douglas-Jones, R., and Cohn, M. (2018). *GDPR: Erasure Poems*. ETHOSLab, IT University of Copenhagen.

Downey, G.L., and Zuiderent-Jerak, T. (2017). Making and Doing: Engagement and Reflexive Learning in STS. In U. Felt, R. Fouché, C. A. Miller, and L. Smith-Doerr (Eds), *The Handbook of Science and Technology Studies*, 4th ed. Cambridge, MA: The MIT Press, pp. 223–251.

Dumit, J. (2017). Game Design as STS Research. *Engaging Science, Technology and Society* 3 (2017): 603–612.

Elliott, D., and Culhane, D. (Eds) (2017). *A Different Kind of Ethnography: Imaginative Practices and Creative Methodologies*. Toronto: University of Toronto Press.

Estalella, A., and Criado, T. S. (Eds) (2018). *Experimental Collaborations: Ethnography Through Devices*. New York: Berghahn Books.

Favero, P. (2017). Tainted Frictions: A Visual Essay. *American Anthropologist* 119(2): 361–364.

Favero, P. S. H., and Theunissen, E. (2018). With the Smartphone as Field Assistant: Designing, Making and Testing EthnoAlly, a Multimodal tool for Conducting Serendipitous Ethnography in a Multisensory World. *American Anthropologist*. Multimodal Anthropologies, 21 February. <http://www.americananthropologist. org/2018/02/21/with-the-smartphone-as-field-assistant-designing-making-and-testing-ethnoally-a-multimodal-tool-for-conducting-serendipitous-ethnography-in-a-multisensory-world/> [accessed 18 September 2019].

Färber, A. (2007). Exposing Expo: Exhibition Entrepreneurship and Experimental Reflexivity in Late Modernity. In S. MacDonald and P. Basu (Eds), *Exhibition Experiments*. London: Wiley.

Fochler, M., and de Rijcke, S. (2017). Implicated in the Indicator Game? An Experimental Debate. *Engaging Science, Technology, and Society* 3: 21–40.

Gabrys, J. (2019). Sensors and Sensing Practice: Reworking Experience across Entities, Environments and Technologies. *Science, Technology and Human Values* 44(5): 723–736.

Gugganig, M. (2011). *hidden practices*. <https://vimeo.com/24065752> [accessed 1 October 2019], 7 min.

——— (2015). *Making Dust Come to Matter: The Scaffolding of Academia*. Visual Essay for Wenner-Gren Workshop 'Hope and Insufficiency: Capacity Building in Ethnographic Comparison'. <https://hopeandinsufficiency.wordpress.com/visual-essay-competition/mascha-gugganig/> [accessed 1 October 2019].

——— (2019). *Exploring Education at a Hawaiian-Focused Charter School, a Food Sovereignty Movement, and the Agricultural Biotechnology Industry*. Visual vignette https://visualvignettes. wordpress.com/exploring-education-by-mascha-gugganig/ [accessed 24 March 2020].

Gugganig, M., and Schor, S. (2020a). Teaching (with) Postcards: Approaches in the Classroom, the Field, and the Community. *Teaching Anthropology* 9(2): 56–65.

—— (2020b). Multimodal Ethnography in/of/as Postcards. *American Anthropologist* 122(3): 691-697.

Howe, S. (2014). A Note About Two Systems. *Law Culture Text* 18: 249–257.

Hyysalo, S., Pollock, N., and Williams, R. A. (2019). Method Matters in the Social Study of Technology: Investigating Biographies of Artifacts and Practices. *Science & Technology Studies* 32(3): 1–25.

Jungnickel, K. (Ed.) (2020). *Transmissions: Critical Tactics for Making and Communicating Research.* Cambridge, MA: The MIT Press.

Kuen, L. (2019). The Freedom of the Forest. Visual vignette. <https://visualvignettes. wordpress.com/the-freedom-of-the-forest-by-laura-kuen-2/> [accessed 26 March 2020].

Larkin, B. (2013). The Politics and Poetics of Infrastructure. *Annual Review of Anthropology* 42: 327–343.

Latour, B. (1988). The Politics of Explanation: An Alternative. In S. Woolgar (Ed.), *Knowledge and Reflexivity: New Frontiers in the Sociology of Knowledge.* London; Beverly Hills: Sage, pp. 155–176.

Law, J. (2007). Pinboards and Books: Learning, Materiality and Juxtaposition. In D. Kritt, and L. T. Winegar (Eds), *Education and Technology: Critical Perspectives, Possible Futures.* Lanham, MA: Lexington Books, pp. 125–150.

Le Bot, J., and Noel, M. (2016). 'Making and Doing' at 4s Meeting (Denver): Let's Extend the Experiment! *EASST Review* 35(1). <https://easst.net/article/making-and-doing-at-4s-meeting-denver-lets-extend-the-experiment/> [accessed 24 March 2020].

Liboiron, M., Ammendolia, J., and Winsor, K., et al. (2017). Equity in Author Order: A Feminist Laboratory's Approach. *Catalyst* 3(2): 1–17.

Lippert, I., and Douglas-Jones, R. (2019). 'Doing Data': Methodography in and of STS. *EASST Review* 38(1). <https://easst.net/article/doing-data-methodography-in-and-of-sts/#_ftn1> [accessed 8 October 2019].

Lury, C., and Wakeford, N. (Eds) (2012). *Inventive Methods: The Happening of the Social.* Oxford; New York: Routledge.

Marcus, G. E., and Fischer, M. M. J. (1986). A Crisis of Representation in the Human Sciences. In *Anthropology as Cultural Critique: An Experimental Moment in the Human Sciences.* Chicago: University of Chicago Press, pp. 7–16.

Mattern, S. (2016). Cloud and Field. *Places Journal.* <https://doi.org/10.22269/160802> [accessed 14 May 2020].

Pandian, A., and McLean, S. J. (Eds) (2017). *Crumpled Paper Boat: Experiments in Ethnographic Writing.* Durham: Duke University Press.

Paper Boat Collective (2017). Introduction: Archipelagos, A Voyage in Writing. In A. Pandian, and S. J. McLean (Eds), *Crumpled Paper Boat: Experiments in Ethnographic Writing.* Durham, NC: Duke University Press, pp. 11–28.

Pink, S. (2011). Multimodality, Multisensoriality and Ethnographic Knowing: Social Semiotics and the Phenomenology of Perception. *Qualitative Research* 11(3): 261–276.

Rose, G., and Tolia-Kelly, D. P. (Eds) (2012). *Visuality/Materiality: Images, Objects and Practices.* Farnham, Surrey: Ashgate Publishing.

Ruby, J. (2000). *Picturing Culture: Explorations of Film and Anthropology.* Chicago: University of Chicago Press.

Rueß, A. (2019). Public Image(s)? – Two Tales of a Nuclear Mono-Culture. Visual vignette. <https://visualvignettes.wordpress.com/public-images-two-tales-of-a-nuclear-mono-culture-by-anja-rues/> [accessed 26 March 2020].

Sanjek, R., and Tratner, S. (Eds) (2015). *eFieldnotes: The Makings of Anthropology in the Digital World.* Philadelphia: The University of Pennsylvania Press.

Schrader, A. (2010). Responding to Pfisteria Piscicida (the Fish Killer): Phantomatic Ontologies, Indeterminacy, and Responsibility in Toxic Microbiology. *Social Studies of Science* 40(2): 275–306.

Star, S. L. (Ed.) (1995). *Ecologies of Knowledge: Work and Politics in Science and Technology.* Albany: State University of New York Press.

—— (2002). Infrastructure and Ethnographic Practice: Working on the Fringes. *Scandinavian Journal of Information Systems* 14(2): 107–122.

Stone, R. (2017). The Trump-Era Boom in Erasure Poetry: How a Poetic Form Gained New Political Purpose Online in 2017. *The New Republic,* 23 October.

Strathern, M. (2006). Bullet-Proofing: A Tale from the United Kingdom. In A. Riles (Ed.), *Documents: Artifacts of Modern Knowledge.* Ann Arbour: University of Michigan Press.

STS Infrastructures (2019). Special Exhibit by the Society for the Social Studies of Science. <https://stsinfrastructures.org/> [accessed 1 October 2019].

Tufte, E. (2003). *The Cognitive Style of PowerPoint.* Cheshire, CT: Graphics Press.

Visual vignettes (2018). Blog. <https://visualvignettes.wordpress.com/> [accessed 1 October 2019].

Watts, L. (2020). This is Not a Poem, This is STS. STS Problems Roundtable, Does STS Have Problems. 4S-EASST Barcelona. https://stsproblems.wordpress.com/2016/10/04/this-is-not-a-poem/ [accessed 15 May 2020].

Watts, L. (2017). The Draukie's Tale. In I. Szeman, and D. Boyer (Eds), *Energy Humanities: An Anthology.* Johns Hopkins University Press.

11

DRONES AS POLITICAL MACHINES: TECHNOCRATIC GOVERNANCE IN CANADIAN DRONE SPACE

Ciara Bracken-Roche

ABSTRACT

THE DEPLOYMENT OF DRONE TECHNOLOGIES ACROSS CONFLICT SPACES AND urban spaces alike (see Jumbert and Sandvik 2017, Pugliese 2015, Wall and Monahan 2011) has been fuelled by a burgeoning surveillance-industrial complex (Hayes 2012), the confluence of economic interests and the securitization of risk (Aradau and van Munster 2011). Drawing on document analysis, from governmental and non-governmental sources, and semi-structured interviews with ~30 drone stakeholders in Canada, I argue that these technologies trouble traditional bounds of state and security (as will be elaborated on with Barry 2001, 2006). Feenberg (2004) argues that 'technical action is an exercise of power' and from their use for intelligence, surveillance, and reconnaissance in international contexts to policing domestic spaces, drones further amplify power imbalances between the operators and the objects of the drone's sensors (Hall Kindervater 2016, Shaw 2016).

While commonly perpetuated discourses across industry groups represent domestic drones as benign sensing technologies as compared to militarized drones (Bracken-Roche 2016, Bracken-Roche et al. 2014), this chapter highlights how security professionals deploy particular narratives about drones to suit economic and political agendas. More so, it highlights how the case of drones (in Canada) represents a technological zone (Barry 2001, 2006). Understanding how this occurs in both civilian and military applications shows how these sensing machines dramatically shape public spaces and impact individuals across various contexts. Based on the data collected, and adding to current debates on drone technologies, boundaries, and materialities, I ask: how is the drone framed by economic and political discourses across an array of sociotechnical spaces? And, relatedly, what roles do drone systems and key actors play in shaping these environments?

INTRODUCTION

It's pretty clear that UAVs didn't come from nowhere, they came from the military. They already came wearing khaki, they're not neutral. That's part of the industry rebranding what were clearly weapons and surveillance equipment as public toys.

Bracken-Roche, Interview 22 – Privacy Advocate, 2018

The rapid expansion of civil drone technologies over the past five to ten years has been met with excitement and trepidation. Commercially, drones are being adopted across a number of industries for dull, dirty, or dangerous jobs, and are positioned as the solution to any problem – or 'like a solution looking for a problem' (Hayes et al. 2014) – with the value of the global drone market expected to reach US$144.38 billion by 2025 (Adroit Market Research 2019). However, many academics, civil libertarians, and privacy advocates are concerned with the privacy and surveillance implications of the widespread adoption of drones due to their sensing, networked, and data collection capabilities (Bracken-Roche 2016; Bracken-Roche et al. 2014; Hayes et al. 2014; Finn and Wright 2012; Wall and Monahan 2011). In the Canadian context, regulations governing drone technologies are set by Transport Canada, the national transportation agency whose primary mandate is safety (Transport Canada 2017). The key actors involved in the regulatory process are government representatives and industry stakeholders, who have particular goals and interests around the rapid deployment of drones. The rapid evolution of drone technologies has spurned a growing drone industry in Canada, which is at odds with the slow regulatory pace (of government), let alone with consultation over public concerns with the technologies. This chapter uses Andrew Barry's (2006) concept of technological zones to demonstrate how the different actors, networks, and regulations engaged with drones in Canada transcend traditional boundaries, and how this results in the interests of industry stakeholders at the fore. As technological zones tend to develop quickly, and with a lot of uncertainty, this limits the opportunity for much public consultation and amplifies imbalances in representation.

The current rules and regulations for drones in Canada are created by a working group at Transport Canada (TC), the national transportation authority, and the membership of this group is comprised of approximately 60% industry actors, 20% military actors, and 20% government actors (Bracken-Roche 2016, Bracken-Roche et al. 2014). The stakeholders from the working group connect to a larger and global network of players that are keen on adopting the technology for various organizational needs, such as within the civil defence arena. This has resulted in the emergence of an increasingly networked group of stakeholders that function more or less the same across corporate and government bodies, including the military, and across allied borders. They test, regulate, and deploy drones together across a number of setting which rests uneasily with the democratic notion of keeping civil and military powers separate, as well as implicating issues of autonomy and sovereignty. It further highlights the ways in which certain groups take privilege in shaping sociotechnical space and systems of security while others are excluded.

One such example of economic/industry interests driving drone development is seen in the case of specific (de)regulation of 'low energy' drones by the TC regulatory group (Gersher 2014a). This decision was based on the lack of harm low energy drones pose to the physical safety of airspace users and the public because of their lower mass and size (Transport Canada 2015). However, while safety is an important consideration and these low-energy drones may pose less of a threat to physical safety because of their low mass and small size, they can still have a number of payloads attached to them for data collection and surveillance purposes and therefore still pose concerns for civil liberties and privacy. What is more concerning is that during the time of these discussions on the regulatory working group, a number of Canadian drone manufacturers were specifically leasing drones in this 'low energy' category to policing agencies. This case shows how the technologies are regulated purely with safety concerns in mind and neglect that the size of drone is irrelevant when it comes to data collection or privacy infringement. Moreover, the actors who directly benefit from this regulation are the same actors who helped implement it, i.e., industry stakeholders. The exemption for this drone category was proposed by industry association representatives who sit on the drone working group and whose members could focus their business on drone development that would fall into the exemption category, and who would directly benefit from less burdensome regulations for their operations (Gersher 2014a). This case demonstrates the impact of power and drone technologies in both physical and regulatory space, where those involved in creating and deploying drone technologies are almost always involved in shaping the rules of their usage. This ultimately reinforces a privilege in the capital gains of particular groups over the political and social security of other groups. This case shows how the blurred lines between actors, agencies, and states perpetuate the adoption of drone technologies with very particular understandings of risk. The particular understandings of the economic, political, and social implications of adopting drones vary greatly depending upon the logics of the various actors and groups.

The stakeholders influencing the growth of drones within the domestic sphere are often the same stakeholders who have developed drones for use internationally in spaces of military engagement. Civil and commercial drones in domestic space raise concerns about safety – as often cited by regulatory agencies and industry manufacturers (Goodyear 2015) – and privacy – the focus of work by academic and civil liberties organizations (Beltran 2015; Bracken-Roche et al. 2014; Stanley and Crump 2011). However, drone stakeholders attend to questions of safety far more than they consider how drones contribute to the increasing digitization of domestic space and thus to the social and political implications of the technologies. The dichotomy between the privacy and safety of drones arises across all stakeholder groups, with each supporting their own position as to why one concern is more relevant than the other. These two concerns – privacy and safety – emerge as competing discourses of risk that permit particular voices as privileged over others in policy making, as well as voicing concerns about the technologies.

This chapter will begin by explicating Barry's (2006) concept of technological zones as they frame the empirical and theoretical approach for this study. The ways in which these technological zones help understand the ways in which drones are transcending traditional state bounds in Canada will be discussed first. This is necessary to see the ways in which various actors and interests shape the space. The next section will discuss the shifting context of the drone from military to domestic space. Thirdly, empirical data on Canadian drone space will be linked to the three prototypes of technological zones as ways of seeing and understanding how this space transcends traditional territorial boundaries. And lastly, the final section will discuss how these technological zones feed the market of drones as surveillance technologies and the related discourses of risk that accompany the growth of the drone market from military to domestic spaces.

(DE-)CONSTRUCTING DRONES: MATERIAL POLITICS AND TECHNOLOGICAL ZONES

Material objects and technologies play a role in assemblages of governance, security, and surveillance (Walters 2014; Aradau 2010; Latour 2005; Barry 2001). These material objects and technologies often exist within spaces which are clearly defined by various norms, and not necessarily limited to traditional state boundaries. That is, they exist within spaces where 'differences between technical practices, procedures and forms have been reduced, or common standards have been established' (Barry 2006: 239). Drones are material objects that are shaped by social actors and spaces, and impact actors and spaces in turn. However, the extent to which certain actors are included and excluded in the making and regulating of drones results in a technological zone that does not address the concerns of certain actors, and this politics of exclusion limits agency and has impacts on sociotechnical spaces as a result of the way drones are operated. Understanding the actors, logics, and regulations that make up the technological zone around drones in Canada (Barry 2001, 2006) provides a lens to understand why some concerns and narratives about drones are stronger than others.

The grand scale adoption of domestic drones has the potential to alter socio-technical environments based on the norms established within the technological zone, without necessarily considering concerns of other stakeholders in the domestic space (see Bracken-Roche 2016; Wall and Monahan 2011). More so, the stakeholder groups driving the deployment of drone technologies are driven by risk narratives that do not address the social implications of drones as surveillance technologies. And so this work looks at not only the way drones are being made and shaped but what it is that they produce and how they act or change spaces (see Bauchspies and Puig de la Bellacasa 2009). The idea of technological zones, 'spaces within which differences between technical practices, procedures and forms have been reduced, or common standards have been established' (Barry 2006: 239), is applied to drones in the Canadian domestic sphere and is exemplified in empirical detail based on fieldwork data on drone regulation in Canada. It gives a macro-level lens for understanding how these technologies shift efficiently from the international realm to the domestic realm as well as informing our understanding of how this zone transcends traditional state borders.

The popularity of drones and their proliferation in the domestic context can be explained in a number of ways. In industry they are promoted as being cost effective, allowing new vantage points of vision, and accomplishing tasks that people and other machines cannot (Jackman 2016; Bracken-Roche, field notes, March 2015 and November 2014). The concept of technological zones (Barry 2006) sheds light on the ways in which political spaces emerge around a new technology 'within which differences between technical practices, procedures and forms have been reduced, or common standards have been established' (239). Technological zones themselves have fairly clear borders, but they do not necessarily parallel the traditional borders of nation-states. In the first instance, technological zones can be seen as spaces that emerge around, and in response to, a new technology or material assemblage (Barry 2001). The spaces, processes, and practices that emerge around a scientific endeavour or a technology are, in Barry's (2001) terms, known as technological zones. Feenberg (1992) further argues that contemporary, industrial society is purely shaped by political power dynamics. And sociotechnical spaces are shaped by the dominant political hegemony, and not by 'technical decisions [that] are significantly constrained by "rationality" – either technical or economic', (Feenberg 1992: 301). Thus, the hegemonic power of the technological zone perpetuates a form of technocratic governance within the domestic realm.

Politics has become preoccupied with technology, in that '[there] is a political preoccupation with the problems technology poses, with the potential benefits it promises, and with the models of social and political order it seems to make available' (Barry 2001: 2). There is an ever increasing importance of technology in shaping relationships of governance, in shaping policy and regulation, and in the way that there are (new) actors involved in affairs that traditionally would have been solely state-run. These technological zones self-define to an extent – based on expertise – but are also determined by measures or, standards that apply to a technology or emerge around it. In this way, the Canadian technological zone around drones is reflexive in that has been shaped by particular logics and proscribed practices but it also adjusts as the technologies change and develop. Understanding technological zones as linked to a new technology helps reveal the ways in which traditional domestic and international demarcations for both stakeholders and institutions are somewhat less significant than the space that emerges around the technology itself, often based on expertise and experience of relevant individuals. Barry (2006) identifies three types of technological zones: metrological zones, infrastructural zones, and zones of qualification. Such technological zones take broadly one of three forms: (1) metrological zones associated with the development of common forms of measurement; (2) infrastructural zones associated with the creation of common connection standards; and (3) zones of qualification which come into being when objects and practices are assessed according to common standards and criteria (ibid.). An example of a metrological zone would be the development of the United States customary units system of measurements prior to their independence from the United Kingdom. Infrastructural zones refer to the common connection standards that integrate production or communication, while excluding producers or consumers who do not adopt the standard. And lastly, zones of qualification refer to objects and practices being assessed and upheld to common standards, such environmental protocols or standardization of transit safety standards.

Barry (2006, 2001) aligns the idea of technological zones with Michel Foucault's (1995) disciplinary institutions – within which practices, bodies, and identities are controlled and determined – as spaces within which the organization of relations between various entities is determined (Barry 2006). Biopower and docility – the way in which control occurs through discourse, regulation, and routine manifest themselves in the individual and render them in particular ways – in Foucault's sense can be seen in technological zones through the normative forces that shape relations within the space, although they are not necessarily disciplinary in nature (ibid.). As opposed to groups of actors emerging because of their role or position within the nation-state, these stakeholders emerge around a new technology because of their expertise and form various groups, policies, and organizations in order to manage this new technology. The emergence of drones in Canada, and within domestic spaces more generally, are prime examples of technological zones.

Like many cases of new technologies being introduced to the public, industry stakeholders see the way the technology will benefit consumers and the economy, and much public concern or resistance is dismissed by stakeholders as being unfounded or unreasonable (Yearly 2005). In the case of UAS (unmanned aerial systems), drone industry stakeholders believe public concerns – which have been related to privacy and civil liberties – are based on a lack of aware-ness and knowledge on the part of the public at large (see Bracken-Roche et al. 2014) as well as perceived media bias. This belief further limits engagement with the public as well as a dismissal of any public concerns more broadly. The introduction of UAS into the domestic realm has been facilitated by funding from government sources, and regulations have been constructed with the aid of key industry stakeholders with limited public consultation – especially in the early iterations of the drone regulations (Bracken-Roche, field notes, February 2016; Bracken-Roche et al. 2015; Gersher 2013). Therefore, the evolution of a technological zone often is the result of particular political and economic interactions, 'and the specificities of the materials, practices, and locations which they transform, connect, exclude, and silence' (Barry 2006: 250). The ways in which drones have transferred from a traditionally military, and international space, will be discussed in the next section.

BEYOND KILLER DRONES: DRONES IN THE DOMESTIC SPACE

The increase in the use of drone technologies in military reconnaissance, domestic policing, and in commercial endeavours is due in large part to drone manufacturers trying to find new markets for their commodities (Bracken-Roche et al. 2014). The cross-pollination and training that has occurred between military and policing agencies in Canada has been a key factor in domestic law enforcement agencies (LEAs) taking up drones for their own purposes (Molnar and Parsons 2013). As is the case with many technologies that transfer from the 'military industrial complex' into domestic policing (Haggerty and Ericson 1999), drone technologies are being developed simultaneously with corresponding policies and practices. As David (1985) argues, there tends to be a small window opportunity – with a number of factors at play – in which a technological zone is open to change. The shifting use of drones from their traditional use in the military sector into the domestic realm for the provision of intelligence and security applications exists within the larger context of the political economy of the UAS industry – and the surveillance-industrial complex more broadly – not only within states, but internationally. The space of the technological zone gives a voice to particular actors over others, in the case of drones in Canada this has meant government, industry, and military stakeholders but generally excludes civil libertarians, privacy advocates and the public. Being privileged within the Canadian drone technological zone as a stakeholder with a voice again relies on one's expertise and experience as it directly pertains to drone technology. Therefore the primary government body regulating drone technologies makes up the UAS working group with military and industry actors because of their technical expertise on drones technologies (Bracken-Roche, Interview 17, 2018).

Analyses of surveillance that permeates our daily lives often 'examine[s] how its practice has become more widespread via technologies used in warfare being diffused into everyday usage by the capitalist enterprise' (Ball 2002: 573). Tracking the historical development of drones and their adoption in the domestic realm shows parallels with military innovation that has occurred with other technologies. Aradau (2010) has argued that artefacts are not neutral or apolitical but that they 'are constituted through intra-action between different material-discursive practices' (499). Therefore, it is likely that the dispositions and logics that accompany drones originating in the military-industrial complex will transfer into their adoption in the domestic realm. This same idea is introduced with the quotation at the beginning of this chapter, where one a privacy advocate states that drones are not neutral but are innately militaristic because that is the primary context from which they've come. As UAS have moved beyond their military uses and spread into the domestic realm a number of civil liberties organizations, privacy commissioners, and members of government have commissioned reports and made recommendations on the key considerations necessary for legislating and regulating the use of UAS domestically (see Hayes et al. 2014; Office of the Privacy Commissioner of Canada 2013; Stanley and Crump 2011).

The extent to which drones permeate the public imagination and daily newsmedia is reflective of their expansion across numerous and multiple sociotechnical spaces but it is increasingly important to understand the social and political spaces that these technologies occupy. No longer found only in war-related contexts, the drone has moved beyond the space of international conflict but it brings with it particular de-territorializing logics (Packer and Reeves 2013). However, drones emerged from a particular historical context that influences their introduction to, and acceptance in, the domestic realm (Bracken-Roche 2016; Shaw 2016; Wall and Monahan 2011). As drones have been adopted for a variety of tasks in the domestic sphere they highlight particular narratives of militarization and surveillance, risk and security (Wall and Monahan 2011). While drone technologies and networks are linked to the state in some ways, in other ways they move beyond traditional state boundaries both in terms of their role in international conflicts (where their legal status is questioned) as well as current proliferation in the domestic sphere. This transcendence of traditional state bounds can be seen in two ways. In the military context, the use of drones overseas has not necessarily been officially acceptable or following traditional capacities. For example the legality of US-led drone warfare in Pakistan has been called into question (see Shaw and Akhter 2012). In the domestic realm, the individual actors and companies that develop and deploy drone technologies are not necessarily limited to one state and a majority tends to have military linkages, past or present, even though their operations are linked to the state in which they are operating and where regulations determine their civil operations.

Looking at the adoption and growth of UAS in the domestic realm and their emergence as surveillance technologies highlights the finding that the same agents who shape the drone market and deploy drone technologies are the same individuals who advocate for particular regulations. UAS manufacturers have proven to be key actors in shaping the UAS market and the way drone technologies are regulated, for example (this will be evident in the interview data discussed later in the chapter; also see Bracken-Roche et al. 2014; Gersher 2014a). The drone industry has worked alongside government to shift the UAS market's focus from (or at least not solely focused on) military applications to those of intelligence gathering and security in the domestic space (Bracken-Roche et al. 2014). And while privileged stakeholders play a dominant role within the drone technological zone, publics are excluded as '[i]n the processes by which structuring decisions are made, different people are differently situated and possess unequal degrees of power as well as unequal levels of awareness' (Winner 1980: 127).

EXAMINING INTEROPERABILITY: LINKING SYSTEMS, STATES, AND AGENCIES

The actors and regulations that emerge around drones not only transcend traditional internal/external agency divisions within states, but also beyond states.

As material objects take on agency, territorial state bounds are no longer the sole determinate of engagement, but instead facilitate the ability to engage with, and around emerging technologies shape new spaces that are instead defined by scientific and technical practices. Documents were obtained through Access to Information and Privacy (ATIP) requests from a number of federal agencies in Canada including but not limited to Transport Canada, the Department of National Defence, and Innovation, Science, and Economic Development. Elite interviews were carried out with 30 stakeholders, and then transcribed. A grounded theory qualitative thematic analysis was the primary method for data analysis. In my approach to the thematic analysis, I conceptualized themes as patterns in the data underpinned by a central concept that organizes the analytic observations, in this case interoperability. Once all of the transcriptions were read and surveyed for preliminary themes, I noted any initial analytic obser-vations about each interview, and then coded for these items across all of the interviews. This was all carried out using QDA Miner, data analysis software.

Following a social constructivist approach, this analysis takes technology as contingent and flexible, that is a co-construction of technology and the social and political sphere is continuously taking place. This approach is important because it highlights the need to carry out empirical research in order to 'inter-rogate surveillance technologies in specific social contexts' (Monahan 2008). Based on the thematic analysis, I focus on the theme of interoperability as it emerged in relation to drone technology, and drone regulations. During inter-views with various stakeholders, themes tended to emerge across particular groups of actors. For many government actors, the focus was on regulations across agencies and to be in sync with the United States. Industry focused on the ability to use different drone hardware and software together seamlessly, which was also a concern for military and policing stakeholders who also highlighted the need for different groups to be able to deploy and operate their technolo-gies side-by-side with ease. Of course, for civil liberties and privacy experts the concern was more focused on data protection when various groups are using drones. Overall, these themes link to integration, or interoperability.

Narratives about interoperability – or integration more broadly – and the ways in which drone technologies and regulations are shaped in order to be compatible across systems, states, and agencies came through in both interviews and document analysis. This emerged in a few different ways among those interviewed but the basic desire for those encouraging interoperability was the same: for drones and their corresponding software systems to be able to work in conjunction with one another across various organizations and spaces. The actual term interoperability was primarily used by current or former military personnel, many of whom have made the transition into the drone industry. However, other stakeholders referred to interoperability in terms of compatibility of regulations, systems, and partnerships between agencies and states. The Canadian government and military have long-standing ties with the Canadian drone industry which has resulted in a 'mutually beneficial relationship where regulators can have technology experts involved in rule making, industry can influence regulations, and military can be involved' in both of these arenas (Bracken-Roche, field notes, January 2016). The ongoing relationships between these various groups have been further intensified through the alignment of drone regulations and technologies. In this sense the examination of the Canadian drone space exemplifies a technological zone in perhaps two of the three ways that Barry (2006) introduces. This notion of interoperability links to infrastructural zones and zones of qualification. In terms of infrastructural zones, within Canada there is a push from various agencies within states to align their drone hardware and software systems to allow interoperability across agencies. The zone of qualification is evident in regulatory terms where Canadian regulation for drones is standardized across the country, and where there is a Canadian-US committee dedicated to regulatory harmonization of drones as part of the Beyond the Border Regulatory Cooperation Council (RCC) (Bracken-Roche, Interview 28, 2018).

This interagency cooperation and regulation in Canada, as well as technological compatibility between systems, has three primary features of interoperability (see Gersher 2014a). The first is that technological systems are being built to communicate with one another, and are in accordance with one another across agencies. This was noted in interviews where numerous stakeholders spoke of OPERATION GRIZZLY as a 'pivotal point for interagency drone cooperation and technological alignment' (Bracken-Roche,

Interview 5, 2018). Additionally, designated Canadian personnel are able to access live video feeds of a United States (US) Predator B drone that is flying along the Canadian-US Border through a handheld device (Gersher 2014a). This highlights the increasing compatibility of technologies and information sharing across agencies and borders and speaks to the 'System of Systems' approached as outlined in primary documents (Gersher 2014a; A-2011-00658). This approach would entail developing drones by Canada's military that would be interoperable and synergetic with a whole collection of sensors, technologies, and data sharing systems (ibid.). This links back to Barry's (2006) conception of infrastructural zones even more so in that the development of the zone is path-dependent (Callon 1995) where particular inter-relations, and circumstances must emerge in order for the zone to development in the way it does. In the Canadian context, OPERATION GRIZZLY seems to play a key role, and was identified across a number of documents, and interviews as being a turning point for the development of drones in Canada. Secondly, an interoperable security system also includes the sharing of information between organizations across and within borders (Bracken-Roche 2018; Gersher 2014a). This is seen above specifically regarding access to drone video feeds and in cross-border law enforcement practices and policies where Canada and the US agencies engage in 'bilateral information and intelligence-sharing' (Gilbert 2012a). The last aspect of interoperability (Gersher 2014a) is the coordination of regulations and standards within and across borders, and across agencies, which demonstrates a zone of qualification in Barry's terms. This regulatory cooperation and synchronization of standards has been demonstrated by the Canadian civil aviation agency working to streamline their domestic regulations with the US as part of the Beyond the Border Regulatory Cooperation Council (RCC) (Bracken-Roche, Interview 28, 2018) and with the International Civil Aviation Organization (ICAO) (attended by Canadian government and industry stakeholders), as well as with Canada's own military (who sit on the transnational working group as well as the Transport Canada UAV Working Group) (ibid.).

These multinational projects extend to Canada's military, who 'work with NATO to standardize regulations to further facilitate interoperability across operations and across the national airspace of other states' (Bracken-Roche, field notes, November 2014). It is because of these partnerships across both civil and military agencies that drone regulations, within Canada and internationally, are becoming increasingly uniform. Additionally, there has been an effort to align information sharing practices in Canada across LEAs and the military (see Abrahamson and Goodman-Delahunty 2014). This is further coupled with recent trends in facilitating Canadian-US cross border law enforcement operations which has resulted in increased information sharing as a result of various economic and security agreements including the Shiprider Agreement and the Beyond the Border action plan (Topak et al. 2015). All of these agreements try to ensure both the technological and bureaucratic alignment across agencies and borders so that data can be collected and shared more efficiently and so that integrated tasks or law enforcement operations can occur outside of their traditional boundaries without posing any jurisdictional issues (Topak et al. 2015; Gilbert 2012b).

However, the interconnectedness and interoperability of these various security and surveillance apparatuses raises concerns about privacy, accountability, autonomy/sovereignty, and the separation of powers. What is even more concerning is that issues of security and surveillance are not wholly administered by state agencies such as LEAs, the military, and relevant government departments. The technologies and apparatuses, regulations, and related data collection and sharing practices are being administered, in part, by (industry) stakeholders who have a vested economic interest in the success of these systems because they 'have skin in the game' (Bracken-Roche, field notes, March 2015). As discussed by Haggerty and Ericson (1999) and Hayes (2012), the result of these public-private partnerships in the realm of security and surveillance is that the logics that shape technologies in the military space are often transported into domestic space alongside the technologies themselves. In practice a number of Canadian drone companies have already benefited from these relationships whether through direct funding from government bodies for research, such as Innovation, Science and Economic Development Canada, or through offering turnkey services for various safety, security, and surveillance procurement contracts (Bracken-Roche, Interview 21, 2018).

When tracing the stakeholders who are involved in the various aspects of creating, regulating, and deploying drones there is a convergence of shared occupational history and expertise across government, industry, and military stakeholders moving between different fields. This revolving door (Hayes 2012) raises concerns about economic interests are prioritized over of the public good. Information that is publicly available online (such as on industry, government, and social media websites) demonstrates how many stakeholders in these three areas exhibit the revolving door at work. One individual who oversaw the Canadian military's drone regulation development and project JUSTAS then moved to a senior role at Transport Canada in their drone civil aviation group, now works for a commercial drone company while consulting for other national and international government bodies and private companies. Another individual, the new USC Executive Director, was formerly a Transport Canada and military employee, while the latest USC Chairman formerly works at the National Research Council of Canada and Industry Canada – all of which are key organizations essential to the success of the drone industry (Bracken-Roche, field notes, April 2016). The revolving door of stakeholders perpetuates a space where interests are narrowed and where power becomes concentrated in certain groups and not others.

Civil liberties and privacy experts referred to concerns about data sharing across organizations or borders, while government spoke to the need to ensure regulations were standardized across various aerospace users within Canada as well as across borders (with the US). So while the use of the word 'interoperability' in and of itself was not entirely widespread, various components that make up or lead to interoperability were addressed across various groups. Industry stakeholders often expressed their desire to ensure their systems would fall into the regulations in both Canada and the US, stating:

> [W]e are working in parallel on both sides of the Canadian and US border and so I manage the production and also the development work on the RND side of things. But in addition to that we have a services branch where we are ourselves a UAV operator and we offer services for different types of industries, so we take care of all the issues that might arise with local regulations. (Bracken-Roche, Interview 25, 2018)

As seen in this quotation, manufacturers focus on emerging drone regulations so that their technologies will be regulated for use in different countries. Government concerns regarding interoperability were primarily in ensuring safety across airspace on either side of the border, from the deployment of drones across and between various state agencies to the broader regulation of their use within particular spaces. In the Canadian case, the regulations were and still are far more advanced than in the US case but as the concerns over privacy increased in the US context, so did the concerns in Canada. A privacy stakeholder from government alludes to this in the following quotation:

> What we were first looking at really was, in fact, the use of the technology by another country which happens to share a border with us [the US], but it was another country. Then we had to come to grips with the state the technology was in then. Then having understood what was going on we started to think about contacting Transport Canada because this is gonna be where you're going to start to see, probably, the first complaints ... (Bracken-Roche, Interview 17, 2018)

The tension that exists in relation to US drones collecting data over Canadian soil is highlighted in this quotation from a privacy stakeholder. Public opinion data (Bracken-Roche et al. 2014) has highlighted The Canadian public's lack of support for any type of data sharing with or data collection by the US The concern over American practices, and regulations on the same processes in Canada is highlighted by this quotation, and was an issue that came up across numerous interviews. While Canadian regulations have allowed for the deployment of drones since 2008, but 'it was only when their use in the US and related concerns with their use came to media attention in 2012' that concerns began to increase in Canada (Bracken-Roche, field notes, November 2014).

Official regulatory cooperation around drones between Transport Canada and the Federal Aviation Authority in the US was implemented in 2011 as part of the Beyond the Border Action Plan for Perimeter Security and Economic Competitiveness (Public Safety Canada 2012) which truly cemented a technological zone around drones in North America. As part of the Regulatory

Cooperation Council, officials from each agency meet regularly and 'share best practices and experiences, and look for opportunities for harmonization where it is practical. It's a more official, structured programme, but we were sharing that information anyway' (Bracken-Roche, Interview 28, 2018). It is since this time that the gap between the Canadian regulations and US regulations has narrowed, with the FAA following Canada's example and trying to open up opportunities for the deployment of drones within their domestic airspace. This was in large part to do with lobbying from various groups who wanted to use drones for particular operations, as well as lobbying from the drone industry and military technology manufacturers who saw a huge market opportunity if the deployment of drones were to be sanctioned within US domestic airspace (Kang 2016).

The question of interoperability and the ability of drones to be deployed across agencies and across borders is a concern for all stakeholder groups, especially when the technology is in a nascent stage. Government officials want to ensure regulatory cooperation to allow their various national agencies to coordinate efforts for cross border enterprises while industry want to ensure a larger market in which to market and deploy their technologies. Privacy and civil liberties advocates question these efforts as cross border deployment of these technologies might mean that the safeguards usually in place in Canada might not exist in technologies coming from the US and being deployed in Canada.

STANDARDIZING REGULATIONS

The standardization of drone regulations between Canada and the US is being overseen by the RCC Air Transport Working Group which includes both national aviation bodies (TC and the FAA) and other relevant stakeholders (Bracken-Roche, Interview 28, 2018). The RCC Air Transport Working Group works to integrate all aerial technologies, safely and seamlessly, across both states (ibid.; Gersher 2014b; Public Safety Canada 2011). However, the cross-border operations have been delayed as well with Transport Canada and the FAA conducting market research before realizing next steps in their joint-regulatory efforts (Transport Canada 2016). Elected officials do not have an opportunity to vote on the regulations as they are introduced and public consultation is limited to a short window of time, and most individuals would not be aware of Canada Gazette's public consultation process anyway. Despite the lack of consultation with elected representatives or the public, this is standard practices for the regulation of new technologies in Canada. More so, it has been the case with drones that unelected government officials, military personnel and drone industry stakeholders have the sole responsibility for shaping the regulations for drones, resulting in a technocratic approach to governance that privileges particular logics and interests over others. Transport Canada draws on industry and military stakeholders because of their expertise but the payloads that are attached to a drone also require assessment and regulation by those who understand the data collection and surveillance implications of these technologies. However, privacy and civil liberties advocates have not been given a seat at the table for regulating drones, even though they understand and aim to protect society from the potentially intrusive surveillance aspects of these devices (Bracken-Roche, field notes, February 2015).

To reiterate the siloing that has occurred during the regulatory process, public consultation only occurs at the end of the process when the regulations are near completion using the Canada Gazette website. This attempt at inclusion and transparency is simply a political strategy for gaining public support without having to change any existing regulations, this is not dissimilar to Barry's ideas around transparency as a technique of governmentality (2013). While transparency is seen as a 'device intended to articulate actions' (Barry 2013: 60) it often contributes to disputes where new activities or information are made public and demonstrate how work has been siloed. When the latest phase of regulations is announced, the TC Working Group will have been assessing the legislation for around fifteen years, while public engagement and consultation typically lasts one month per round of regulations. This lack of consultation seems purposely limited so as to reduce public engagement but this speaks to the exclusionary logics that exist within such technopolitical spaces.

The tracing of the regulatory processes for drones reveals how and why particular stakeholder groups are privileged in their involvement while other groups are excluded from shaping policies that have real consequences in Canada's sociotechnical space. The reasons for excluding other groups is said to be for reasons of expertise, and many of these other groups would say this is valid to the extent that they do not know the intricacies of Canadian aviation regulations or civil aviation operations (Bracken-Roche, Interview 17, 2018). However, these groups do understand the implications of these technologies and their various payloads in terms of privacy and surveillance. TC argues that safety is all they can address under their mandate, but ostensibly privacy threats and surveillance concerns can manifest as safety issues. The prioritization of economic interests over the public good is exemplified in regulation building that lacks larger democratic input, especially when those creating the regulations have a vested interest in their deployment, as with most stakeholders engaged in the revolving door. As seen in the case mentioned in the introduction, there is a drive to create less restrictive regulations on the part of industry.

CONCLUSION

The shift from drone use in the military context to their use in the domestic realm has a particular history, and drone technologies are in many ways constrained and guided by their origins. Perhaps it is the association with killer drones in the Middle East and elsewhere that individuals recall when they think of surveillance drones (Bracken-Roche et al. 2014), or perhaps is it because more population groups have felt subject to increasingly pervasive surveillance in the post 9/11 era (Monahan 2012). This research has demonstrated that technocratic governance is a feature of technological zones, and is exemplified in Canada's drone space. Power relations and representation of particular economic and political interests result in the regulatory space developing in a particular way, highlighting how a zone of qualification emerges for drone technologies within Canada and across the border with the US (Barry 2006). Those who take up positions of power in organizations shaping the technological zone control the concerns and the conversation to the exclusion of those who do not possess the right capital or expertise to engage in governance. However, many refute

(Feenberg 1992, 2004; Winner 1980) rationality and expertise as valid reasons for excluding publics and secondary actors from the technological zone governing drones. What is concerning in the context of the (potential) widespread adoption of (interoperable) drones is that they are being regulated with almost no consideration for their sensory capabilities, and that the technological zone is being pushed forward by (government, industry, and military) actors who have a vested interest in economic growth. The privacy and security implications are a last consideration despite the data collection and sharing capabilities offered by drones.

This chapter has assessed the relationships that have been forged around the development and regulation of drone technologies in Canada drawing primarily from the interview data and primary documents to highlight how we see the emergence of a technological zone. The specific focus on the interoperability of drone technologies and regulations across agencies and across state boundaries exemplifies infrastructural zones and zones of qualification. The findings in this chapter are important because they reveal the way that drones and drone regulations are developed in ways that accommodate inter-agency and inter-state cooperation. This further demonstrates the impact of technologies in social and political spaces where new political circumstances come about specifically in response to drones, in this case. The actors and regulations that emerge around drone technologies not only transcend traditional internal/external agency divisions within states, but also go beyond states. The technological zone that encompasses drone integration in Canada highlights a form of technocratic governance where expertise and economic interests shape the space.

The regulation of drones by Transport Canada demonstrates how, and possibly why, public-private partnerships might benefit from a particular type of expertise and logic. However, this is at the great expense of other equally important social and political concerns that the key stakeholders cannot address or understand. As drones become a familiar sight in Canada, it is increasingly uncertain how inappropriate designs and uses of drones by various individuals and organizations will be curbed. More so, as drones become capable of capturing and collecting more data, inappropriate data collection and storage are of increasing concern and as seen in the above assessment of regulation, these capabilities of drones are not sufficiently addressed. The question asked by those concerned with privacy and civil liberties is how to engage in forward looking, safety and privacy sensitive, regulation in order to prevent unrestricted surveillance. Transport Canada's Working Group attends to only one part of the regulations: safety. Physical safety is important in the context of flying machines technologies, but privacy and civil liberties concerns are equally important due to the data collection capabilities of drone payloads. And so even if it would be impossible to open up regulatory oversight more directly to elected officials and the public, the presence of privacy and civil liberties advocates would ensure a more balanced approach to understanding and regulating drones in our sociotechnical space.

Despite the current trend around drones in Canada, the oversight and regulation of these technologies is not just a technical issue for aviation and engineering experts. It is a social and political issue that calls for a broader spectrum of stakeholders who can adequately assess all aspects and implications of drone deployment. The social processes that govern these relations are passed off as rational, bureaucratic processes but are instead shaped by the logics of stakeholder groups whose status allows access to the technological zone of drones. And thus, instead of a democratic and transparent regulatory process, power asymmetries are further concentrated.

REFERENCES

Abrahamson, D. E., and Goodman-Delahunty, J. (2014). Impediments to Information and Knowledge Sharing Within Policing: A Study of Three Canadian Policing Organizations. *Sage Open*: 1–17.

Adroit Market Research (2019). <https://www.globenewswire.com/news-release/2019/05/10/1821560/0/en/Drones-Market-will-grow-at-a-CAGR-of-40-7-to-hit-144-38-Billion-by-2025-Analysis-by-Trends-Size-Share-Growth-Drivers-and-Business-Opportunities-Adroit-Market-Research.html>.

Aradau, C. (2010). Security That Matters: Critical Infrastructure and Objects of Protection. *Security Dialogue* 41(5): 491–514.

Ball, K. (2002). Elements of Surveillance: A New Framework and Future Directions. *Information, Communication & Society* 5(4): 573–590.

Barry, A. (2001). *Political Machines: Governing a Technological Society*. London: Athlone Press.

——(2006). Technological Zones. *European Journal of Social Theory* 9(2): 239–253.

——(2013). *Material Politics: Disputes along the Pipeline*. Oxford: Wiley-Blackwell.

Bauchspies, W. K., and Puig de la Bellacasa, M. (2009). Re-Tooling Subjectivities: Exploring the Possible with Feminist Science and Technology Studies. *Subjectivity* 28(1): 227–28.

Beltran, D. (2015). The Privacy Commissioner of Canada Comments on Proposed UAV Regulation. CyberLex: Insights on Cybersecurity, Privacy and Data Protection Law, 3 November. <https://www.canadiancybersecuritylaw.com/2015/11/the-privacy-commissioner-of-canada-comments-on-proposed-uav-regulation/>.

Bracken-Roche, C. (2016). Domestic Drones: The Politics of Verticality and the Surveillance Industrial Complex. *Geographica Helvetica* 70: 285–293.

Bracken-Roche, C., Lyon, D., Mansour, M., et al. (2014). Privacy Implications of the Spread of Unmanned Aerial Vehicles (UAVs) in Canada. Surveillance Studies Centre. Research project for the 2013–2014 Contributions Program of the Privacy Commissioner of Canada, Ottawa, April 30.

David, P. (1985). *Clio and the Economics of QWERTY*. American Economic Review 75(2): 332–7.

Department of National Defense Canada. (2011). A-2011-00658.

Feenberg, A. (1992). Subversive Rationalization: Technology, Power, and Democracy. *Inquiry: An Interdisciplinary Journal of Philosophy* 35(3–4): 301–322.

——(2004). Critical Theory of Technology. https://www.sfu.ca/~andrewf/books/Critical_Theory_Technology.pdf [accessed 22 August 2016].

Foucault, M. (1995). *Discipline and Punish: The Birth of the Prison*. New York: Vintage Books.

——(2003). *Society Must Be Defended: Lectures at the Collège De France, 1975–76*. New York: Picador.

Gersher, S. (2013). Canada's Domestic Regulatory Framework for RPAS: A call for public deliberation. *Journal of Unmanned Vehicle Systems* 2(1):1–4.

—— (2014a). Drone Surveillance is Increasing in Canada. *Ottawa Citizen*, April 10. <http://ottawacitizen.com/news/drone-surveillance-is-increasing-in-canada>.

—— (2014b). Eyes in the Sky: The Domestic Deployment of Drone Technology and Aerial Surveillance in Canada. Master's thesis, Carleton University, 2014.

Gilbert, E. (2012a). Harper's Border Deal Expands the National Security State. Rabble, 1 February. <http://rabble.ca/news/2012/02/harpers-border-deal-expands-national-security-state>.

—— (2012b). The Canada-US Border Deal. Perspectives, Fall. <https://www.uc.utoronto.ca/magazine/canada-us-border-deal>.

Goodyear, S. (2015). Drones Get More Popular, and the Rules Are Getting Stricter. CBC News, 9 November. <http://www.cbc.ca/news/technology/canada-u-s-drones-rules-1.3280065>.

Graham, S. (2013). Foucault's Boomerang: The New Military Urbanism. Open Democracy, 14 February. <https://www.opendemocracy.net/opensecurity/stephen-graham/foucault%E2%80%99s-boomerang-new-military-urbanism>.

Haggerty, K., and Ericson, R. V. (1999). The Militarization of Policing in the Information Age. *Journal of Political and Military Sociology* 27(2): 233–255.

Hayes, B. (2012). The Surveillance-Industrial Complex. In D. Lyon, K. Ball and K. D. Haggerty (Eds), *Routledge Handbook of Surveillance Studies*. London: Routledge, pp. 167–175.

Hayes, B., Jones, C., and Töpfer, E. (2014). Eurodrones Inc. Report for the Transnational Institute and Statewatch, February. <http://www.statewatch.org/news/2014/feb/sw-tni-eurodrones-inc-feb-2014.pdf>.

Jensen, O. B. (2016). Drone City: Power, Design and Aerial Mobility in the Age of Smart Cities. *Geographica Helvetica* 71(2): 67–75.

Jumbert, M.G. and Sandvik, K.B. (2017). Introduction: What does it take to be good?, in Sandvik, K.B., Jumbert, M.G. (eds) *The good drone*, London, New York: Routledge, 1–25.

Kang, C. (2016). F.A.A Introduces Commercial Drone Rules. *New York Times*, 22 June. <https://www.nytimes.com/2016/06/22/technology/drone-rules-commercial-use-faa.html>.

Latour, B. (1987). *Science in Action: How to Follow Scientists and Engineers Through Society*. Cambridge, MA: Harvard University Press.

—— (1999). On Recalling ANT. In Law and Hassards (Eds), *Actor Network Theory and After*. Oxford: Blackwell Publishers, pp. 15–26.

—— (2005). *Reassembling the Social: An Introduction to Actor-Network-Theory*. Oxford: Oxford University Press.

Molnar, A., and Parsons, C. (2013). Watching Below: Dimensions of Surveillance-by UAVs in Canada. *Block G Privacy and Security Report* (November).

Monahan, T. (2012). Surveillance and Terrorism. In D. Lyon, K. Ball, K. D. Haggerty (Eds), *Routledge Handbook of Surveillance Studies*. London; New York: Routledge, pp. 285–291.

Office of the Privacy Commissioner of Canada (OPC) (2013). Drones in Canada. OPC. Last modified 21 November 2013. <https://www.priv.gc.ca/en/opc-actions-and-decisions/research/explore-privacy-research/2013/drones_201303/>.

Packer, J., and Reeves, J. (2013). Romancing the Drone: Military Desire and Anthropophobia from SAGE to Swarm. *Canadian Journal of Communication* 38(3): 309–332.

Pugliese, J. (2015). Drones. In M. B. Salter (Ed.), *Making Things International: Circuits and Motion*. Minneapolis: University of Minnesota Press, pp. 222–240.

Public Safety Canada. (2011). Beyond the Border: A Shared Vision for Perimeter Security and Economic Competitiveness. Public Safety Canada. Last modified 18 September 2017. <https://www.publicsafety.gc.ca/cnt/brdr-strtgs/bynd-th-brdr/index-en.aspx>.

—— (2012). Beyond the Border Implementation Report. Public Safety Canada, 14 December. <https://www.publicsafety.gc.ca/cnt/rsrcs/pblctns/archive-2012-bynd-brdr-mplmntn/archive-index-en.aspx#Integrated>.

Shaw, I. G. R. (2016). The Urbanization of Drone Warfare: Policing Surplus Populations in the Dronepolis. *Geographica Helvetica* 71(1): 19–28.

Shaw, I. G. R., and Akhter, M. (2012). The Unbearable Humanness of Drone Warfare In FATA, Pakistan. *Antipode: A Radical Journal of Geography* 44(4): 1490–150.

Stanley, J., and Crump, C. (2011). Protecting Privacy from Aerial Surveillance: Recommendations for Government Use of Drone Aircraft. American Civil Liberties Union, December. <https://www.aclu.org/files/assets/protectingprivacyfromaerialsurveillance.pdf>

Topak, Ö. E., Bracken-Roche, C., Saulnier, A., and Lyon, D. (2015). From Smart Borders to Perimeter Security: The Expansion of Digital Surveillance at the Canadian Borders. *Geopolitics* 20(4): 880–99.

Transport Canada. (2017). Transport Canada 2017–2018 Departmental Plan. Transport Canada. Last modified 10 July 2019. <https://tc.canada.ca/en/transport-canada-2017-2018-departmental-plan>.

—— (2016). Guidance Material for Operating Unmanned Air Vehicle Systems Under an Exemption. Advisory Circular (AC) No. 600-004, 22 December. <https://www.tc.gc.ca/eng/civilaviation/opssvs/ac-600-004-2136.html>.

Wall, T., and Monahan, T. (2011). Surveillance and Violence from Afar: The Politics of Drones and Liminal Security-Scapes. *Theoretical Criminology* 15(3): 239–254.

Walters, W. (2014). Drone Strikes, Dingpolitik and Beyond: Furthering the Debate on Materiality and Security. *Security Dialogue* (2): 101–118.

Winner, L. (1980). Do Artefacts Have Politics? *Daedalus* 109(1): 121–136.

Yearley, S. (2005). *Making Sense of Science: Understanding the Social Study of Science*. London; Thousand Oaks; New Delhi: Sage Publications.

SENSING EUROPEAN ALTERITY: AN ANALOGY BETWEEN SENSORS AND HOTSPOTS IN TRANSNATIONAL SECURITY NETWORKS

Annalisa Pelizza and Wouter Van Rossem

INTRODUCTION

The topic of this book carves a distinctive space in a promising dialogue between sensor technologies and the performativity of security devices. On the one hand, literature on the design of sensor networks has pointed out how it challenges established features of traditional computer networks. Sensing networks require *ad hoc* architectures to respond to at least two key requirements: support for large numbers of unattended autonomous sensor points and adaptation to environmental conditions (Estrin et al. 1999; Dargie and Poellabauer 2010). Such requirements shape not only the technical infrastructure, but also divisions of labour across nodes.

On the other hand, the recent debate between Security Studies and Science and Technology Studies (STS) has produced accounts proposing an 'analytics of security devices' (Amicelle et al. 2015), questioning identification techniques as sociotechnologies of insecurity production (Suchman et al. 2017), wondering how surveillance and security systems shape power and regulatory dynamics (Vogel et al. 2017), investigating how systems shape legal expertise (Leander 2013). Security Studies scholars most actively engaged in a dialogue with STS have embraced the notion of performativity to challenge the naturalness of security actors and of stabilized enunciating subjects (Aradau 2010; de Goede et al. 2014). Such achievements have made sense of security as sociotechnical agency being shaped but also shaping institutional orders and organizations (Dijstelbloem and Pelizza 2019). Security devices, in particular, (de)stabilize 'the power balance between organizational segments by altering communication patterns, roles relationships, the division of labor, established formats for organizational communication, and taken-for-granted routines' (Manning 1996: 54, quoted in Amicelle et al. 2015: 302).

The attempt to launch a dialogue between the sensor and security scholarships has thus the merit of focusing attention on the entrenchments between the performativity of infrastructures for data production and the alleged obduracy of institutionalized agency. With a few exceptions (e.g., Pelizza 2016; Witjes and Olbrich 2017), the interplay between data infrastructures and order institutionalized through laws has received ambivalent consideration in Science and Technology Studies. The spotlight on security sensing infrastructures thus allows recovering an interest in how sociotechnical orders crystallized in laws and regulations can mutate. Sensors can provoke institutional tensions (see Chapters 4 and 5 in this book). They can trigger changes in nation states and international organizations. These, in turn, can shape knowledge production by stabilizing sensing practices.

Following similar concerns, this chapter aims to conduct an experiment. The experiment is finalized to test the tension between the performativity of data infrastructures and the obduracy of institutionalized agency by adopting the rhetorical figure of analogy. Such rhetorical experiments are not new to the history of technology (Agar 2003), and we wish to extend them to current affairs. As it is known, analogy does not require a full overlap between items to be compared. It does not claim that they are *ontologically* equivalent. Less pretentiously, it singles out some common features of the two elements to be compared and *opportunistically* explores the extent to which such comparison can reveal new aspects of the second item, before reaching the limits of the analogy itself.

The experiment we propose to conduct in this chapter explores the extent to which an analogy between architectures of sensor networks and trans-national security orders can have heuristic consequences and reveal new aspects of the latter term of comparison. As Ian Hacking (1983) has recalled, experiments' goal does not pertain to the realm of discovery, but to that of creation. To what extent can an analogy between data and institutional architectures provide new insights for inquiry?

The two elements of the proposed analogy are sensor data infrastructures and trans-national security networks for migration management. Not only do security networks rely upon data infrastructures, they also articulate trans-national orders which 'hit the ground' at distinctive, state-bound locales. One type of such locales are the 'Hotspots': migrant registration and identification centres set up at the external borders of Europe in 2015, in replacement of former, less technologically equipped centres (European Commission 2015b). Following literature on sensor architectures, we propose to consider four relevant features in order to unfold the analogy: the topological position of sensors as input devices, their ability to produce knowledge that would not otherwise exist, separation of concern and data reduction as design criteria.

In conducing this experiment, we also propose a methodological and epistemological challenge. Most sociologists who feel the pressure to imitate the natural sciences might find a textual experiment – a book chapter, in this case – unorthodox. However, such scholars would be at risk of overseeing two issues. First, they would confuse an objectivist style with an analysis that allows objects to *object* about what is said about them (Latour 2005). This is exactly what we do in the last part of this chapter, where the proposed analogy is followed to the point of reaching its own limits. Second, they would underestimate the insight that 'textual accounts are the social scientist's laboratory' (Latour 2005: 127). A well written text is a laboratory in that it makes the production of realism and objectivity progressively more complicated by constantly listening to the objections exerted by humans and artefacts.

Such 'listening to objections' has taken place through the analysis of regulation, through the collection of data during fieldwork at Hotspots in the Hellenic Republic in 2018, as well as through the analysis of information systems and technical documents developed by Hellenic and European authorities. In particular, the data analysed in this chapter have been collected from March to October 2018 during a multi-sited ethnography at four registration and identification facilities (i.e., three 'Hotspots' on the Hellenic islands and one identification centre on the Hellenic-Turkish border) through observation of border crossers identification procedures, in-situ interviews with officers from the Hellenic Asylum Service, the Hellenic Police and the Hellenic Reception Service, further off-site interviews – including with European officers, analysis of web interfaces of the Hellenic Register of Foreigners, procurement calls issued by the Hellenic Government, analysis of European regulation and other technical documents made available by both Hellenic and European authorities.

As a result of such 'listening', we suggest that migrant registration and identification centres can be understood as 'sensing nodes of equivalence'. On one hand, they might be conceived of as 'sensors' of European infrastructures for the 'processing of alterity' (Pelizza 2019). Hotspots have been designed by European agendas and practices as input devices for data collection and risk detection, producing information that wouldn't otherwise exist. On the other hand, registration and identification centres are not only input 'points' of European migration management architectures: they are also 'nodes' of equivalence in global security networks.[1] We suggest that Hotspots are nodes tasked with making non-European standards and procedures linguistically and materially equivalent to national ones.

In what follows we discuss how furthering an analogy of Hotspots as sensors (section 2) allows making sense of specific divisions of labour across organizational roles (section 3) and European authorities (section 4). However, we also test the limits of such analogy and suggest that the role of registration and identification centres cannot be only that of input *points* in European alterity processing networks. They also implement global security standards and practices that have become dominant worldwide (section 5). As such, we argue, Hotspots constitute *nodes* at which European data infrastructures and transnational security networks not only metaphorically, but materially intersect.

All in all, testing the analogy of Hotspots as sensing nodes of equivalence allows opening incursions in current debates about the materiality of security regimes. Such understanding suggests new questions and research directions both to an emergent strand in Science and Technology Studies concerned with sociotechnologies of insecurity and to Security Studies proposing an analytics of security devices.

TWO EARLY FEATURES OF SENSOR NETWORKS

Sensor networks present characteristics that partially distinguish them from traditional computer networks. First, sensors are usually deployed in large numbers in peripheral or otherwise unreachable areas. Second, their deployment is unattended, and sensors are subjected to the caprices of weather, hostile animals (including hostile humans), energy shortages, disasters. Third, sensing devices interact with the physical environment and therefore experience a significant range of task dynamics (Estrin et al. 1999).

These characteristics have suggested distinctive architectures for sensor networks. Early architectures for sensor networks were based on a centralized model, with individual sensors communicating their data to 'a central node, which then performs the computation required for the application' (Estrin et al. 1999: 265). As scholars have stressed, 'most deployed sensor networks involve relatively small numbers of sensors, wired to a central processing unit where all of the signal processing is performed' (Estrin et al. 2001: 2033). More recently, however, the key requirement to assure energy efficiency has prompted different architectures, in which high-level pre-processed information – instead of raw data – is transferred (Elson and Estrin 2004).

These recent architectural developments will be discussed in more details in Sections 3 and 4; now we would like to stress two features of early sensor devices. First, sensors are input devices, tasked with measuring phenomena and encoding information that is then transferred to centres of calculation (Latour

1987). As such, sensors tend to occupy a distinctive position in the topology of measurement networks, namely a peripheral one. This division of labour between input devices and centres of calculation is allowed by the distinctive character-istic of sensors: the ability to operate unmanned and unattended. Sensors are delegated the task of replacing human beings in conducting measurements which would otherwise be limited in time and/or in space. Given these features, in early architectures sensors were conceived as input *points* – black boxed units for data collection, without processing power. Points are distinguished from nodes – unfolded sociotechnical assemblages whose inner working is accessible. This distinction will turn out useful in Section 5.

Sensors' capability to operate unattended introduces the second feature. Sensing devices are first and foremost tasked with producing information of phenomena that would otherwise remain invisible and unknown. In remote desert areas, on mountain peaks or on a 24h shift, human ability to know depends on sensing artefacts. In such situations, data would not only remain invisible: they *would not exist without sensors*. Such performative ability can find an echo in recent work about sensors as individuating devices: 'sensors can be described as engaged in processes of individuating by creating resonances within a milieu, where individual units or variables of temperature and light levels, for instance, are also operationalizing environments in order to become computable' (Gabrys 2016: 11, see also Gabrys 2019).

Hotspots as European sensors

Elaborating on the above-mentioned early features of sensing devices, we wonder to what extent Hotspots can by analogy be compared to sensors in European networks for alterity processing. While to our knowledge we are the first to propose such an analogy, we do not claim that we are 'discovering' it. Rather, as any analogy, it is a heuristic act of arbitrary association by the authors, that is nevertheless expected to open new research questions and directions.

Let's look at the first technical feature of sensors: they act as peripheral input points in sensing networks. Centres tasked with migrant reception and management functions had been established already in the 1990s at the external borders of Europe. They proliferated as a consequence of the adoption of the Schengen Convention in combination with subsequent European treaties addressing 'irregular migration' and asylum (Balch and Geddes 2011). Being established at the external borders of Europe, such centres were geographically peripheral with respect to the rest of the Schengen Area.

However, informational input functions became a priority especially with the introduction of the 'Hotspot approach' (Pelizza 2019). In spring 2015, the European Commission issued a European Agenda on Migration, which announced the introduction of 'Hotspots' as an immediate action to address the challenges faced by frontline Member States (i.e., Member States at the external European border) involved in the increasing arrival of migrants (European Commission 2015a). The 'Hotspot approach' tackled primarily informational needs: 'The operational support provided under the Hotspot approach, will concentrate on registration, identification, fingerprinting and debriefing of asylum seekers' (European Commission 2015b: 1). The goal of the new approach was indeed 'to swiftly identify, register and fingerprint incoming migrants' (European Commission 2015a: 6). To achieve such goal, the approach foresaw the secondment to frontline countries of European officers from the European Asylum Support Office (EASO, with asylum support functions), European Border and Coast Guard Agency (Frontex, with policing and screening functions), Europol and Eurojust (with policing functions). Frontex and Europol are tasked with conducting mainly risk detection activities. Frontex's debriefing interviews, for example, are aimed at identifying trafficking networks and other risks.

Hotspots' characterization as informational input points emerged even during our multi-sited ethnography.[2] At Hotspots, people on the move are registered and identified against a plethora of national and European information systems utilized to verify previous asylum requests (Eurodac system), check previous criminal activities (SIS II system), establish identity, family relations, health conditions and other events (various national and international databases). Their data are inputted by national and European officers according to a strict division of labour (see next Section). Data on European systems are then accessible by European and national authorities Europe-wide.

Such data architecture shapes a distinctive division of labour. Hotspots can be seen acting as input points, 'sensors' tasked with data collection and risk detection functions. On the other hand, European and national asylum and police agencies act as centres of calculation, users of data collected at the border. As a consequence of this division of labour, Hotspots are peripheral, but not only in the geographical sense.[3] Hotspots are *topologically* peripheral because in the European migration data network they are tasked only with inputting functions and no processing power.[4] As such, they lie at the periphery of the security network.

The second technical feature of sensors is their ability to produce knowledge that would not otherwise exist. Here, too, the analogy seems to hold. As we have just seen by means of the regulation, the introduction of Hotspots was mainly aimed at improving data collection, thanks to the support of European officers. The European Commission rationale was that frontline states did not consistently comply with European regulations in the field of identification and registration. As a matter of fact, in 2015 the European Commission adopted measures against frontline states (European Commission 2015c).

Under similar circumstances, border crossers did not formally exist for European authorities and non-frontline member states, as their data did not exist on European databases. It was thanks to the introduction of Hotspots – with their personnel seconded by European agencies – that information could be produced, which would have otherwise remained unknown to centres of calculation. This is another sense in which Hotspots can be conceived of as sensors producing information that wouldn't exist without them.

Having suggested an analogy between sensing architectures and European networks for alterity processing, in the following two sections we further test the consistency and heuristic usefulness of the analogy by discussing two design criteria proper of sensor networks: separation of concern and data reduction. We also analyse the consequences of adopting those design criteria in the deployment of Hotspots for the division of labour in institutional security orders.

SEPARATION OF CONCERNS AS DESIGN CRITERION

Separation of concerns is a well-established design criterion within software engineering. It emphasizes a modular way of designing software by separating and encapsulating different functions of a system (i.e., 'concerns'), as a type of 'divide and conquer' strategy to manage the complexity of software development (Laplante 2007). We may find examples of separation of concerns in the way data produced by a sensor network are stored and processed.

Gibbons (2018) distinguishes three approaches for storing data in a sensor network, each of which has its own trade-offs. Data can be stored locally at production nodes in the sensor network, externally at points outside of the sensor network, or at other nodes. Storing data at a site external to the sensor network has historically been the most chosen option. This approach is an example of the separation of concerns, since it allows separating data collection from storage and processing functions carried on at external points. This form of separation is desirable because, while the sensor network is good at collecting data, points outside the sensor network usually have more resources available for storage and processing. Transmitting raw data outside the sensing network, on the other hand, has also some downsides. In the next section we will see how this issue factors into our analogy through the design criterion of data reduction.

System components designed according to separation of concerns are said to be 'modular'. Modules are self-contained, as they encapsulate their functions and data, so they can work independently and become interchangeable (Taylor 2009). In a sensor network, this modularity makes it possible for nodes to independently manage the processes for capturing data, and for external nodes to use the data without knowing how they were captured (Yick et al. 2008: 2293).

Separation of concerns at the Hellenic Hotspots

To what extent can we observe separation of concerns in the organization of Hotspots? What could be the heuristic consequences? Observations of practices of use of the Hellenic Register of Foreigners at the Hellenic Hotspots suggest that the analogy between sensor architectures and security networks could hold even in this case. Notably, parts of the registration and identification procedure work in a similar way as 'software modules' which encapsulate functions and data addressing specific concerns. This is revealed more clearly once we compare the front and back-end designs of the Hellenic Register of Foreigners.

The Hellenic Register of Foreigners[5] was developed between 2011 and 2013 by the Hellenic Police and is used to identify and register persons who arrive at the border and other control points in Greece. As emerged during interviews with officers and observation of registration and identification practices mediated by the Register, different personnel roles – such as police, administrative clerks and asylum officers – use the system to input and retrieve migrants' personal and biometric data. Each personnel role has restricted access to data, according to their functions. These restrictions materialize in the graphical user interfaces used for registration and identification, in the form of tabs and fields available for some personnel and not others (Figs 12.1 and 12.2).

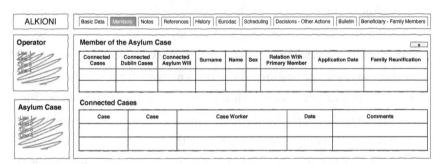

FIG. 12.1 Authors' elaboration of the original graphical user interface of the Hellenic Register of Foreigners, as accessible by the Hellenic Asylum Service.

FIG. 12.2 Authors' elaboration of the original graphical user interface of the Hellenic Register of Foreigners, as accessible by the Registration and Identification Service (i.e., administrative civil personnel).

As a comparison between Figs 12.1 and 12.2 shows, some tabs and fields are accessible to asylum officers (i.e., 'References', 'Scheduling', 'Decisions', 'Bulletin', 'Beneficiary'), but not to administrative personnel, who have access to additional tabs (i.e., 'Verification', 'Vulnerable Groups', 'Limitation of Freedom'). Furthermore, different functionalities are accessible inside the same tab by different roles. For example, the tab 'Members' allows different tasks for each role. The information available for the asylum service relates to connections with other cases (i.e. family members). Differently, the registration and identification service can only access functions about the identification of individual applications through Eurodac.

Further evidence that supports the analogy with separation of concern is provided by back-end integration. While most tabs in Figs 12.1 and 12.2 link to data stored in and fields prompted by the Hellenic Register, the 'Eurodac' tab is loosely integrated with the European Eurodac information system.[6] The Eurodac component supports the fingerprinting process. When officers choose the Eurodac tab, the system opens up a separate software application that allows collecting and storing applicants' fingerprints on external databases, as well as checking whether asylum seekers have already lodged an asylum application. As it has emerged from technical document analysis and interviews with technical developers, the system then sends the fingerprints to the Hellenic Police Criminal Department. This Department in turn sends the fingerprints to the European Eurodac database and receives the hit or no-hit back. In this data flow it is important to note that Eurodac does not receive information about the contextual conditions of fingerprints collection. By doing so, modules have little direct knowledge of how each of them works and instead function in a self-contained and reusable manner.

In summary, both the interface design of the Register of Foreigners and its back-end integration with Eurodac show evidence of a separation of concerns between the Hotspots as sensors that collect data and the centres of calculation that use the data. Following the analogy with the design of software systems, the Hotspots data infrastructure uses a modular approach to separate and encapsulate different concerns, or functions.

This evidence triggers the question of how the separation and encapsulation of concerns in the Hotspot data infrastructure shapes the division of labour in European migration networks. Our on-field observations and interviews suggest that the separation of concerns in Hotspot data infrastructures entails a strengthening of epistemic divisions between different personnel roles. Such divisions are especially visible between national and European officers tasked with fingerprinting functions at Hotspots and expert officers at centres of calculation. Interviews with IT developers who work on the Register of Foreigners in Athens suggested that system design is explicitly expected to elicit boundary work. When asked about how the Hellenic Register of Foreigners integrates with the European systems, IT developers described the role of fingerprinting officers as having to be only concerned with doing the correct steps. They even specified that fingerprinting officers shouldn't know where data is transferred to.

Furthermore, the separation of concerns and ensuing encapsulation of functions can make work at the Hotspots invisible, as fingerprint data that are uploaded do not contain any metadata of how they were captured. Recalling Bowker and Star (1999), what information is recorded matters. In this case, separation of concern as a design criterion makes invisible the efforts needed to make bodies machine-readable and to produce data of acceptable quality. As Kloppenburg and Ploeg (2018: 15) explain: 'Accuracy, speed, and security are not inherent characteristics of biometric systems: a lot of work is continually required to achieve these outcomes in actual operational settings.'

All in all, the analogy between separation of concerns and the design of the Hellenic Register of Foreigners allows highlighting new forms of division of labour and production of knowledge, not only between input points and centres of calculation, but also between different personnel roles. From a software development perspective, the separation of concerns is a strategy to manage the complexity of systems: separate modules can be organized independently and become reusable. In the European security and migration network, encapsulating modules and functions can shape how knowledge is produced and circulated across different types of labour.

DATA REDUCTION AS DESIGN CRITERION

A distinctive requirement of sensor networks is the need to maximize energy efficiency. As in unattended and exposed sensor networks energy is the most precious resource, sensor networks need to reduce energy consumption as much as possible. Recent developments have marked new paradigms in this regard. In last generation sensor networks, energy efficiency is often achieved by converting raw data into high-level information as upstream as possible: 'A perfect system will reduce as much data as possible as early as possible, rather than incur the energy expense of transmitting raw sensor values further along the path to the user' (Elson and Estrin 2004: 10).

The design criteria of 'data reduction' establishes that in sensor networks it is not necessary to provide a complete record of every sensor measurement, but rather to provide high-level syntheses. To achieve reduction and synthesis, most recent sensors are thus designed to pre-process raw data at each node in the network: data are aggregated, and redundant information is filtered, before being transferred to the centre of calculation.

Hotspots pursuing data reduction

To what extent can data reduction be observed at Hotspots, and with which heuristic consequences? Our analysis of registration practices, technical documents and interfaces about migrant data exchange between Hotspots and European agencies has evidenced a design criterion similar to data reduction. Notably, during registration and identification at Hotspots a vast and heterogeneous amount of data is collected by officers in spreadsheets and national databases. However, only a minor part of those data is inputted in European systems. Most data are only inputted in national systems and never made available Europe-wide.

This is not due to some form of governmental data jealousy (Bekkers 2007), but to system design underpinned by legal principles of necessity and proportionality. Data reduction, or filtering, between national and European databases used at Hotspots becomes evident if only one takes into account data models (i.e., classification systems) implemented nationally by the Hellenic Register of Foreigners (Fig. 12.3), and Europe-wide by Eurodac (Fig. 12.4).

As Fig. 12.3 shows, the Hellenic Register of Foreigners collects a range of standard basic data: name, nationality, gender, ID, photo and date of birth. On top of that, it also includes less standard categories, like name of father and mother, religion, ethnic group, educational level and languages spoken, profession, family situation and number of children, members of the family who already reside in Greece, socio-cultural ties with Greece. Furthermore, separate sections accessible only to specific profiles (e.g., physicians) collect health and vulnerability data.

BASIC DATA			PERSONAL DOCUMENTS		
Surname	Mother's name	Photo of	Type of	Identification	Accom-
Name	Mother's surname	the person	document	no of the doc	panied
Father's name	Country of birth		Passport		files
Nationality			Residence		
Estimated nationality			permit		
Estimated date of			Other		
birth					
Declared date of					
birth					
Sex/Gender					
Religion	Ethnic group	Education	Marital status	Additional info	
Profession	Communication	level	Contact details		
	language	Languages			
	Mother tongue	(other)			
OTHER DATA					
Sent to Eurodac	Expression of	Bed of alien	Member of		
Yes/No	interest for	Defined/	family		
Last place of staying	application of	not defined			
(country)	international	Date of			
	protection	departure			
	Yes/No				
	Expression of inter-				
	est for voluntary				
	return				
	Yes/No				
Valuables Kind		No of Asylum will			
(pieces)					
Withholding of					
objects					

FIG. 12.3 Basic data collected on the Hellenic Register of Foreigners, as accessible by the Registration and Identification Service (source: authors' elaboration from system interface).

DATA COLLECTED ON EURODAC

(a) fingerprint data

(b) Member State of origin, place and date of the application for international protection

(c) sex

(d) reference number used by the Member State of origin

(e) date on which the fingerprints were taken

(f) date on which the data were transmitted to the Central System

(g) operator user ID

(h) date of the arrival after a successful transfer

(i) date when the person left the territory of the Member States

(j) date when the person left or was removed from the territory of the Member States

(k) date when the decision to examine the application was taken.

FIG. 12.4 Data collected on Eurodac (source: European Regulation (EU) No 603/2013 of the European Parliament and of the Council of 26 June 2013). Some categories of data are only recorded when applicable.

Differently, Fig. 12.4 shows data collected on Eurodac. As it clearly emerges, Eurodac collects very few types of data. What is not in the system is relevant here, especially if compared to the Hellenic Register of Foreigners: religion, ethnic group, educational level and languages spoken, profession, family situation and links within Greece, socio-cultural ties with the Hellenic Republic. Furthermore, most data are system native: they did not exist before the person was recorded in the system (e.g., place and date of the application for international protection). In other words, Eurodac creates a self-referenced digital index, in which information acquires meaning in the context of the system itself, and is functional to pursue its main goal: compare fingerprints with asylum requests.

Comparison between data models implemented in the Hellenic Register of Foreigners and in the European Eurodac database suggests that a sort of 'data reduction', or filtering, takes place in the exchange of migrants' data from frontline Member States to European agencies. Such exchange indeed concerns only a few basic and biometric data. It should also be noted that national and European databases are not interoperable, but integrated only through unique identifiers, what we called indexing data (e.g., Eurodac unique number). Furthermore, neither European agencies nor non-frontline Member States can access data on national systems. Consequently, most personal data about migrants are 'filtered' at the national level.

This evidence further grounds our analogy between sensor networks requiring upstream data reduction and European security and migration networks filtering most part of data collected at Hotspots. The analogy triggers new questions, as well. We have seen how in recent sensor networks the distinction between input devices and centres of calculation corresponds to a specific division of labour. Data reduction partially re-distributes tasks by pre-processing raw data before they are transferred to centres of calculation. Extending the analogy, we can ask how division of labour in European security networks is re-arranged.

Indeed, the practices of data filtering just described suggest a *de facto* division of labour between frontline countries and the rest of Europe. As any Member State and most European agencies involved, frontline countries are tasked with policing functions. To this end, basic and biometric data are paramount. However, through its Register of Foreigners the Hellenic Republic also collects data about family composition, education, religion, ethnic group, health, linguistic and professional skills, family links and socio-cultural ties with Greece. That is, data necessary to fulfil a broader set of functions, like accommodation, family reunification, health care, asylum, integration into the job market and in society at large.

We can conclude that a division of labour between frontline Member States and European agencies and non-frontline members is performed by filtering data collected at Hotspots. A division of labour in which all institutional actors are tasked with some sort of policing functions. On top of that, functions like accommodation, family reunification, health care, asylum and integration are mainly delegated to countries hosting Hotspots. It would indeed be difficult to design integration policies without data about family composition, professional and linguistic skills.[7]

As a last note, it should be noted that such division of labour does not take place because of geographical location, but because of epistemic differences in how the Other is made legible. Through its Register of Foreigners, Greece enacts people on the move as long-term foreigners, while European systems like Eurodac enact them as irregular foreigners. In other words, different ways of processing alterity correspond to different ways of institutionalizing security order.

HOTSPOTS AS GLOBAL NODES OF EQUIVALENCE

Up to now the tentative analogy between architectures of sensor networks and Hotspots as 'sensors' of European security and migration networks has seemed to hold. Like sensors, Hotspots work as input devices, retaining a peripheral position in the European security networks, and they enact information that wouldn't otherwise exist. Furthermore, as for sensing networks, design criteria like separation of concerns and data reduction can be seen at work. Following such analogy has also allowed us to pose new questions about division of labour between input points and centres of calculation.

However, analogy should not be mistaken for ontological sameness. As in any experimental laboratory, we have to be ready to acknowledge the limits of analogy. We have to be prone to 'listen to objections' moved by human actors and objects. In our case, the analogy between sensor networks and European security networks shows its limits when the global scale enters the picture.

Hotspots are not only involved in European migration networks. They also take part in global security networks. Yet their role in global networks is not the same as in European ones: they do not act as input *points* – black boxed units for mere data collection and risk detection, without processing power, but as *nodes* – unfolded sociotechnical assemblages at which technical standards and practices developed outside Europe are made equivalent to European ones.[8]

We have already seen in the previous Section that the most recent developments in sensor networks have endowed sensors with some processing power. On the other end of the analogy, when analysed in a broader transnational context, Hotspots acquire other roles than mere input points: as (re)users or clients. This is revealed more clearly when registration and identification centres are considered in a context that includes technical and economic elements, besides strictly security ones.

Methodologically, one way to pursue this epistemic enlargement consists in analysing formal documents released for standardization goals in procurement practices. Such sources can reveal more heterogeneous relationships than those commonly assumed as part of security networks. A case in point is provided by a procurement call issued in 2011 by the Hellenic Agency for Information Society, a governmental body. The call concerned hardware and software provisions of electronic identification and authentication services – including fingerprint-ing – for citizens and foreigners. It mentioned the following specifications for the automated fingerprint identification system (AFIS):

1. The proposed AFIS solution must have implemented at least one (1) working AFIS system at a National, State or Federal Level worldwide over the past five years (5).

2. The proposed AFIS solution must have at least one implementation in a criminal AFIS that supports database with at least four (4) million ten-fingerprints, one (1) million palm prints, and has a minimum daily volume of a thousand (1,000) ten-fingerprints uploaded into the system. (Hellenic Republic Ministry of Citizens Protection 2011: 139)

This excerpt asks for three distinctive requirements: 1) that software is imple-mented worldwide and then reused in Greece; 2) that it is a reuse of criminal implementations; 3) that it can handle rather large-scale amounts of data. On top of that, fingerprint scanners must be FBI-certified (Hellenic Republic Ministry of Citizens Protection 2011: 144). Furthermore, the AFIS interface with INTERPOL should use the ANSI/NIST-ITL -1-2000 Data Format for the exchange of fingerprints, facial images and scars, marks, or tattoos (SMT) information (Hellenic Republic Ministry of Citizens Protection 2011: 40–41).

By posing such requirements, the procurement call positions any agency, registration centre or Hotspot using identification and authentication services in Greece at the intersection of multiple global networks. First, according to the call the AFIS software must have been implemented worldwide, thus positioning Hellenic registration and identification centres as *(re)users of global travelling software* (Pollock and Williams 2009).[9] Second, the AFIS software must have been implemented in criminal contexts, thus positioning Hellenic centres as *(re)users of security software*. Third, the large scale of the required system positions the Hellenic Agency for Information Society as *client of incumbent software suppliers*. Fourth, by asking that fingerprint scanners are FBI-certified, Hellenic authorities *delegate certifying functions* to the US Federal Bureau of Investigation. Finally and similarly, choices about the interconnectivity format to be used between Hellenic authorities and INTERPOL are *delegated* to US government organizations developing the ANSI/NIST standard.[10]

In this division of labour, the utilization of software, equipment, practices and standards developed and implemented outside Europe carves for Hotspots a more complex role than mere European input points for data collections. Rather, registration and identification centres are conceived of by Hellenic authorities issuing the call as nodes in global security networks. In such position, centres are expected to create equivalences between European and non-European elements. Locally-acquired ink fingerprints must be made equivalent to AFIS-encoded high-resolution digital prints. Database entries for 'mother's name' on the Hellenic Register of Foreigners is expected to be made equivalent to 'اسم الأم' in the words of the Arabic interpreter. Spreadsheets generated for internal use among Hotspot officers must be made equivalent to travelling software produced by transnational corporations. While this work of making equivalences can be successful or not, what is important to stress here is that – when the global scale is taken into account – Hotspots act as nodes at which work of equivalence between standards and practices developed in and outside Europe is ceaselessly carried on.

Two further aspects are important. First, from these examples drawn from our fieldwork it results that equivalence can be established between diverse languages (the second case) as well as between diverse materialities (the first and third case). Second, it goes without saying that in this activity of creating equivalences, power relations are affected. Equivalence always entails betrayal and pronouncing 'mother's name' in Arabic is not the same as pronouncing it in English or Greek. Reading ink fingerprints does not include the same actors as reading digital scans. In both cases, some actors are excluded because they do not speak English or do not have access to the digital system.

CONCLUSION: HOTSPOTS AS SENSING NODES OF EQUIVALENCE

As mentioned at the beginning of this chapter, the heuristic potential of any analogy lies in opening new spaces for questions and directions of research. This is the case even with the analogy between architectures of sensor networks and transnational security networks. The analogy has allowed us to ask novel questions on the division of labour in European security networks, and to focus on the new distribution of roles between frontline and non-frontline Member States.

However, such analogy intended to test the tension between data and institutional infrastructures has shown its limits in not being able to account for extra-European connections. As in any experimental laboratory, we had to leave our analogy when we realized that sticking to it would have brought us in a misleading direction. To account for the roles that Hotspots can undertake in global security networks, we conceived of them as 'nodes of equivalence'. Such switch has helped in acknowledging the major work of establishing equivalences that is conducted daily by national and European officers, as well as by migrants and interpreters, at centres for the identification and registration of people on the move to Europe.

Such new questions and research directions appeal both to Security Studies proposing an analytics of security devices, and an emergent strand in Science and Technology Studies concerned with sociotechnologies of insecurity. In the first case, they solicit Security Studies scholars to move their attention from devices to infrastructures. Hotspots are not only points, but nodes integrating European alterity processing infrastructures and transnational security infrastructures not only metaphorically, but also materially. In the second case, they urge Science and Technology Studies concerned with identification practices and infrastructures to consider how their object of analysis can throw light on emergent transnational constructions of order.

Finally and related to the last point, conceiving of Hotspots as sensing nodes of equivalence suggests a further question, to be investigated in future work: what organizing logics of authority emerge from the peculiar positioning of Hotspots at the intersection of European alterity processing infrastructures *and* global security networks? Like early Modern city leagues (Tilly 1990), Hotspots articulate a trans-local topology, in which they are nodes in global security networks characterized by non-contiguity. However, differently from city leagues, they do not articulate an isotropic geography, in which they are supposed to be the centre of a local economy. Rather, they remain at the periphery of European security and migration networks, whose core are the centres of calculation at European and national level. For sure, such topological arrangement requires further investigation, both in relation to European, global and to national centres.

ACKNOWLEDGEMENTS

In writing this chapter, the authors acknowledge the 'Processing Citizenship' project (2017–2022), which has received funding from the European Research Council (ERC) under the European Union's Horizon 2020 research and innovation programme under grant agreement No 714463. Both authors would like to thank Ermioni Frezouli for her work as coordinator of the Project's fieldwork in the Hellenic Republic. If she is not included as co-author, it is because of her doctoral commitments, which have not allowed her to engage in this writing endeavour. The authors would also like to thank Aristotle Tympas. For the sake of scientific attribution, Wouter Van Rossem has written the section entitled 'Separation of concerns as design criterion', while Annalisa Pelizza has authored the main argument and the other sections. The work has nevertheless benefitted from joint discussions, supervision meetings and collaborative analyses.

NOTES

1 As it will become clearer in what follows, in the context of this chapter we distinguish between 'points' and 'nodes'. We conceive of the first as folded devices tasked with an inputting task; the latter as unfolded actors which translate different sources into each other.

2 Here, 'our' includes also Ermioni Frezouli, in her capacity as temporary collaborator of the *Processing Citizenship* Project. Ms. Frezouli however decided not to participate in this chapter as co-author.

3 As a matter of fact, Hotspots ought not to be deployed exclusively in frontline countries. While they eventually were only implemented in Greece and Italy, originally the European Agenda foresaw their potential deployment in any Member State that required them (European Commission 2015b).

4 The shift from geographical to topological remoteness has mostly gone unnoticed by literature on 'fortress Europe' and borders. However, it is crucial to study the relationship between data infrastructures and institutional orders.

5 In Greek, Χαρτογράφηση Κυκλοφορίας Αλλοδαπών.

6 The Eurodac (i.e., European Dactyloscopy) system was first introduced in 2003 to support the application of the Schengen Treaty and Dublin Convention. It stores the digital fingerprints of every person claiming asylum in one of the European Member States. By doing so, it intends to univocally identify asylum seekers, so they cannot apply in more than one Member State. Eurodac was developed by European authorities and is now run by the European Union Agency for the Operational Management of Large-Scale IT Systems in the Area of Freedom, Security and Justice (eu-LISA).

7 It should be noted, however, that in some cases non-frontline Member States receive such data through international organizations. That non-governmental and non-European organizations act as intermediaries of European relations is indeed an important topic of analysis, and is addressed in forthcoming work by Pelizza, Loschi and Lausberg.

8 In the STS field, we are well aware of the topological meaning of equivalence as translation, that is, making to things that are different occupy the same position (see e.g. Latour 2005).

9 Following our observation on field and analysis of the procurement call, similar considerations could be made for hardware.

10 The ANSI/NIST standard can be considered the dominant standard worldwide for exchange of biometric and forensic information. The American National Standards Institute/National Institute of Standards and Technology – Information Technology Laboratory (ANSI/NIST-ITL) defines the content, format and units of measurement for the exchange of biometric and forensic information utilized to identify and authenticate individuals. The first version of the standard for the interchange of fingerprint, facial and biometric information was published in 1986 by the then called 'United States National Bureau of Standards'. Its goal was to support electronic fingerprint submissions from US state and local authorities to the FBI (Wing 2013). The standard is now used by law

enforcement, homeland security, military and other authorities in 71 countries in all continents.

REFERENCES

Agar, J. (2003). *The Government Machine: A Revolutionary History of the Computer.* Cambridge, MA: The MIT Press.

Amicelle, A., Aradau, C., and Jeandesboz, J. (2015). Questioning Security Devices: Performativity, Resistance, Politics. *Security Dialogue* 46(4): 293–306. <https://doi.org/10.1177/0967010615586964>.

Aradau, C. (2010). Security That Matters: Critical Infrastructure and Objects of Protection. *Security Dialogue* 41(5): 491–514. <https://doi.org/10.1177/0967010610382687>.

Balch, A., and Geddes, A. (2011). The Development of the EU Migration and Asylum Regime. In H. Dijstelbloem and A. Meijer (Eds), *Migration and the New Technological Borders of Europe. Migration, Minorities and Citizenship.* London: Palgrave Macmillan UK, pp. 22–39. <https://doi.org/10.1057/9780230299382_2>.

Bekkers, V. (2007). The Governance of Back-Office Integration. *Public Management Review* 9(3): 377–400. <https://doi.org/10.1080/14719030701425761>.

Bowker, G. C., and Leigh Star, S. (1999). *Sorting Things Out: Classification and Its Consequences.* Cambridge, MA: The MIT Press.

Dargie, W., and Poellabauer, C. (2010). *Fundamentals of Wireless Sensor Networks: Theory and Practice.* John Wiley & Sons.

De Goede, M., Simon, S., and Hoijtink, M. (2014). Performing Preemption. *Security Dialogue* 45(5): 411–422. <https://doi.org/10.1177/0967010614543585>.

Dijstelbloem, H., and Pelizza, A. (2019). The State Is the Secret: For a Relational Approach to the Study of Border and Mobility Control in Europe. In de Goede, M., Bosma, E., and Pallister-Wilkins, P. (Eds), *Secrecy and Methods in Security Research: A Guide to Qualitative Fieldwork.* London: Routledge, pp. 48–62.

Elson, J., and Estrin, D. (2004). Sensor Networks: A Bridge to the Physical World. In C. S. Raghavendra, Krishna M. Sivalingam, and Taieb Znati (Eds), *Wireless Sensor Networks.* Boston, MA: Springer US, pp. 3–20. <https://doi.org/10.1007/978-1-4020-7884-2_1>.

Estrin, D., Govindan, R., Heidemann, J., and Kumar, S. (1999). Next Century Challenges: Scalable Coordination in Sensor Networks. In *Proceedings of the 5th Annual ACM/IEEE International Conference on Mobile Computing and Networking – MobiCom 1999,* pp. 263–70. Seattle, WA: ACM Press. <https://doi.org/10.1145/313451.313556>.

Estrin, D., Girod, L., Pottie, G. and Srivastava, M. (2001). Instrumenting the World with Wireless Sensor Networks. In *2001 IEEE International Conference on Acoustics, Speech, and Signal Processing. Proceedings (Cat. No.01CH37221),* pp. 2033–36. Salt Lake City, UT: IEEE. <https://doi.org/10.1109/ICASSP.2001.940390>.

European Commission (2015a). The Hotspot Approach to Managing Exceptional Migratory Flows. <https://ec.europa.eu/home-affairs/e-library/multimedia/publications/the-hotspot-approach-to-managing-exceptional-migratory-flows_en>.

—— (2015b). Communication from the Commission to the European Parliament, the Council, the European Economic and Social Committee and the Committee of the Regions. A European Agenda on Migration. Brussels. <https://eur-lex.europa.eu/legal-content/EN/TXT/?uri=CELEX:52015DC0240>.

—— (2015c). Refugee Crisis: European Commission Takes Decisive Action – Questions and Answers. <http://europa.eu/rapid/press-release_MEMO-15-5597_en.htm>.

Gabrys, J. (2016). *Program Earth: Environmental Sensing Technology and the Making of a Computational Planet*. University of Minnesota Press.

—— (2019). Sensors and Sensing Practices: Reworking Experience across Entities, Environments, and Technologies. *Science, Technology, & Human Values* 44(5): 723–36. <https://doi.org/10.1177/0162243919860211>.

Gibbons, P. B. (2018). Data Storage and Indexing in Sensor Networks. In Liu, L. and Tamer Özsu, M. (Eds), *Encyclopedia of Database Systems*. New York: Springer New York, pp. 850–53. <https://doi.org/10.1007/978-1-4614-8265-9_112>.

Hacking, I. (1983). *Representing and Intervening: Introductory Topics in the Philosophy of Natural Science*. Cambridge: Cambridge University Press.

Hellenic Republic Ministry of Citizens Protection. (2011). Διακήρυξη Ανοικτού Διαγωνισμού Για Το Έργο «Ηλεκτρονικες Υπηρεσιες Ταυτοποιησης Και Αναγνωρισης Πολιτων (E-Ταπ)» (Open Call for the Project 'Electronic Identification and Identification Services (E-Tap)').

Kloppenburg, S., and van der Ploeg, I. (2018). Securing Identities: Biometric Technologies and the Enactment of Human Bodily Differences. *Science as Culture* 0 (0): 1–20. <https://doi.org/10.1080/09505431.2018.1519534>.

Laplante, P. A. (2007). *What Every Engineer Should Know about Software Engineering*. CRC Press. <https://doi.org/10.1201/9781420006742>.

Latour, B. (1987). *Science in Action: How to Follow Scientists and Engineers Through Society*. Harvard University Press.

—— (2005). *Reassembling the Social: An Introduction to Actor-Network Theory*. Oxford: Oxford University Press.

Leander, A. (2013). Technological Agency in the Co-Constitution of Legal Expertise and the US Drone Program. *Leiden Journal of International Law* 26(4): 811–31. <https://doi.org/10.1017/S0922156513000423>.

Manning, P. K. (1996). Information Technology in the Police Context: The 'Sailor' Phone. *Information Systems Research* 7(1): 52–62. <https://doi.org/10.1287/isre.7.1.52>.

Pelizza, A. (2016.) Developing the Vectorial Glance: Infrastructural Inversion for the New Agenda on Governmental Information Systems. *Science, Technology and Human Values* 41(2): 298–321. <https://doi.org/10.1177/0162243915597478>.

——(2019). Processing Alterity, Enacting Europe: Migrant Registration and Identification as Co-Construction of Individuals and Polities. *Science, Technology and Human Values* 45 (2): 262–288. <https://doi.org/10.1177/0162243919827927>.

Pollock, N., and Williams, R. (2009). *Software and Organisations: The Biography of the Enterprise-Wide System or How SAP Conquered the World.* Routledge Studies in Technology, Work and Organisations 5. London; New York: Routledge.

Salter, M. B. (2008). When the Exception Becomes the Rule: Borders, Sovereignty, and Citizenship. *Citizenship Studies* 12(4): 365–80. <https://doi.org/10.1080/13621020802184234>.

Suchman, L., Follis, K., and Weber, J. (2017). Tracking and Targeting: Sociotechnologies of (In)Security. *Science, Technology, & Human Values* 42(6): 983–1002. <https://doi.org/10.1177/0162243917731524>.

Taylor, R. N. (2019). Software Architecture and Design. In S. Cha, R. N. Taylor, and K. Kang (Eds), *Handbook of Software Engineering.* Cham: Springer International Publishing, pp. 93–122. <https://doi.org/10.1007/978-3-030-00262-6_3>.

Tilly, C. (1990). *Coercion, Capital, and European States, AD 990–1992.* Oxford: Basil Blackwell.

Vogel, K. M., Balmer, B., Weiss Evans, S., et al. (2017). Knowledge and Security. In U. Felt, R. Fouché, C. A. Miller, and L. Smith-Doerr (Eds), *The Handbook of Science and Technology Studies.* Cambridge, MA: The MIT Press, pp. 973–1001.

Wing, B. J. (2012). The ANSI/NIST-ITL Standard Update for 2011 (Data Format for the Interchange of Fingerprint, Facial and Other Biometric Information). *International Journal of Biometrics* 5(1): 20–29. <https://doi.org/10.1504/IJBM.2013.050731>.

Witjes, N., and Olbrich, P. (2017). A Fragile Transparency: Satellite Imagery Analysis, Non-State Actors, and Visual Representations of Security. *Science and Public Policy* 44(4): 524–34. <https://doi.org/10.1093/scipol/scw079>.

Yick, J., Mukherjee, B., and Ghosal, D. (2008). Wireless Sensor Network Survey. *Computer Networks* 52(12): 2292–2330. <https://doi.org/10.1016/j.comnet.2008.04.002>.

13

SENSING DATA CENTRES

A.R.E. Taylor and Julia Velkova

FIG. 13.1 The exterior of a hyperscale data centre in Finland operated by Yandex, a major Russian Internet platform (credit: Julia Velkova)

DATA CENTRES UNDERPIN AND ENABLE THE INCREASINGLY UBIQUITOUS sensor infrastructure that makes and shapes transnational security formations. These network buildings facilitate and make possible the work of sensing media, the tracking, collection and aggregation of digital data and the production of metric cultures. Yet they remain curiously absent in discussions of contemporary sensor-driven security. Offering an alternative vantage on data infrastructures and the security sensing practices they enable, this Visual Vignette draws on empirical fieldwork conducted inside the buildings that store the vast volumes of sensor data now produced on a daily basis. Data centres are at once nodes in planetary-scale information networks but they are also meaningfully emplaced in specific locales. While data is persistently imagined in terms of 'flows', such imaginaries overlook its situatedness and the static, unmoving sites of digital information storage and accumulation where different technologies of sensing – human, animal, mechanical and digital – intersect, with the aim of ensuring the uninterrupted continuity of data-based capitalism. Playing with the rich polysemy of 'sensing' as a conceptual and empirical mode, we adopt a sensory ethnographic approach, with each image in this vignette providing an entry-point for a more detailed sensory exploration of these high-security sociotechnical environments. In doing so, we seek not only to enfold the architecture of 'cloud' computing into discussions of sensor-driven security but to draw attention to the role that sensors play in the production and quantification of space and time in the data centre, configuring these buildings as anticipatory sites for the preemption and detection of imminent but sub-visible failure events.

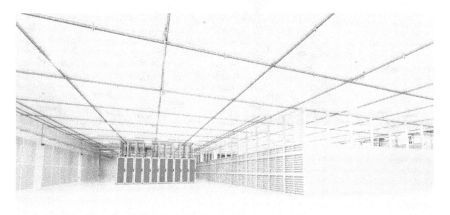

FIG. 13.2 The whitewashed interior of the cloud (credit: A.R.E. Taylor)

SPACES OF SECURITY

Data centres form the core of the globally interconnected infrastructure that is commonly known as the 'cloud'. At its most basic, cloud computing describes an infrastructural shift from desktop computing (where files and applications were stored on the local hard drives of our computers) to a form of online computing (where these are stored in data centres accessed remotely 'as a service' through the Internet). A significant consequence of this, as Peter Jakobsson and Fredrik Stiernstedt (2012: 103), among others, have highlighted, is that 'increasingly more information, as well as the means to process that information, becomes centralised resources in the hands of a few, large actors'. The emergence of cloud computing, coupled with developments in wireless technologies and the aggressive (though uneven) deployment of computing and sensor infrastructure throughout the biosphere (Gabrys 2016), has enabled for new cyber-physical ecologies of data circulation in the form of the 'Internet-of-Things', the 'smart city' and the 'sensor society'. As architectures of industrial-scale data storage, data centres are now essential to emerging forms of data-driven security and intelligence (Amoore 2018). The pooling of vast volumes of data that cloud-based storage enables, promises to provide security agencies and government authorities with new capacities to 'discover, access and share critical information in an era of seemingly infinite data' (Konkel 2014).

FIG. 13.3 Biometric sensors such as fingerprint and retina scanners regulate access throughout data centres (credit: A.R.E. Taylor)

SENSORSCAPES

A hyper-illuminated corridor leads to an armour-plated security door. The guard's steel-toecapped footsteps are absorbed by the polyethene flooring as he walks. The corridor is empty and odourless. Fluorescent lights on the ceiling glare against the PVC wall cladding. The interior of this data centre is divided into a nested series of securitized areas that are electronically regulated by multiple access control systems. Here, the production of security is inseparable from the production of space. A biometric sensor next to the security door digitally reconstructs the guard's identity as he places his fingerprint to the scanner. The door unlocks with an electronic whirring noise and opens slowly. A rush of cold air leaks from the room as the roar of air conditioning units becomes audible. At the base of the door, a dust trap collects the dirt from shoes. This is the data hall where hundreds of servers are located. It is on the hard drives of servers that data centres store their digital information. Data centres do not only underpin sensor societies but are highly specialized sensing environments themselves.

FIG. 13.4 Sensors fitted to server cabinet doors enable data centre operators to detect anticipated events potentially emerging within the quantified space of the data hall (credit: A.R.E. Taylor)

Equipped with a multitude of sensing technologies, the data hall is a highly metricated space. Motion sensors, smoke detectors and humidity sensors are positioned throughout the room. 'Fires, floods, intrusion, you name it, we've got a sensor for it', the guard informs visitors. The sensor-regulated environs of the data hall are a decidedly non-human space, configured and calibrated for the sole purpose of providing optimal conditions for computation. An ambient room temperature of around 20–23°C and a humidity level of 45–55% must constantly be maintained to ensure that the servers are not damaged by moisture or overheating. The server cabinets are arranged in symmetrical aisles, with cold air distributed through fans beneath the raised flooring. Thermal sensors monitor the air flows and the temperature of each server cabinet, while humidity sensors monitor air moisture levels. Sensors attached to the server cabinets immediately alert operators in the data centre control room if a door has been opened and whether it was opened with or without authorization.

SENSING FAILURE

Data centre security does not only work as a productive force that constitutes and acts through material spaces, but it also involves the production and detection of future failure events on which to pre-emptively act. In this sterile, dustless world of brushed metal surfaces, sensors enable a specific temporal configuration of security that is anticipatively orientated towards occurrences and activities that might (or might not) become events. These devices work as sentinels for the pre-evental detection of threats that arise beyond the threshold of human sensory perception, constructing the data hall as an elusive threat-space filled with potential events that can range from equipment failures, intrusions or other disaster scenarios. This is a realm beyond risk, an anticipatory space orientated towards events that have events that have yet to materialize but that can hopefully be detected and diagnosed in their micro-visible and sub-visible forms of emergence through sensor assemblages. Data centre operators can then act upon these instances before they become events. Guided by logics of preparedness, preemption and redundancy, measures are in place to ensure the continued functionality of servers in the event of a blackout or other failure scenario. Mechanical devices like flywheels, weighing 4000kg and rotating at 3300rpm in helium atmosphere, perform crucial functions in maintaining sensor operationality. As sources of kinetic energy storage and production, flywheels work to keep sensors and other computing equipment running even if diesel and electrical systems fail. As technologies that have been used since antiquity, flywheels appear strangely anachronistic in these high-tech landscapes.

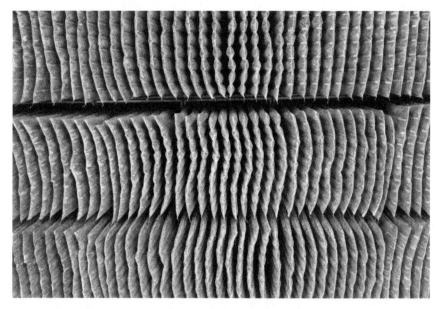

FIG. 13.5 Dust filters on data centre rooftops ensure that the air for computer room cooling is not contaminated with particulate matter (credit: Julia Velkova)

PARTICULATE MATTER

Organic and inorganic particulate matter, such as dust, plant pollens, human hair, liquid droplets and smoke from cigarettes and nearby traffic can interfere with the fragile drive mechanisms of data storage media. Dust is perceived by data centre professionals as a threat to the data centre that could disturb the sociotechnical order required for data processing. For this reason, dust filters are sometimes placed on data centre rooftops to ensure that the incoming cold air used for cooling computing equipment does not contain hazardous particles.

Photoelectric sensors are positioned at strategic points along the ceiling of the data hall to detect smoke particles or other particulate matter. The data hall is thus a highly controlled environment and the startling whiteness gives the space a sterile appearance. The well-lit, white surfaces serve to make visible any 'foreign matter' that may have entered the facility. Here, the data centre 'whitescape' (Taylor 2018) joins 'the doctors white coat, the white tiles of the bathroom, the white walls of the hospital' (Wigley 1995: 5), amongst other surfaces that have mobilized the colour white 'in the construction of the concept of cleanliness' (El-Khoury 1996: 8). In addition, on a daily basis employees wipe off any dust from the diesel generators in order to check for any leaks. The shiny epoxy floors of the data hall are regularly vacuumed, eliminating dust particles that may threaten to short-circuit computer electronics and cause disruption. Dirt is perceived both as a threat to securing the uninterrupted work of machines in the data centre, and as a sign of negligent maintenance that threatens to destabilize the image of the data centre as a futuristic and sterile architecture of control. The concern with cleanliness, sanitation, air and water provision configures the climate-controlled data hall as a space of preemption under constant threat of contamination, an environment that needs to be equipped with sensors in order to cater for its support systems.

FIG. 13.6 Data centre security is often outsourced to private security firms. Their contractors patrol the perimeter of the data centre, inspecting the security of infrastructure (credit: anonymous data centre security officer, via Julia Velkova)

THE CARE OF THE DATA

The sensing work of data centre security is not only conducted by technical equipment. Human beings play a central role in taking care of the data stored and processed in these buildings. Acting as living, human sensors, technicians and security guards routinely patrol data centre facilities. Technicians inspect the data hall while security guards monitor the multiple CCTV cameras, check office buildings and test locks multiple times a day to ensure their proper functioning. Security guards also conduct regular inspections of the razor wire fences that surround these facilities and inspect the on-site water purification systems and power transformers. Security guards collect and report data about the state of the fences, doors, surveillance infrastructure and other aspects of the site. Here, security is produced as an observational, embodied, sensory regime within the larger circuitries of 'surveillance capitalism' (Zuboff 2015). Security is not only the remit of trained professionals. Electricians, engineers, technicians, receptionists, cleaners and other employees are encouraged to 'listen and look' for sensory abnormalities – uncommon noises, leaked diesel, suspicious passers-by or obviously broken technology – as they wander around the site to ensure the uninterrupted processing of global data. The work of human sensory vigilance often takes place in an environment that is not designed for human comfort. Rather, the security guards, electricians and other technicians must adapt to the sensory environment of the computing machines. In order to secure the optimal thermal conditions for server functionality, the corridors through which humans move are drafty and the temperature in them alternates between too cold and too hot, ranging between 10°C and 35°C. The background noise of computing servers, air conditioning systems and diesel generators provides the soundscape for everyday human labour in the data centre. Loud noises from this industrial equipment amplify in the vast open spaces inside, requiring workers to wear noise protection gear, in addition to thick clothing to withstand the wind of the air conditioners and the cold temperatures that define the data centre workplace. The sociopolitical importance of maintaining global data capturing and processing regimes exceeds the human scale, with the needs of servers prioritized over human needs for fresh air and thermal comfort.

The prioritization of data over those who care for data was highlighted during a week-long data centre management training programme one of the authors attended in London in 2017. On the first day, the course tutor announced to the class: 'The data centre is not a people space. This needs to be made clear up front as it can lead to serious consequences and costs if it is overlooked. The primary aim must always be to support the IT assets which, in turn, support the business need'. As such, the needs and affects of the humans working in these buildings are rarely incorporated into their design: 'We all work for the machines, this is why we are all here, but I am used to that', one of our interlocuters explained.

HUMAN-ANIMAL-MACHINE

In these sanitized and regulated environments, animals might at first appear as a form of 'matter out of place' (Douglas 2002). Yet guard and detection dogs are a valuable part of data centre security work, helping to sense threats or detect illicit substances, such as explosives, arms or contraband electronics that dangerous actors might try to smuggle on site. As well as providing the

FIG. 13.7 Guard and detection dogs often operate as non-human sensors in data centre securityscapes (credit: A.R.E. Taylor)

security guards with support, they also provide companionship. But dogs are not the only animals entangled within data centre sensor security assemblages. Rabbits, rodents and hedgehogs are frequent night visitors. As they traverse the open gravel spaces outside of the data centre in search of food, their presence is sensed by infrared cameras, alerting the guards on shift. Motion sensors detect illicit human and non-human movement around the data centre compound while infrared sensors police the invisible region of the electromagnetic spectrum. Sensing technologies thus monitor and control who enters different areas of these securitized compounds, as well as non-humans that range from particulate matter to rodents. The wildlife that is tracked, sensed and visualized also creates new objects of vigilance in the form of holes in or around fences or damage to buildings. In the same way that data centres enfold longer-standing socio-spatial tactics of security, such as the fortified wall, with more recent digital technologies, they also draw together diverse human and non-human actors into larger configurations of surveillance and control. Data centre security is thus produced through different sensory modes, calling forth new assemblages of human-animal-machine.

FIG. 13.8 The data centre control room (credit: Julia Velkova)

QUANTIFIED SECURITYSCAPES

The metrics generated by the distributed human and non-human sensors on site are gathered and monitored in the control room. The control room aligns and visualizes the functioning of different environments within the data centre. On one screen, a weather map provides anticipatory knowledge of changing climate conditions outside the artificially climatized inner spaces of the data centre. The weather map alerts control room operators of approaching storms that are conceived as a potential source of threat to electrical infrastructure. Colourful LEDs placed behind the monitors provide bias lighting that reduces eye strain and fatigue for extended periods of screen surveillance. Myriad other screens display the environmental and operating conditions of the computing rooms and data halls that have been converted by sensor assemblages into quantified geographies of pre-eventual emergence. On the screens in the control room, we thus find a representation of the data centre as a quantified securityscape. Monitoring, logging, mapping, sorting, ordering and tracking, sensors generate new spatialities and temporalities in which to anticipate, detect, diagnose, pre-empt and respond to security threats. The daily actions that make up the ordinary work of data centre security thus unfold along the ambiguous spatiotemporal plane between the event and the potential event. This analysis has drawn attention to sensor-driven data centre security as a productive force that constitutes and acts through space and time in an attempt to render equipment failure and other threatening futures visible and knowable before they become events. Within contemporary security landscapes, sensors increasingly enable the quantification of space for the pre-eventual detection and control of potentially threating occurrences, irregularities or abnormalities. As a critical infrastructure underpinning the ongoing push towards ubiquitous sensing, the data centre is thus both an ensensored technological system and an architectural model of a quantified world where events can be pre-emptively securitized and acted upon through sensor-driven practices of anticipatory governance and control.

REFERENCES

Amoore, L. (2018). Cloud Geographies: Computing, Data, Sovereignty. *Progress in Human Geography*, 42(1): 4–24.

Douglas, M. (2002 [1966]). *Purity and Danger: An Analysis of Concept of Pollution and Taboo*. London and New York: Routledge.

El-Khoury, R. (1996). Polish and Deodorise: Paving the City in Late-Eighteenth-Century France. *Assemblage* 31: 6–15.

Gabrys, J. (2016). *Program Earth: Environmental Sensing Technology and the Making of a Computational Planet*. Minneapolis: University of Minnesota Press.

Jakobsson, P., and Stiernstedt, F. (2012). Time, Space and Clouds of Information: Data Centre Discourse and the Meaning of Durability. In G. Bolin (Ed), *Cultural Technologies: The Shaping of Culture in Media and Society*. New York: Routledge, pp. 103–117.

Konkel, F. (2014). The Details about the CIA's Deal with Amazon. *The Atlantic*. 17 July. <https://www.theatlantic.com/technology/archive/2014/07/the-details-about-the-cias-deal-with-amazon/374632/>.

Taylor, A. R. E. (2018). The Technoaesthetics of Data Centre 'White Space'. *Imaginations: Journal of Cross-Cultural Image Studies*. Special Issue: Location and Dislocation Global Geographies of Digital Data, 3(8-2): 42–54.

Wigley, M. (1995). *White Walls, Designer Dresses: The Fashioning of Modern Architecture*. Cambridge, MA: The MIT Press.

Zuboff, S. (2015). Big Other: Surveillance Capitalism and the Prospects of an Information Civilization. *Journal of Information Technology* 30(1): 75–89. DOI: 10.1057/jit.2015.5.

14

HACKING SATELLITES

Jan-H. Passoth, Geoffrey C. Bowker, Nina Klimburg-Witjes and Godert-Jan van Manen

THIS IS NOT A REGULAR PAPER, BUT AN EXPERIMENT IN COLLABORATION and conversation, turned into an experimental paper as a way of giving and balancing voices. It is based on a conversation that started two years ago when we, a group of scholars/professionals in STS, Computer Science and Critical Security Studies, practical politics, hacking and IT security speculated about the possibility of hacking satellites, a core component of contemporary security infrastructures. Why not admit it here? It *was* some kind of challenge from the social scientists, asking the hacker if he can do it. '*Sure*', he said, '*hacking a satellite is not a big deal, it has been done before and I am pretty sure I can do it.*'

Two years later, at the workshop on 'Sensor Publics: On the Politics of Sensing and Data Infrastructures' at the Technical University of Munich organized by some of us and filled with meaning by others, (and the event from which the idea of this whole book emerged), participants were then treated with a real time experiment in hacking a satellite. And indeed: We witnessed an impressive and very nerdy presentation of the steps necessary and the security issues exploited in each step, that was constantly switching back and forth between fancy slides and a black and green command line window. Much later the presenter admitted: '*I showed how to sniff that; which – from the hacker point of view – is not really attacking or hacking the satellite, but just listening in to what is already replayed there.*'

But when he fired up that SSH[1] terminal and hooked up and configured the network interface of (at least what could have been) a satellite to his Linux machine, he seemed to be very serious that what we were witnessing now was a live satellite hacking event.

After the talk, the four of us started an experiment in extended conversations about the sociotechnical security infrastructures. Our aim was (at least) two-fold: First, we wanted to explore novel ways of listening to, and discussing and engaging with people inside and outside of academia – yet explicitly not in a sense of extracting knowledge and information, that is almost always at risk of patronizing or exploiting the expert engineer, but as a form of mutual exchange of perspectives, questions, and issues. Or, as one of us, in a moment of disciplinary identity crisis said: *'we are all trained in very specific fields. And of course, you get that specific expertise that makes you the person you are in a way.'*

Second, we aimed at experimenting with and developing novel formats for integrating these engagements into an academic publication while being sensible to the different work logics as well as the different disciplinary logics of crediting (academic) work and the challenges that bear for traditional processes of academic peer-review.

For us as writers and you as readers this is a challenge since *'if you are really stubborn – like this table is straight – well, you might think it is straight… if you turn it like this moves his hands quickly sideways, it* (replaceable with any form of knowledge) *looks different.'* That is exactly what we did (and you might do) with this text: turn it like this, sideways or upside down. This text is the preliminary result of this experiment. Over the course of our conversation which took place, amongst others, at a University in Germany, a restaurant in Amsterdam, onboard several trains across Europe, at Long Beach California, and in a bar in New Orleans, via skype, email, drawings and sketches, phone calls and text messages, we almost forgot *'who is speaking on whose behalf and who is the useful idiot'* (see Stengers 2005). We recorded and transcribed our conversations and decided to treat ourselves as authors symmetrically by citing all of us, and none of us specifically.

Going back to a long tradition of experiments with dialogue and conversation in anthropology after 'writing culture' (Clifford and Marcus 2010), we believe that although fieldwork, encounters and especially interviews are never really symmetrical, at least the text itself can try to infra-reflexively (Latour 1988; Passoth and Rowland 2013) introduce various symmetries and asymmetries. All of us will speak in what follows, and all us will be spoken about – from different angles and shifting positions, but we will intentionally just appear as 'we' – and in *italics*.

INFRASTRUCTURAL LEGACIES

Back to hacking satellites – and to a conversation about (IT) security that turned out to be all about passion, protection and trust, less about technical fixes than about constant attention, responsibilities and care. Of course: the most obvious thing to discuss was this: if what we saw was not an actual hack, was it all just a big show? Something *'to scare those social scientists a little bit'*? Could we have seen a real satellite hack, if we all would just have dared to operate one from an official university IP address?

The answer to that is as simple as it is boring: yes, of course, there were quite a number of instances in the last decades – *'out there since the 90s, and also, the last one where someone in China took over two satellites'.* But the reason why this is possible in the first place is far less boring and it has to with some interesting characteristics of many, if not all large-scale infrastructures: what looks like a rigid security regime from the outside (or: from below as in the case of satellites), is quite often a patched together, partially upgraded, selectively maintained complex arrangement of old and new technologies, practices and organizations. Infrastructure *'is not only [the things?] that we have just built, but it is also something that would go ten years back, or 50 years back. And it is a whole complex of – or a whole arrangement of – systems that are maybe too big to shut down. And [that] we have to deal with an existing infrastructure already, and not just rethink our way of communicating with the sky from scratch, and we cannot start with a blank slate.'* Our technical world is built on such legacies. Marissa Cohn has argued very convincingly that despite our modern fascination with innovation and shiny new toys, such a progressivist account of technology and technological change is not very helpful when it comes to dealing with large scale systems (Cohn 2013), but not even when it comes to rapidly updated software (Cohn 2019). Satellites are a very good example for such legacy systems as '*these systems were designed to be put up and to run for 30, 40 years. They are way, way over their expiration date, but they still run*'.

A lot of them are in orbit for quite a long time and even if a security issue is discovered and someone bothers to write a patch for it, it is still increasingly complicated to update them from the ground. Satellites are not Android phones, there is no update guarantee. In fact, it is not even a reasonable idea to think of something like a regular update and patching cycle: A satellite, in orbit for more than just a few years, is basically a very simple (and old) computer with quite a specific set of hardware.

'*I mean, if some programmer in Fortran[2] makes the operating system for satellites – Fortran is a really specific programming language, and also very old – and makes a mistake, then yeah, satellites would come crashing down, and no one would know that these lines of code accidentally made the satellite go left instead of right.*' In the regular software world, there are protocols, modules and pieces of code that are so widely spread across the globe that once a bug is detected and a patch released, that patch – at least in theory – can be applied to all kinds of systems like a cure.

But in the case of satellites? Not that there are just a few of them, but compared to regular home computers or widely used embedded systems, most of them are pretty unique. And they last. Once up in orbit, they continue to work until they break (or fall) down or become space debris. Nevertheless, they are one backbone of contemporary telecommunications and security infrastructures (Witjes and Olbrich 2017). They are meant to last, but are not well cared for.

PATCHING WITH PASSION, ADDING CONTAINMENTS, CIRCLES OF TRUST

Such infrastructures are not only legacy systems that require maintenance to prevent them from breaking down, but also a lot of care to make sure that they do not turn into security risks. How could one care for them? By comparing the case of satellites with others, we collectively identified three forms of care – patching with passion, adding containments and circles of trust – that are embedded in open source software practices, secure data centre management and cybersecurity/network security practices. Patching is a very passionate activity. Auditing and testing pieces of code is part and parcel of the work in small- and large-scale open source communities, but it is also often voluntary, unpaid and honorary work. '*People would do the checking like voluntarily?*', we wondered, '*just because they can?*' *Well, yes and no* – '*from the open source world, in practice, we know that this is not going to happen (...), there are times that we thought that people are auditing these codes, but it never happened.*' Just because the source code is out in the open does not make it more secure, a free license does not automatically spark interest – and of course: '*The sky is filled with proprietary software.*'

As Chris Kelty has argued in his account of the history and practices of free and open software (2008) they are based on a reorientation of practices and relations of power that drive the design, circulation and maintenance of software. What is true for new software projects fuelled with the thrill of new beginnings is even more true for the tedious task of updating and the pesky job of searching for and fixing bugs. Patching requires 'arts of noticing' (Tsing 2015: 17–19), the kind of mixture of attentiveness, responsibility, competence and responsiveness, that Tronto and Fisher (1990), identified as core elements of an ethics of care.

While it might seem strange, maybe even inappropriate to use such concepts and sensibilities of care in a field so dominantly (and correctly) associated with 'white boys with cherry coke' (thanks to Noortje Marres for this wonderful image), they allow us to not only to counter today's progressivist technology narrative (in line with Marisa Cohn's work), but also to identify and highlight some of the mostly hidden and far less accounted for practices and sensibilities that keep today's digital infrastructures running and prevents them from – in the case of satellites even literally – crashing. Such practices are attentive in a way that they start with a recognition 'of a need and that there is a need that (needs) to be cared about' (Tronto 1993: 127) – a need for others, human and non-human. They are rooted in a felt responsibility, leading both to a pressing obligation and an understanding that 'something we did or did not do has contributed to the needs for care, and so we must care' (Tronto 1993: 132). They also require those involved not only to feel responsible, but also to be able to care – patching a bug in a piece of old FORTRAN code needs a very specific competence. And they require those who care to be responsive, to care when needed, not only when there is time. Patching and caring for security is therefore a form of response-ability – an ability to respond.

And as in other fields of practice requiring care, quite often the attempt to organize it more thoroughly paradoxically results in having less time, space and options for caring. *'If you are like – let's say I am the Dutch government and I think it is really important to [...] have a certain amount of time for security and justice [...] you could also think as a government and say "We need to do something about it and fix this code before someone else fixes it for us."'* Instead of relying on attentiveness, responsibility, competence and responsiveness, security is often organized and institutionalized very strictly, and the way that is done is by adding levels and more levels of containment. The way that highly protected data centres are managed are a good example for this (see also Chapter 13 by Taylor and Velkova, this volume).

To seal a part of the data handling and compute powers delivered by a huge data centre used by many different actors so that a part of it is highly protected, the most common option is: *'build a black box. So, in the data centre, there is a black box. (...) Everything that comes out of the black box must be encrypted. And if you cut one line, it would go onto the other line, and another one, should the last one fail. And if someone were to put their head into the black box, to see what is there, how it is functioning, police should be immediately alarmed.'*

A need for care for security is handled by securitization, into an extraordinary, but still banal loop of analysing and managing risks and thereby creating *'new security risks by solving old ones'*. Edwards has reconstructed this 'politics of containment' approach in his account of the cold war history of information technology and has highlighted very convincingly that once the construction of such 'closed worlds' (Edwards 1996) starts, there is no real limit on how far down to the micro level and how far up to the global level it can scale. *'[...] If somebody has to go in, they have to go through multiple security measures;*

(here should have been some detailed information about the different security measures which we unfortunately cannot disclose due to the sensitivity of this particular data centre) *so there are multiple authentication factors. [...] And then, [once you are] in that black box, you have three different cages; depending on your authorization, you can go into one, or two, or three cages. And then in those cages, you have [...] with computers, and of course, backup power, and all that.*' And for each level, more and more security measures add up: from password to physical tokens, from biometric details to time-restricted access, from contracts and non-disclosure agreements to military grade vouching and screening procedures.

A '*layered trust model security*', one of us notices, based on a '*hierarchy of mistrust*', another one replies. But containment has side effects, in fact: effects that often directly oppose the way security is achieved. A closed world is also a world with restricted access, on purpose.

But by protecting one part of an information infrastructure formally – for example by locking up a data centre in national security containers equipped with cages and sealed black boxes – another part of the information infrastructure – its protocols, the bits and pieces of firewall software packages – are sealed off, too, and thereby effectively barred from maintenance, patching and care. On a level of bugs and vulnerabilities, such containments create interesting conundrums: what to do with a detected vulnerability? Publishing it very quickly and openly increases the chanced of a rapid fix, but it also increases security risks as long as the vulnerability is not fully understood. A common problem only one actor knows about is only an issue for that actor. As long as no one else knows, it can even be used as an advantage or weapon. But it also creates a new risk: if one actor found a vulnerability, chances might go up that someone else – someone careless or with criminal intentions – might also find it. So it might be better to fix it quick – and to fix it quick, it might make sense to tell others – at least others one can trust.

But who might be trusted and why? Again: those who care, those with that mixture of attentiveness, responsibility, competence and responsiveness. The formal hierarchy of mistrust is countered with informal circles of trust based, again on an infrastructure of services, technologies and vouching practices.

The circles have their own platforms and their own (trusted) communication channels, a system of closed worlds to bridge the closed worlds of organized containment, based on a simple question: *'We (…) have a big problem. (…) Does anybody see where this can come from?'*

Those who already trust each other help each other to identify those who might care and might be trustworthy: to join the circle (the platform, the mailing list, the professional secret network), someone already on the list acts as a sponsor and at least two other people on that list need to vouch for someone they trust, based on previous experiences with that person: *'if they screw up, this means I am screwed'.*

CARING AND RESPONSE-ABILITIES

Security infrastructures are relational, just like you would expect from infrastructures: one's devices are another's work, one´s solutions are another's problems – to use a paraphrase of Star's aphorism (1999: 180). What looks like a regime of securitization (Burgess and Balzacq 2010; Buzan, Wæver and Wilde 1997) or a dataveillance architecture from one angle (Amoore and De Goede 2005; Dijck 2014) turns out to be a messy patchwork of standards, exploits, firewalls, log files, careless users and annoying script kiddies from the other. In principle, this should come as no surprise for scholars in STS or critical security studies, but in practice, such sensibilities for symmetry or multiplicity are far from being standard practice. Whether this is a result of a certain preference for critique, an effect of packaging the bits and pieces of contemporary security infrastructure into official machineries and decorating them with uniformed humans, clean interfaces and maps, or just a matter of conceptual ancestry (*Foucault, we can hear you*) is not important. But the lack of responses from those involved and accounts of the work they provide to build, maintain and, well, care for security infrastructures leaves us with a lack of accountability and response-abilities (Kenney 2019) – a lack of 'cultivation through which we render each other capable, that cultivation of the capacity to respond' (Haraway and Kenney 2015: 230–31). Can we foster this capacity?

To whom or to whose interests, issues, standards, or requirements do we (as security engineers, as hackers, as scholars studying security, as citizens…) respond to – and how? Our conversation began with hacking satellites, it led us to infrastructure, legacies and care. Infrastructures such as satellite communication networks are not only systems and technical as well as institutional legacies that require maintenance to prevent them from breaking down. They first and foremost need attention, shared responsibilities, rare and specific competencies and responsiveness – an ability, availability and readiness to respond. Satellites cannot be updated and keep running on 1980s protocols, p2p protocols can be turned against their users by hackers and security experts alike, the massive investment in protecting server racks in a physical data centers create the need to keep up a constant routine of security checks for all those involved. Such care cannot be delegated to additional (tech) components or 'standard' politics. Care is instead delegated to those informal networks of trust – *I know who I need to call at company X* – or an army of 'human sensors' (see also the Visual Vignette by Mayer and Iblis Shah, this volume). Also (or even more so) as a more practical, organizational or even political consideration of how to manage the various response-abilities: To whom or to whose interests, issues, standards, or requirements do we (as security engineers, as hackers, as scholars studying security, as citizens…) respond – and how? How to open 'up possibilities for different kinds of responses'? (Schrader 2010: 299) Engaging is this conversation was exciting, challenging, time-consuming, fun and sometimes annoying, leaving at one point or the other, each of us wondering how many languages a group of four can actually speak.

Creating an inclusive, mutually respectful conversation amongst those who seldomly cross path and practising the translation of the different meanings of responsibility across different communities might be a first step for taking-care.

NOTES

1   Modern operating systems offer graphical user interfaces (GUI) to control and administer them to run applications with clicks, drag and drop. Below the surface, there is still a level of immediate control, the command line (see Stephenson 1999). In its iconic form it sometimes appears in popular culture as a black window with green typography, in the lived reality of computer culture it is accessed by starting a so-called 'shell' to communicate with the computer. An encrypted secure version of this is the secure shell or SSH.

2   Fortran is a programming language, in fact, the first programming language ever implemented. Before that, computers were programmed in machine code (such as START ST:MOV R1,# ... MOVE R2,#1.END), after that in a more accessible form. Fortran (or FORmula TRANslation) was designed in 1957 and it is still in use in e.g. scientific and numeric calculations, although the number of people who can code in Fortran is decreasing constantly.

REFERENCES

Amoore, L., and De Goede, M. (2005). Governance, Risk and Dataveillance in the War on Terror. *Crime, Law and Social Change* 43(2): 149–173.

Burgess, J. P., and Balzacq, T. (2010). *Securitization Theory: How Security Problems Emerge and Dissolve* (New.). Milton Park, Abingdon, Oxon; New York: Taylor & Francis Ltd.

Buzan, B., Wæver, O., and Wilde, J. D. (1997). *Security: A New Framework for Analysis* (UK ed.). Boulder, CO: Lynne Rienner Publishers.

Clifford, J., and Marcus, G. E. (Eds). (2010). *Writing Culture: The Poetics and Politics of Ethnography* (25th Anniversary Edition edition). Berkeley, CA: University of California Press.

Cohn, M. (2019). Keeping Software Present: Software as a Timely Object for Digital STS. *Digital STS: A Field Guide for Science & Technology Studies*: 423–446.

Cohn, M. L. (2013). *Lifetimes and Legacies: Temporalities of Sociotechnical Change in a Long-Lived System*. Dissertation thesis.

Dijck, J. van. (2014). Datafication, Dataism and Dataveillance: Big Data Between Scientific Paradigm and Ideology. *Surveillance & Society* 12(2): 197–208.

Edwards, P. N. (1996). *The Closed World: Computers and the Politics of Discourse in Cold War America*. Cambridge, MA: The MIT Press.

Haraway, D., and Kenney, M. (2015). Anthropocene, Capitalocene, Chthulhucene. Donna Haraway in Conversation with Martha Kenney. In H. Davis and E. Turpin (Eds), *Art in the Anthropocene: Encounters among aesthetics, politics, environments and epistemologies*. London: Open Humanities Press London, pp. 255–269.

Kenney, M. (2019). Fables of Response-ability: Feminist Science Studies as Didactic Literature. *Catalyst: Feminism, Theory, Technoscience* 5(1): 1–39.

Kelty, C. M. (2008). *Two Bits. The Cultural Significance of Free Software*. Durham; London: Duke University Press.

Latour, B. (1988). The Politics of Explanation: An Alternative. In S. Woolgar (Ed.), *Knowledge and Reflexivity, New Frontiers in the Sociology of Knowledge*. London: Sage, pp. 155–176.

Passoth, J.-H., and Rowland, N. J. (2013). Beware of Allies! Notes on Analytical Hygiene in Actor-Network Account-Making. *Qualitative Sociology* 36(4): 465–483.

Schrader, A. (2010). Responding to Pfiesteria Piscicida (the Fish Killer): Phantomatic Ontologies, Indeterminacy, and Responsibility in Toxic Microbiology. *Social Studies of Science* 40(2): 275–306.

Star, S. L. (1999). The Ethnography of Infrastructure. *American Behavioral Scientist* 43(3): 377–391.

Stengers, I. (2005). The Cosmopolitical Proposal. In B. Latour and P. Weibel (Eds), *Making Things Public: Atmospheres of Democracy*. Cambridge, MA: The MIT Press.

Tronto, J. C., and Fisher, B. (1990). Toward a Feminist Theory of Caring. In E. Abel, and M. Nelson (Eds), *Circles of Care*. Albany, NY: SUNY Press, pp. 36–54.

Tronto, J. C. (1993). *Moral Boundaries: A Political Argument for an Ethic of Care*. New York: Routledge.

Tsing, A. L. (2015). *The Mushroom at the End of the World: On the Possibility of Life in Capitalist Ruins*. Princeton: Princeton University Press.

CPSIA information can be obtained
at www.ICGtesting.com
Printed in the USA
BVHW010544021121
620520BV00002B/11